INTELLECTUAL LEADERSHIP
IN EDUCATION

INTELLECTUAL LEADERSHIP
IN EDUCATION

by

J. Patrick Conroy

KLUWER ACADEMIC PUBLISHERS
Boston / Dordrecht / London

Distributors for North, Central and South America:
Kluwer Academic Publishers
101 Philip Drive
Assinippi Park
Norwell, Massachusetts 02061 USA
Telephone (781) 871-6600
Fax (781) 871-6528
E-Mail <kluwer@wkap.com>

Distributors for all other countries:
Kluwer Academic Publishers Group
Distribution Centre
Post Office Box 322
3300 AH Dordrecht, THE NETHERLANDS
Telephone 31 78 6392 392
Fax 31 78 6546 474
E-Mail <services@wkap.nl>

 Electronic Services <http://www.wkap.nl>

Library of Congress Cataloging-in-Publication Data

Conroy, J. Patrick.
    Intellectual leadership in education / by J. Patrick Conroy.
       p. cm.
    Includes bibliographical references (p.) and index.
    ISBN 0-7923-8658-2 (alk. paper)
    1. Educational leadership. 2. Education--Philosphy. I. Title.

  LB14.7 .C653 1999
  370'.1
                          99-047096

Printed on acid-free paper.
Printed in the United States of America

To

Barbara Jonte Conroy

Contents

Preface xiii

1 Introduction 1
  Education's Most Fundamental Intellectual Error   3
  Familiar Epistemologies   6
    Science and The Scientific Method   6
    The Epistemology of Mathematics   7
    Historiography, The Epistemology of History   8
    Anti-Epistemologies   9
  Epistemology in Education   11

Part I A Brief History of Western Knowledge

2 Christianity, The Foundation of Western Culture 17
  The Dark Ages   19
  The Attraction of Christianity to the Germanic People   25
    Clever Christian Leaders Neutralize the Opposition   25
    The Church's Contribution to Germanic Rulers   26
    The Christianization of the Heroic Myth   28
    Church Respect for Folk Ways   30
    Christian Respect for Labor   30

3 Intellectual Life in the Middle Ages 33
  Augustine's Complex Influence on Western Knowledge   36
    Platonic-Augustinian Idealism   36
    The Augustinian/Manichaean Controversy   37

The Epistemology of the Early Medieval University   39
St. Thomas, Rationalism, and the Scholastic Tradition   41
    Aquinas Makes the West Safe for Reason   41
    Aristotelian/Thomistic Rationalism   43
    The Restructuring of the Medieval University   47
    The Polarization of Medieval Theology   48
    Moral Philosophy vs. Moral Theology   53
Rationalism's Achievements, Rationalism's Failure   56

4 The Collapse of the Medieval World   59
    Human Suffering in the 14th & 15th Centuries   60
        Church Corruption   60
        Laymen Strive to Save the Church   61
    The High Middle Ages in Germany   64
    The Protestant Reformation   65
        Martin Luther   65
        John Calvin   67
        Henry VIII and The Church of England   68
        The Unavoidable Mix of Religious and Political Conflict 68
    The Thirty Years War   69
        Entangled Interests that Drove the War   70
        The Peace of Westphalia   71
        The Impact of the Thirty Years War On Western Culture 72

5 The Birth of the Modern Era   77
    Independent Authority of the Scientific Community   79
        Restructuring Empiricism as The Scientific Method   81
        The Contributions of Isaac Newton   82
        The Institutionalization of Scientific Inquiry   85
        Scientific Achievements   87
        Two Major Challenges to the Independence of Science 87
        The Compatibility of Theology and Science   90
    Achievements of 17th Century Secular Philosophy   91
        Major Political Events in 17th Century England   92
            The Redefinition of the Monarchy   93
            The English Bill of Rights   94
            Habeas Corpus   95

Thomas Hobbes (1588-1679)   96
   Hobbes' Source of Knowledge: Natural Man   96
   The Social Contract, Its Purpose and Terms   97
John Locke (1632-1704)   98
   Locke Redefines the State of Natural Man   99
   Locke Redefines the Terms of the Social Contract   101
Evaluating the Achievements of Locke and Hobbes   102

6 The Devolution of Secular Philosophy 105
  The Problematic Strand of Kant's Work   107
  Classical vs. Post-Kantian Realism   109
  Encyclopaedia   113
   Encyclopaedia's Source of Knowledge   114
    Intellectual Affirmation of the Continuous Progress
     of History   115
    Religious Support for Encyclopaedia   116
   Encyclopaedia's Methodological Claims   118
   Manifestations of Encyclopaedia in Western Intellectual
    Life   122
    19th Century Encyclopaedia   123
    20th Century Encyclopaedia   125
  Genealogy, The Anti-Epistemology   129
   Genealogy's Source of Knowledge   129
   Genealogy's Method of Inquiry   130
   Genealogy's Place in History   131
   Post-modernism: Genealogy's Progeny   133
    Hermeneutics   137
    Critical Theory   139
  Analytical Philosophy   142
  Conclusion   147

Part II An Epistemology for Education

7 The Source of Knowledge 155
  Resolving the 700 Year Old Problem   157
   Two Kinds of Material Knowledge: Physics and Ethics   159
   The Indispensability of Ethics to the Social Sciences   162

Developing Mature Secular Moral Reasoning   164
   Aristotle's Ethical System   165
   Kohlberg's Theory of Moral Development   166
   Kohlberg's Levels of Moral Development   168
   Ethical Development vs. Materialistic Ontology   171
   Kant's Categorical Imperative   173
   Winning Consensus to a Secular Ethical Canon   176
   Opposition to Ethical Inquiry in the Social Sciences   179
Teaching Mature Secular Ethics in Education   183
   Teaching Ethics to Educators   185
   Teaching Secular Moral Reasoning and Ethics in Public
      Schools   186
   Opposition to Ethics in Public Education   189
Education's Source and Standard of Knowledge   192

8 The Integration of Research and Practice   197
Research and Practice   201
   The Formal Integration of Research and Practice   201
   Scientific Paradigms   203
   From Chaos to Order in Education   203
   Articulating Theoretical Models in Education   205
Paradigms and Theoretical Models in Education   207
   Fundamental Assumptions   209
   Advantages and Disadvantages that Children Bring to
      Learning   211
   Methodology   214
   Instrumentation   216
Cognitive and Social Development   217
   The Application of Theoretical Models in Education   220
   Members of the Educational Community   222
   The Character of Professional Commitment   223

9 Institutionalizing Intellectual Authority   227
Research Methodology in Education   228
   The Role of Deductive Reason in Education   228
   Adapting the Scientific Method in the Social Sciences   229
   The Integration of Qualitative and Quantitative Analysis   231
Intellectual Authority in Natural Science   235

Research and Development in Natural Science and
Commerce   236
Financial Support of Commercial Research and
Development   240
Competition and the Market Place vs. Competition in
Society   241
Intellectual Authority in Education   245
Research and Development in Education   246
Competition in Education   250
Sophisticated Financial Support for R & D in Education   252
Re-Thinking Change in Education   254
The Irrational Context in Which Change is Attempted   255
How Education's Epistemology Accommodates Change   258

10 Conclusion 261

Bibliography 275

Index 285

Preface

I must say that to a great extent I did this work alone, but even I cannot tell if I am bragging or complaining. Obviously, I had to have some support, and the most consistent, unwavering, and indispensable help came from my wife Barbara Conroy. In addition to a spouse's support, she provided invaluable intellectual assistance. She taught me about Kohlberg and how his work helps educators understand the social and psychological development of children, especially in secondary schools. And she persuaded me to revisit Kant, whose work I did not admire. In following her suggestion, I discovered the strand of his work that provides one of the most important solutions in this text.

During various stages of research and writing, I sought feedback from professional educators, but most were reluctant to speak to my work in depth. Some pointed out that they did not have the background in philosophy and others were quite frank about not having the time. Interestingly, everyone I contacted who took the time to help, contributed in a way that I had not anticipated.

Bruce Barnett, director of Educational Leadership Policy Studies, University of Northern Colorado, and Tom Bellamy, dean of the school of education, University of Colorado at Denver read early drafts and helped me make decisions regarding what to include and what to exclude.

Henry Levin and I exchanged e-mail. He disagreed with nearly everything I wrote to him, but he responded so kindly that he had an enormous impact on my thinking. Henry made it clear that I had to be decisive regarding my claim that ethics are indispensable to inquiry in education and the social sciences. That approach caused me considerable unease. Richard McCormick and Charles Curran, moral theologians at the

University of Notre Dame and Southern Methodist University respectively, convinced me that trying to second guess any group's reaction to my work would be counter productive. They helped me develop the courage to adopt the attitude I express regarding secular ethics as opposed to religious ethics. Robert B. Sloan, president of Baylor University and Mike Beaty, director Baylor's Institute for Faith and Learning, spent considerable time discussing the challenge of integrating religious ethics with the social sciences and business schools in a religious university. Jehuda Reinharz, president of Brandeis University, discussed the role of ethics in private, secular universities that have roots in a religious community.

Alasdair MacIntyre had no time to give, but he took time to allow me to check major assertions that I dared not be wrong about. Alex Kozulin helped me understand the relationship between Vygotsky and Feuerstein, and also discussed some of the translation problems in *Thought and Language*. Dorothy Singer was quite frank about how she and Revenson elaborated Piaget's work so that I did not have to read all of Piaget in order to verify inconsistencies I had noticed. Ed Dean, a friend since college, spent considerable time providing quality assurance to my thinking about the history and epistemologies of natural science and mathematics. Ed has two degrees from the University of California, a Ph.D. in nuclear science and an M.S. in architecture.

Fairly late in the project, I began to communicate with Dan Stufflebeam who has an international reputation for his contributions to the evaluation of programs and personnel. Dan encouraged my work because of its potential to help educators build prior agreement to criteria for the evaluation of programs and personnel. In addition, it was through the Evaluation Center that I met Kamil Jbeily who heads the Texas Regional Collaboratives for Excellence in Science Teaching at the University of Texas. I visited Kamil in Texas during December, 1998, and met with science educators from throughout the state of Texas. When I returned home, I expanded chapter 9 to emphasize the completeness of programs that research and development must deliver to teachers and teacher trainers.

Preparing the final manuscript is a major task. I am deeply indebted to Wes Apker, Ellen Conroy, Kerry Case, and Carol Irwin for the hours they spent reading and commenting on the text. The errors that remain are mine, but they removed many and vastly improved the text's clarity.

Protecting a manuscript is always a concern, and typically unfamiliar ground. John Moye, another friend since college, provided me with his and his firms assistance.

In the text, I am somewhat critical of the media. In fairness, I should mention support I received. *The Economist* provided intellectual companionship which was quite important to my development. And CSPAN brought live coverage of influential events into my home. Imagine watching Cardinal Bernadin's last public address and seeing George Soros scold the Economic Club of New York without leaving Colorado's mountains.

I also wish to thank publishers for permitting me to use quotations from their works.

"Trends in Recent American Philosophy" and "A Half Century of Philosophy Viewed from Within;" *Daedalus:* Journal of the American Academy of the Arts and Sciences, from the issue entitled, "American Academic Culture in Transformation: Fifty Years, Four Disciplines;" Winter, 1997, Vol. 126, No. 1.

The University of California Press for quotations from Sir Isaac Newton; *Mathematical Principals of Natural Philosophy and System of the World*; edited and translated by Andrew Motte, Copyright 1934 and 1962, Regents of the University of California.

The University of Note Dame Press and Alasdair MacIntyre for quotations from Alasdair MacIntyre; *Three Rival Versions of Moral Enquiry: Encyclopaidia, Genealogy, and Tradition*, and John Henry Newman; *An Essay in Aid of A Grammar of Assent.* Doubleday, a division of Random House, Inc. for a quotation from Christopher Dawson's *Religion and the Rise of Western Culture.*

Orbis Books for a quotation from Leonard Boff's *The Path to Hope: Fragments from a Theologian's Journey.*

The Crossroad Publishing Company for a quotation from Edward Schillebeeckx's *Jesus: An Experiment in Christology,* Herbert Hoskins translator.

MIT Press for a quotation from Lev Vygotsky's *Thought and Language*, Alex Kozulin translator.

1

Introduction

Educated citizens who are interested in their country and their children have little difficulty describing the kind of public schools they would like. A school should be a place where kids are safe, enjoy their childhood, and prepare for successful and meaningful adult lives. Professional educators might add to these general goals a more specific list that addresses particular problems that many schools face. Such a list might include:

> Each year, virtually all children become better students, increasing their intellectual skills, knowledge, values, and habits.

> Poverty, ethnicity, and other social factors influence program design but do not determine student achievement.

> Teachers and administrators commit to the same goals for children and work together to achieve them.

> Staffs use instructional programs that work and abandon programs that do not work.

> Parents praise their schools and express gratitude both that their children attend these schools and that the professionals treat them with so much respect.

These statements describe what professional educators might want from schools. Much of the knowledge needed to develop or invent such schools exists today. It may not be easily identified or widely known, but it exists. And yet, many students languish in the early grades, more begin to underachieve in the middle grades, and even more leave high school unprepared for further schooling or rewarding work. As Margaret Donaldson explained in her book *Children's Minds*, the gap in the ability to benefit from schooling that exists between well prepared and unprepared students in first grade grows as students get older. Educators are not able to reduce these gaps. Rather, they watch them widen.

Importantly, I am not blaming anyone. I am merely saying that what educators must achieve as a group and what we do achieve are too far apart. Furthermore, the gap between what we can do and what we must do is somewhat new. In recent years, society has experienced significant changes, some of which have made it necessary for public schools to change their mission. The knowledge and skills that adults must have to participate in the world economy go far beyond what most students have attained. This change alone explains the urgency of the crisis in education. It explains why leaders from virtually every intellectual, economic, political, and social perspective list the improvement of education as one of their country's greatest challenges.

Not surprisingly then, the failure of public schools adequately to educate children has caused deep concern throughout society. Teachers, administrators, and university professors have been accused of indifference and inertia. That is an unfair criticism because it is wrong. The profession's response has been anything but indifferent and inert. Indeed, there has been an almost overwhelming inundation of both instructional and structural innovations in education. Which raises an important question: If there is wide spread agreement that education must change, and agreement regarding what children should know and be able to do when they leave school (and at various grades along the way), and if educational researchers and practitioners are dedicated to improving the education of children, what is the problem? Can't we just leave educators alone and let them do the work that everyone agrees needs to be done? Unfortunately, it is not that simple.

In recent years, educational researchers have developed some excellent innovations, some practitioners have implemented them, and some schools have shown remarkable improvement. However, other innovations have been advanced that make bold claims but are quite flawed. Most important, professional educators in universities and public schools have great difficulty distinguishing genuine solutions from pretenders. Of course, there are educational researchers who are confident that they can distinguish quality research from nonsense. The problem is that professional educators cannot agree *as a group* regarding what constitutes quality research and what constitutes inferior research. Clearly, any discipline whose members cannot distinguish quality research from nonsense suffers from some sort of intellectual problem. The challenge educators face is not to agree that we have intellectual problems or even that intellectual problems require intellectual solutions, for both are quite evident. What we must agree to is that educators are capable of finding intellectual solutions to the challenges that face us. That assumption is not at all evident.

Education's Most Fundamental Intellectual Error

We can begin to understand the intellectual challenges in education by answering a rather simple question: How do principals and teachers resolve important intellectual differences? At first, we talk them through. We conduct rational discourse expecting to find rational answers to difficult questions. Admittedly, this is a theoretical state in most public schools. Probably not since the mid 1960's have public school faculties been able to discuss intellectual problems optimistic that they would reach rational conclusions shared by all. On the other hand, many educators have personally experienced a stage of professional innocence in which they expected rational conduct from themselves and their colleagues, but virtually everyone has lost that innocence. The events that result in the loss of intellectual optimism tell us more about the intellectual changes we must make than does anything that occurs within our pessimistic intellectual conduct. Therefore, it is necessary to notice what causes our loss of intellectual optimism.

During the best moments in the stage of innocence, disagreement among principals and teachers is followed by respectful discourse which clarifies the contradictory positions that define the conflict. Then, being optimistic, practitioners agree to check the research. But when practitioners turn to research, what do they find? They find contradictions. There is virtually no topic that educational research describes in a consistent, coherent fashion. For virtually any topic, educational research provides conflicting views, and sometimes it provides many deeply conflicting views. When principals and teachers reassemble after checking the research they are more likely to encounter intensified, research based conflicts than research based clarity and agreement.

Ironically, educational researchers do not even try to overcome these contradictions and integrate research, except in rather small groups that happen to agree with one another. Why? Because the current condition of inquiry in education makes that task impossible.

On the other hand, faced with growing demands for accountability, principals and teachers must attempt to improve instruction in their schools. Clearly, improving instruction requires research regarding how children learn and how best to teach. Therefore, *principals and teachers* must figure out how to use research which means that they must figure out how to study, integrate, and evaluate research. But the nature of the task of integrating research does not change because practitioners rather than researchers attempt it. The intellectual barriers to the integration of research that make that task impossible for researchers make it impossible for practitioners.

As a practical matter, when principals and teachers use research as the basis for discussions about how children learn and how best to teach, they find themselves locked in redundant, unresolvable arguments that may become loud, contentious, and even mean. Confronted with intensifying conflicts, teachers and principals declare a truce by agreeing to disagree. They accept the fact, We are never going to agree! Optimism is replaced by a sense of utter futility and the loss of intellectual innocence.

As in other kinds of personal development that require the loss of innocence, the loss of intellectual innocence in education is an important event. But is it an important *achievement*?

Sometimes the loss of innocence is inseparable from the achievement of maturity. For example, children often believe that good things just happen. That is a kind of innocence, and losing it typically involves recognizing that nothing good comes our way without work. We lose our innocence about work at the same time we discover the satisfaction that hard work offers. In this case, growth occurs as a single event.

On the other hand, the kind of innocence many young people bring to the task of building intimate relationships not only must be lost, but also replaced. Innocence in relationships typically consists of assuming that others feel and behave the way we do. But then we find out that our feelings cannot predict the other person's feelings and that our sincerity and trustworthiness cannot assure the same from others. We experience betrayal. Most of us do not require a lot of examples of betrayal before we lose our innocence. However, some of us take a lot of time moving past the stage of lost innocence into a wiser, more empowered, more responsible stage of relationship building. Some adults wallow in their misery for ever, convinced that they have found the truth about relationships. They declare to themselves and the world that intimacy can only lead to pain and that friendships always fail, leaving them more lonely than before. One is better off accepting loneliness than subjecting oneself to inevitable disappointment. But most of us develop some form of the old saying, First time, shame on you; second time, shame on me. We accept responsibility for figuring out whom we can trust and how to build trust and commitment in our relationships. We replace the pain and disappointment we feel when we have lost our innocence with the skills and attitudes that provide the capacity to build and sustain relationships.

What about the loss of intellectual innocence in education? We reach the point where we realize that we are never going to agree. Have we made an important intellectual discovery that will now guide educational inquiry and practice? Or, have we merely lost our innocence? Is our despair the equivalent of discovering that we must work, a discovery that not only leaves our innocence behind but also contains a solution? Or have we merely closed the door to one room and entered another where we must figure out how to conduct our intellectual lives?

These questions go to the heart of what we believe about knowledge in education. I argue that the loss of intellectual innocence is an important event in education but that it is not an important intellectual achievement. It merely opens the door to a new level of understanding about the nature of inquiry in education. It does not *describe* the nature of inquiry in education.

Unfortunately for education and educators, we have treated the loss of innocence, the conclusion that we cannot agree on anything, as the truth about knowledge in education. We have decided, however consciously or unconsciously, that *the nature of knowledge* in education is such that different educators may agree on various issues, even deep intellectual issues, but that agreement is the result of accident. *We believe* that when educators disagree, there is nothing that can be done.

We must begin to question this conclusion. When we claim that we cannot agree and treat that claim as if it were the truth about knowledge in education, we take a specific philosophical stand. We say: There is no such thing in education as truth. There is nothing that can be said about anything that is true about it, that describes the nature of the thing. Rather, truth is only true from each individual's point of view. Our greatest, most defining intellectual stand is the conclusion that we can never agree on anything.

There is an important point to be remembered about rational arguments in the *social sciences*, whether inductive or deductive. Regardless of the structure of the argument and weight of evidence, rational conclusions may be rejected solely on the grounds that they are ethically or intellectually unacceptable.[1] That we can never agree on anything is an unacceptable conclusion in education. It must be rejected on ethical grounds because of the consequences it carries for children and society. And it must be rejected on intellectual grounds because of the consequences it carries for our discipline. But rejecting this conclusion is not the problem. It must be replaced. We must invent a more powerful way of conducting research and a capacity to integrate research and practice. We need an epistemology for education.

Familiar Epistemologies

To my best recollection, every educator with whom I have used the term *epistemology* has demonstrated discomfort. Therefore it will be useful, before we begin the work at hand, to allow the reader to notice that we are quite familiar with various epistemologies and can easily become comfortable with the term. Many educators earn undergraduate and graduate degrees in disciplines other than education, especially secondary teachers. We have degrees in English or math or physics or history or whatever. Although some of these disciplines enjoy highly developed epistemologies, we rarely study their epistemologies as such. Rather, we simply use the epistemology of our major without really thinking about it or other epistemologies. As a result, we do not gain useful knowledge of the term. By considering some of the epistemologies we use and noticing their similarities and differences, we begin to understand epistemology in general and why we must use different epistemologies in different disciplines.

Science and The Scientific Method

Part of learning any discipline includes learning how to think in the discipline. In science, students must learn the content of the sciences, but

---

[1] Natural scientists cannot reject conclusions that are established by the scientific method whether they like them or not. But it is a fundamental necessity in the social sciences that we be able to reject conclusions that are ethically reprehensible. In chapters six and seven I establish and use this point. For now I ask the reader to give it sympathetic consideration.

just as important, students must learn to use the scientific method, to think in the logic of science. Most educators and much of the general public can describe the scientific method, at least in its basic structure: identify a problem, form an hypotheses, test the hypotheses, and draw a conclusion. Furthermore, most of us know that prior to the invention of the scientific method (in the 17th century), inquiry in science was quite a mess. However, to appreciate the mess science was in prior to the 17th century, we need to know a lot more about the epistemology of science. We need to know what it is, how it came about, and especially what it rejected (how science was conducted during the Middle Ages).

One of the fundamental epistemological questions that must be answered in every discipline is, What is our source of knowledge? The source of knowledge in science is nature, the physical world, and by extension, the laboratory where physical experiments are conducted to verify or reject scientific hypotheses. The method of inquiry is what we call the scientific method. The question regarding the source of knowledge has been so completely resolved in science that most of us would not identify *nature as the source of knowledge* as an essential component of the epistemology of science. However, the importance of that solution was quite evident and controversial during the 17th century. This topic receives considerable attention in Part I and Part II.

The Epistemology of Mathematics

When we learn mathematics we learn the content of mathematics: mathematical terms, rules, functions, proofs, and so on. We also learn to use deductive reason and to think in the logic of mathematics. More of us know that we learned the scientific method in science than that we learned deductive reason in mathematics, but when deductive reason is described in mathematical terms, most of us can recognize the connection. However, deductive reason merely provides the method of inquiry in mathematics. What is the source of knowledge in mathematics? Mathematics is very different from science. We do not prove mathematical statements in nature. Mathematics has no source of knowledge other than the community of mathematicians around the world who either confirm or reject the validity of mathematical statements.

External, physical phenomena cannot alter the truth of mathematical statements even when used in science. For instance, physicists are currently interested in working out the physics involved in stabilizing quantum mechanics sufficiently to permit quantum computing. They want to free computers from the limits of on-off electronics and replace it with the multiple dimensions of quantum physics. There is little evidence that physicists can solve the problems they have taken on, but mathematicians have already solved the mathematical problems that must be solved in order for quality control to be assured. It does not matter to the mathematicians whether physicists can solve their problems or not. The mathematicians have already done their work. That mathematicians can solve mathematical problems related to physical phenomena that may or may not actually exist has led some scientists to refer to the virtual reality of mathematics.

However, the independence of mathematics from physical verification should not be confused with the absence of rigorous intellectual authority. Mathematical conclusions must be supported by mathematical proofs, and those proofs must withstand rigorous review within the mathematics community. When a proof has been accepted, it is accepted everywhere in the world. Refutation of an existing proof must meet the same standards of verification as the original proof, must include its own evidence, and must withstand rigorous review within the community. "Well, be that as it may, I just disagree" is an impossible statement in science and mathematics. It would be immediately recognized as having no meaning and no validity. No scientist or mathematician could say that about an accepted scientific or mathematical statement. They could dedicate themselves to proving it wrong, but they could not conduct science or mathematics as if it did not exist.

Historiography, The Epistemology of History

The epistemology of history is probably even less understood than the epistemology of mathematics. Only if we had very good history teachers, might we have learned both historical facts and the method of developing historical knowledge or historiography. Unlike mathematics, the source of knowledge in history is fairly easily described: primary and secondary sources, the historical record. Historical method is less clear, more varied, and accounts for the lack of agreement that attends many historical conclusions.

Historians use logic fairly consistently. Indeed, an invaluable book on logic is D.H. Fischer's *Historians' Fallacies: Toward a Logic of Historical Thought*. Regardless of what other methods historians use, they rely on generally accepted standards of logical analysis. On the other hand, historians develop different points of view which greatly influence how they select and focus their attention on historical sources. Some use the great person theory of history. In this view, the direction that history has taken has resulted from the defining acts of great people. Other historians consider economic forces to have had defining influence on historical events; therefore, they focus their attention on economics.[2] Obviously, once historians have adopted a particular point of view, it will greatly impact their interpretation of history. By adopting different perspectives, historians produce very different historical conclusions. In that way, history lacks intellectual authority. However, any historical view is deemed to have failed if it violates standards regarding the proper use of historical sources or logic.

Sociology and anthropology are particularly interesting to educators thinking about epistemology. Each discipline has members who conduct research that is very much like historical research, and they must make responsible use of sources and logic. Others study social phenomena as they currently exist. They often conduct research in a very scientific way, using the scientific method to help them identify the underlying forces that drive social and anthropological phenomena.[3] However, when members of either discipline stop asking historical questions (How have societies formed?) or current questions (What makes these societies function?) and begin to ask how societies and social institutions *ought* to be formed so as best to serve the community, they face the same epistemological problems that educators face. One of the major tasks of this text is to demonstrate that historical and scientific methods do not work for that kind of inquiry.

Anti-Epistemologies

Of course, not all disciplines enjoy these levels of agreement regarding epistemology. For instance, artists may be required to learn various rules, but great artists have a way of redefining those rules. I find it useful to think of art as defined by expression rather than inquiry. Aesthetics is probably more useful to artistic criticism than epistemology. If that is a problem, it is one I am completely unprepared to address.

[2]See M. Bloch, *The Historian's Craft.*

[3]See Burrell, G. and G. Morgan; *Sociological Paradigms and Organizational Analysis: Elements in the Sociology of Corporate Life.*

Literary criticism inevitably confronts historical and aesthetic issues, and again, resolves them in individual and group opinions, but has very little of what anyone could call intellectual authority. Indeed, both art and literary critics must compete with the compelling opinions of the market place. It seems to me that these disciplines are best understood as being guided by aesthetics rather than epistemology and need have no positive or negative attitude toward epistemology.

The major source of anti-epistemological thinking comes from moral philosophy. In Part I, I discuss individualism as a tradition grounded in the work of Friedrich Nietzsche. In this introduction it is interesting to notice that Cardinal John Henry Newman, a 19th century theologian and educator, defended individualism and defined its limitations. In *An Essay in Aid of A Grammar of Assent*, Newman argued that each individual can defend his or her faith merely by claiming to believe, based upon individual experience. He called this personally grounded, individually derived belief *assent*. Because assent is fundamentally a way of knowing that is dependent upon individual experience, it is indistinguishable from individualism and can be considered an anti-epistemology. An epistemology describes how a group of intellectuals agrees to conduct inquiry. Any claim about the nature of knowledge that describes inquiry as fundamentally an individual issue produces an anti-epistemology.

I do not claim that all individuals in living their private lives require an epistemology. I agree with Newman and the entire Western liberal intellectual tradition that honors the individual and acknowledges and defends individual liberties in private matters. And as I mentioned above, I do not suggest that literature or the arts would benefit from epistemology. Indeed, I must stress that I make no attempt to include literature, the arts, or criticism in this discussion. My point is that the social sciences, and in particular education, cannot develop the intellectual foundations, knowledge, and practice we require to accomplish our mission if we conduct inquiry using methods appropriate to private individuals. Newman described the problem for us when he wrote:

> Real assent . . . is proper to the individual, and as such thwarts rather than promotes . . . intercourse . . . It shuts itself up, as it were, in its own home, or at least in its own witness and its own standard; and . . . it cannot be reckoned on, anticipated, accounted for, inasmuch as it is the accident of this man or that, (p. 82-83).

Any method of inquiry that is grounded in the views of individuals and opposes community methods and standards of inquiry ultimately frustrates discourse. Rather than establishing shared standards, it produces and validates individual views, however contradictory. That is the condition of inquiry in education today.

One problem with this condition is fairly obvious once we begin to question our assumptions about inquiry in education. Educators reach conclusions more through assent than rigorous, overt inquiry or discourse. We cling to our conclusions and to our right to conclude anything we personally feel is correct even though that method and standard of inquiry produces enormous barriers to building powerful knowledge in theory and practice.

Individualism has ancient roots, but has only been treated seriously since the 19th century. Secular moral philosophers in major universities have developed elaborate arguments for the view that none of us can agree on anything. They insist that all morality and all truth are subject to the experiences and dispositions of individuals. Educators and other social scientists have assented to this anti-epistemology. They have adopted this view from a group of intellectuals who are unlikely to provide authoritative knowledge about anything. Clearly, it is worthwhile to visit this topic and challenge such conclusions.

Epistemology in Education

Educators cannot avoid two distinct sets of epistemological issues. First, educators need to understand the epistemologies of the disciplines they teach and of the disciplines that others teach. This issue is especially important in secondary schools (middle schools, junior high schools, and high schools) where teachers are almost always required to have degrees in the academic disciplines they teach, frequently teach only one discipline, and often are organized in departments defined by different disciplines. Secondary teachers obviously must help students learn the epistemologies that guide the disciplines they teach. As we have noted, students benefit from knowing that when they learn science, they must learn the scientific method; when they learn mathematics, they must learn deductive reasoning; and when they learn history, they must learn historiography.

In addition, as educators, we all belong to a distinct discipline. Education has its own purpose and intellectual problems and must have its own epistemology. Our epistemology must permit us to integrate research as well as to integrate research and practice. It must permit us to conduct discourse that leads to agreement, commitment and action.

Secondary principals find building cohesive staffs more difficult than do elementary principals. Understanding education's epistemological problems helps us understand the challenges that secondary principals face. Teachers do not adequately know the epistemologies of their own disciplines, and frequently they reject as inferior the epistemologies and content of other disciplines. Furthermore, virtually all teachers reject educational research methods and knowledge. One cannot blame secondary principals for selecting any goal other than trying to build a learning community in their schools.

When a secondary principal calls a faculty meeting, at a minimum two groups show up: 1) the teachers whose disciplines follow highly developed (but different) epistemologies: natural science, math, and history teachers; and 2) teachers whose disciplines have no epistemology at all or anti-epistemologies: art, music, English, and social science teachers. Even before a principal and faculty encounter the contradictions contained in educational research, their initial attempts at discourse can become polarized by the application of conflicting epistemological habits developed in their disciplines. If they express overt disdain for the intellectual methods and knowledge of their colleagues, they deepen the polarization and raise the temperature of conflicts.

Faced with such intractable conflicts, principals and teachers resort to the same solution they use when confronted by research based conflicts: they declare a truce. Everyone agrees that they can never agree on anything. They resort to individualism. Clearly individualism has an important place in Western societies. Democracy and market economics both rely on principles of individualism. So do many of the advanced forms of psychology and human relations and communication skill programs: they start with the assumption of the rights of the individual, including to be a bit quirky or even wrong. In relationships and the voting booth and the market place, *how I feel* is the ultimate source of truth. But in a discipline and profession such as education, where children and society depend upon our attaining powerful knowledge and integrated theory and practice, it is impossible to allow *how I feel* to operate as the final source of truth. Individualism, for all its benefits at the personal and even political levels, cannot guide research or practice.

If we are going to solve these intellectual problems, we must change how we think about epistemology in general and we must solve epistemological problems in education. In Part I below, we study epistemology so that we can think about how we think in general and think about how we think in our various disciplines. We study epistemology formally. In Part II, we do epistemology. We invent an epistemology that permits educators to integrate research, integrate research and practice, and conduct discourse that leads to agreement, commitment, and action.

The most troublesome epistemological question we ask is What is our source of knowledge? What we discover in Part I is that this question presents a 700 year old problem in education and the social sciences. In answering this question in Part II, we discover that ethics plays an indispensable role in our epistemology and inquiry. But in Part I, we will have discovered that moral theology and religious moral philosophy (two terms we learn to distinguish) cannot guide ethical discourse in a pluralistic society's public square or university. We realize that we must develop and use mature, *secular* moral reasoning as a fundamental intellectual skill if we are to provide intellectual leadership in education.

A second important but not nearly as intractable epistemological question has to do with the structure and method of inquiry. We find that this question is impossible to address until we have resolved the source of knowledge problem. We also discover that the most essential question regarding the *method* of inquiry asks, What is the formal architecture of knowledge in education? We must be able to think about how we think and that requires that we develop formal cognitive operations specific to education.

Intellectual leadership, we discover, must come from those who serve as researchers, university teaching faculty, classroom teachers, and school administrators. But leadership requires intellectual authority, and intellectual authority must be located primarily in the community of researchers and practitioners, not in individuals. In this text, we establish that in order to develop *intellectual leadership*, educators must develop *intellectual authority*, and to do that we must attend to our *intellectual development* first as a community and then as individuals.

We find that intellectual development in the social sciences has three essential components: ethical development, cognitive development, and community development. Ethical development requires the development and use of mature *secular* moral reasoning. Cognitive development requires the design and use of a formal cognitive architecture that guides inquiry and structures knowledge in education. Community development is grounded in ethical and cognitive development but makes the leap from the development of the individual to the development of the community.

We turn now to part one which provides a brief history of Western knowledge. Chapter two discusses the Dark Ages, a period of virtually no intellectual activity. Consequently, it deals with very little intellectual history, which may seem off point. However, it is a brief chapter in which I describe the complete conquest of the western Roman Empire by the Germanic people and the astonishing conversion of the conquerors by the religion of Rome. Those events provided the roots of the cultural and intellectual development of Europe and America and a description of them had to be contained in either very long footnotes or a very short chapter.

Part I

A Brief History of Western Knowledge

2

Christianity, The Foundation of Western Culture

Without arguing why the Middle Ages have been ignored, it is important to note why they should not be. The Middle Ages are best understood as two very different periods. The first is often called the Early Middle Ages or the Dark Ages. It began with the fall of Rome (c. 476) and lasted until around 1050. The second is called the High Middle Ages and began around 1050 and lasted until the 17th century. The Middle Ages are important because they are the earliest periods of what has come to be recognized as the distinctive Western culture that combined ancient, especially Roman, influences with Christianity and Germanic tribal traditions.

Rather than beginning this study with Rome, I start with the Dark Ages. This decision is largely expedient, for a competent discussion of Rome's influence on Western culture would necessarily be quite long. In addition, it is helpful to think of Rome as part of the ancient world. It was an Eastern Mediterranean culture, an extension of Egyptian and Greek influences, and it was pagan until its last 150 years. In the West, Rome was conquered by Germanic tribes and its fall cleared the way for the development of a new, distinctively Christian and Germanic culture. The much praised Renaissance brought Eastern[1] traditions and achievements back into the mainstream of Western culture. However, the West's unique Christian and Germanic influences were already institutionalized and ingrained in the psyche of central and western Europe.

Even if the modern era witnessed the complete replacement of Christianity and theology in the university, politics, and civil society; we would still need to know a great deal about this period. For every culture must be able to answer questions regarding the ultimate meaning of the lives of individuals and the ultimate meaning of society. In order for society to develop and flourish, individuals must work toward that end. The energy used to work depends upon our finding lasting meaning in our lives. If we believe that our individual lives and all human life end in complete, final, obliterating death, we suffer disillusionment and despair

---

[1]By Eastern I refer to Eastern Mediterranean cultures. I refer to the far east as Asian.

that sucks energy out of us. If every life ultimately ends in complete, obliterating death, why should we strive to build society? It is no small matter that Christianity provided Western civilization with eternal answers to those questions. Intellectuals thinking about society at the turn of the second millennium face these same questions without the universal and eternal assurances that Christianity provided in the first millennium. It is puerile to assume that without religion and without alternative, eternal answers to these questions, individuals and society can continue to grow and act with the same hope and determination as they did in the past. It is naive to assume that the psychological and ethical dilemmas raised by the question of death can be overcome by ignoring them.

Ironically, William James, the pragmatist, made this very point in lectures delivered at Harvard university in 1907. Pragmatism excludes religion and metaphysics from its methodology. Members of the audience noticed their absence and pushed the question about the existence of God. Finally James responded that he must believe in God as a practical necessity, for without God, he quoted Balfour:

> The energies of our system will decay, the glory of the sun will be dimmed, and the earth, tideless and inert, will no longer tolerate the race which has for a moment disturbed its solitude. Man will go down into the pit, and all his thoughts will perish. The uneasy consciousness which in this obscure corner has for a brief space broken the contented silence of the universe, will be at rest. Matter will know itself no longer. "Imperishable monuments" and "immortal deeds," death itself, and love stronger than death, will be as if they had not been. Nor will anything that is, be better or worse for all that the labor, genius, devotion, and suffering of man have striven through countless ages to effect.[2]

James declared his preference to believe in God, but the status of God in Western *intellectual life* has diminished since the early 1900's and virtually disappeared in the last years of this century. It seems that the work that must be done to build individual lives and societies requires more than a vague, impersonal, but comforting eschatology. We must

---

[2] In James, *Pragmatism*, (p. 76); from Balfour, *The Foundations of Belief*, (p. 30).

work which means that our vision of the ultimate meaning of humanity must be strong enough to activate the energy in our lives. In addition, and this is a point that has significant consequences throughout this work, our eschatology or ultimate, metaphysical purpose, like any goal, does not reveal the specific tasks that must be done to achieve it. We must figure out what work we ought to do and what work we ought to avoid. We must develop personal and social ethics; but ethics, like God, have substantially disappeared from Western *intellectual life*.

This work does not attempt to resolve the psychological dilemmas created by the demise of religion among Western intellectuals. That task is left to theologians, religious leaders, and psychologists. However, we cannot leave ethics to moral theologians or religious moral philosophers. That point is not self-evident, but it is one of the major conclusions established in part one. It is no secret that orthodox Christian activists in the West have recently attempted to fill the vacuum created in political and civil life by the decline of secular personal and social ethics. What is not so clear is that the decline in interest in ethics generally has so eroded the capacity of secular intellectuals to conduct rational ethical discourse that they cannot assert and teach mature secular ethics; therefore, they sound decidedly unpersuasive when they oppose orthodox Christian activists in the public square. In part one, I describe the different traditions that have divided moral theology and religious moral philosophy, forcing each other out of the university and the public square. I also trace the collapse of secular moral philosophy which has left it silent in the university and the public square. At first we reacquaint ourselves with the central role of Christianity in medieval Europe and then we notice how *Christians* forced Christianity out of the center of civil and political life. Although we give considerable attention to the role of Christianity in the Middle Ages, our purpose is secular, as becomes evident when we move past the Middle Ages.

The Dark Ages

The contemporary reader does not have to look far for images of life in Europe after the fall of Rome. We can bring to mind life in the Balkan States after the collapse of the Soviet Union, or we can focus on the central nations of Africa during the late 1990's. There was no rule of law. There was no economy. Most lives were marked by continuous misery:

hunger, cold, fear, and violence. Mercifully, lives were short, but the period was not. It lasted nearly six hundred years.

The source of the misery is obvious but important to note. For hundreds of years prior to the fall of Rome, the Roman legions forced the Germanic peoples (barbarians) to remain north of the Rhine and Danube rivers. When they finally defeated their Roman enemies, they swept across Europe, completely destroying the Roman empire's institutions and culture. People living during the Dark Ages suffered an almost constant state of war as tribes from the north migrated south, plundering and killing along the way. Towns were destroyed. Homes were destroyed. Everything Roman was destroyed.

Amazingly, amidst the complete destruction of the Roman Empire, virtually the whole network of Christian bishoprics, which were established in western Europe during the last 150 years of Roman rule, survived. With no law, order, or economy to support the church, the lives of bishops were sparse, harsh, and sometimes violent, yet their institutional place survived, and some lived quite well.

Far more vulnerable than the bishops were the people. The marauding tribes sought a better life, better climate and land. If the people living in their path were lucky enough to survive, they lost either their land and everything they possessed, which meant they had to leave, or they were robbed of the food and supplies the tribes needed to support their journey. In any case, people had to endure enormous risk, and were constantly forced to fight or flee. Every winner produced losers and those who survived moved on to destabilize other regions. Whether they had been settled in an area for generations or just a year, people lived under fear of another invasion. Plant a field or build a hut, and your work would probably be stolen or destroyed.

Occasionally a particularly strong leader would assemble fierce warriors and determined peasants and would establish a measure of stability. What developed were essential ingredients of feudalism: the warrior leader and fierce warriors protected the peasants. These relationships grew over time as did the areas that were stabilized, but feudalism was not systematized until early in the 9th century, after the death of Charlemagne.

All of this makes sense to the modern reader, except the length of time these conditions continued. A hundred years, even a couple hundred years seems possible. But 600 years! How could Europe's ancestors not have established economic and political order sooner? Having destroyed Roman culture, leaders had to invent new laws and forms of governance. That took time. In addition, ancient problems such as how to assure the orderly transfer of power from one generation to the next were especially disruptive during this period of general instability. But most importantly, invasions by northern peoples did not cease for over 400 years. And not only did the tribal migrations cause chaos throughout the West, they proceeded chaotically. There were no leaders who planned the assaults. The Visigoths and Ostrogoths did not get together and decide who would take which regions. Various tribes warred with each other as well as the indigenous people.

Consider Italy. The Visigoths invaded Italy in 410 and the Huns (who were not even Germanic) in 451. The Ostrogoths waged war in Italy from 488 until 493, when they established their rule but it lasted for only 33 years. When the Visigothic king died, the country fell into disarray; and the Byzantine Emperor, always longing to reunite the empire, launched an invasion that won some small territories but did little for the people living on the peninsula. In 568, the Lombards conquered Italy although they were so few in number that they never took Rome or Naples.

From 410 to 568 Italy was in a nearly constant state of war, but to what end? The Lombards established a capital at Pavia, the pope retained the capital of Christianity in Rome, and the Byzantine Emperor installed a capital at Ravenna. Not only was the Roman Empire destroyed, the peninsula was partitioned. None of the three conquerors could grasp control, so they all, but most significantly the popes, began years of political intrigue in which they attempted to establish alliances that would provide a final advantage. This strategy was at the heart of the close ties of the Church to the Franks.

The Franks, who settled around the lower Rhine during the 4th century were unique for two reasons. They were the first Germanic tribe to expand their territories rather than migrate. In addition, they were the only major Germanic tribe that converted to orthodox Christianity rather than Arianism. However, the pope and especially some Frankish bishops worked very hard for that conversion. Led by Clovis, who the French consider their first king, the Franks established what was known as the Merovingian Empire which from 507 included what is now France and parts of Germany. The Visigoths lost southern France to Clovis in 507 but controlled what we now call Spain from then until 711. It would appear that the West had secured enough stability to see the end of the Dark Ages. Each story, early medieval France and early medieval Spain, provides archetypes of political inadequacy.

By the time Clovis moved his capital from Soissons to Paris, the Merovingian Empire seemed ready to provide vast stability, but one of the great political inadequacies of the world weakened and ultimately destroyed it. The Merovingians had no system of succession. Upon his death, Clovis's four sons established four capitals. One son, Lothair, survived his brothers and re-united the Merovingian Empire; but his four sons created three kingdoms: Austrasia, Neustria, and Burgundy. This pattern continued. Strength was always located in the person, whether Clovis or Lothair or Lothair II. Ultimately, personal frailty and legal inadequacy led to decentralization and collapse. The same pattern was followed by the Carolingians who began with Charles Martel (c. 689-741) whose army defeated the Moslems which limited their expansion in western Europe to Spain. His son, Pepin the Short, who defeated the last of the Merovingian kings, was followed by Charlemagne (742-814) whose empire was so vast and powerful that it appeared to have ended everything dark in the Dark Ages. But the greatness of the Carolingian Empire merely reflected the greatness of their leaders, and Charlemagne's sons were normal. In 787, 27 years before Charlemagne's death, the first recorded raid by Danes occurred in England, and in 856 the Danes launched a full invasion of Europe. Even if the Carolingian line had continued to produce great leaders, the Viking invasion would have extended the Dark Ages for 200 years.

The Vikings engulfed Ireland and established rule in England north of the Thames and Leu Rivers (878). Because the Vikings ruled the sea, they were able to invade the continent via sea ports and major rivers. They took Utrecht, Paris, Nantes, Bordeaux, Hamburg, and Seville. They entered the Mediterranean (843) from the west and Swedes from Russia invaded Constantinople.

Feudalism was systematized in France as an attempt to bring enduring order to this final, devastating chaos. Not surprisingly, this new political system bound people to the land which ended the migrations, but it did so in ways that also defined each family's permanent place in society. It established rules of inheritance, but in ways that destroyed wealth. The system's goal was to establish peace and security in a time of constant war. Understandably, kings, lords, and peasants benefitted from this system and accepted the loss of liberty. When trapped in a state of constant war, liberty seems less important than peace and security. However once peace and security were established, the long struggle for liberty began.

Because Spain played an enormous role in mediating the relationship between medieval Europe and the Moslem world, it is important to note Spain and Islam's development. In addition, medieval Spain and Islam provide images of what Europe would become. And medieval Europe provides images of what Spain and Islam would become.

In 466, 10 years before the fall of Rome, the Visigoths began their rule of what is now southern France and Spain. At the time, Spain was populated by the old Gallo-Romans, Christians, Jews, and the survivors of early Germanic migrations, the Vandals, Sueves, and Alans. In 507, the Merovingian king Clovis drove the Visigoths over the Pyrenees. Nonetheless, from 507 until their defeat by the Moslems in 711, the Visigothic kings provided considerable stability, especially after 587 when they and their people converted to orthodox Christianity from Arianism. This conversion permitted the integration of Spanish culture and the emergences of a common Latin based language. Although Spain did not flourish under the Visigoths, it faired better than most of Europe and enjoyed enough stability to produce the greatest intellectual of the Dark Ages, Isidore of Seville.

Isidore of Seville (560-636), was a bishop, theologian, historian, and scientist. If any Christina intellectual who lived after the 4th century should be declared a Doctor of the Church, Isidore should probably be included. He wrote the most important surviving history of the Visigoths, but his greatness was assured by his major work, *Etymologiae*. Today we would call this work an encyclopedia. Structured as lexical analysis, it compiled the inherited knowledge of his age. It was, without a challenge, the greatest intellectual achievement in the West during this period and for 500 years provided the major textual link between medieval European intellectuals and the ancient (Greek, Roman, and Arabic) world.

In 600 (13 years after converting to orthodox Christianity) the Visigothic rulers forced Spanish Jews to accept Christian baptism. Just as Visigothic Spain was taking shape, it manifested its greatest weakness and the Moslem world that would replace it was being born.

Mohammed was born in 570, and committed to a religious life in 610. The first year of the Moslem era is 622. From 632 to 738, Islam expanded beyond Arabia, conquering Spain in 711. Early on, Islam was open, curious, rational, and tolerant. The Moslems (*Moriscos* or Moors,) permitted Spanish Jews to flourish and treated Christians far better than they had treated the Jews. Intellectual life, especially philosophy, mathematics, science, and medicine flourished as they did throughout Islam. Because Charles Martel's army halted Moslem expansion into Europe, Spain did not participate in the Western experience during the late Dark Ages and early High Middle Ages. Consequently, we do not discuss Spain again until we begin to review the Thirty Years War in chapter four. We might conclude here our review of their medieval history.

In the late 900's Islam began an inexorable decline that saw it become as closed and religiously ideological as medieval Christianity and far more politically passive than Christians and Germanic peoples. Eventually, the light went out in Islam. Thus weakened, the Moors lost their control of Spain.

In 1478 the orthodox Catholic monarchs, Ferdinand V (1452-1516) and Isabella I (1451-1504), established the Spanish Inquisition.[3] They used it as a tool to expel the Jews (1492) and Moors (1502) from Spain. They believed that the unity provided by a single, national religion would maximize their authority. But the expulsion of the Jews and Moors left Spain so impoverished intellectually, economically, and technologically, that it largely destroyed Spain's future. The history of Spain and Islam has made it clear that dogmatic religions (whatever their names) cannot provide the principles of government that assure justice and safety in public life.

Enduring political solutions marked the *end* of the Dark Ages in the rest of Europe and therefore do not provide the major topic of interest to our discussion of the period. After noting the widespread political chaos and economic disaster that created the Dark Ages, we turn to the definitive achievement of the Dark Ages, Christianity. In spite of the well founded modern inclination to distrust organized religion, more often than not we are supported psychologically by a faith, however vague, that human life and work are not doomed to ultimate obliteration. We benefit from Christianity's victory over the ultimately dissatisfying pagan

---

[3]Astonishingly, the Spanish Inquisition persisted as an official extension of the Spanish monarch's authority until 1834.

explanations of the meaning of life. We might be interested in how that victory was won. Even more important to our purpose, we must note that Christianity provided vital answers to personal and political ethical questions.

The Attraction of Christianity to the Germanic People

One of the great achievements of Christianity was inherited from the Jewish tradition, the Ten Commandments. What was so unique about the Ten Commandments was not that they were issued by God but that only the first three commandments instructed humans regarding how they were to act toward God in order to stay on good terms. The next seven commandments instructed humans regarding how they were to treat one another in order to retain God's favor. These rules were not written by attorneys or politicians. There were no loop holes. Humans were not instructed, Thou shalt not steal, unless you encounter fools in which case you are obligated to separate them from their wealth. The command was clear, direct, and unequivocal. It applied to everyone: Thou shalt not steal. It is impossible to overestimate the impact of the Ten Commandments as ethical imperatives that advanced the humanization of Western culture. Everyone is responsible and everyone is protected. The Jewish and Christian traditions provide the intellectual and ethical *foundation* for the notion of the dignity and worth of every individual.

In addition, Christianity provided social and spiritual teachings that went far beyond the capacity of pagan religions. Among the most important were: the church's contribution to secular rule, the Christianization of the heroic myth, and the dignity that Christianity placed on labor. But before we look at those achievements, it is important to notice that church leaders were careful and skillful when dealing with their conquerors.

Clever Christian Leaders Neutralize the Opposition

Central to the relationship between Christian leaders and their Germanic conquerors was the Christian orientation toward what Augustine of Hippo[4] called the city of God as opposed to the city of man. Early Christianity concerned itself far more with eternal life, the hereafter,

---

[4]Saint Augustine of Hippo (354-430) was born in North Africa, educated in the classics, and converted to Christianity as an adult. A Doctor of the Church, few rival his impact on Christian theology.

than the physical and political world. In their initial relationships with Germanic leaders, church leaders were very cautious. In addition, Augustine had taught that the authority of both church and state leaders flow from God. Rather than challenge the authority of Germanic leaders, Church leaders provided them with a new, religious source for their authority.

Christianity was born in the Roman Empire: proud, powerful, pagan, and cruel. During the first three centuries of Christianity's existence, Christians were frequently executed. However, during the fourth century, the Emperor Constantine first tolerated (313) then gave full support to Christianity (c. 324). Christian martyrdom ended and martyred men, women, and children became heroic figures in Christian lore. But to my knowledge there is no record of Christians longing for a new martyrdom. When Rome fell to the Germanic peoples, the church lost the support of Roman rule and the Roman legions. Church leaders fully understood the dangers they faced and quickly shifted their allegiance from Rome to their Germanic conquerors.

As Roman rule collapsed, church leaders exercised considerable skill placating the conquerors. One can speculate with confidence that had the bishops exhibited the arrogance toward the Germanic rulers, warriors, and people during the Dark Ages that they exhibited during the Renaissance, Christianity would have gone the way of Roman law and political institutions. The caution and accommodation that Christian bishops showed toward the Germanic people, especially during the early centuries of the Dark Ages, provides an important contrast between early Christianity and the Christianity that ushered in the Protestant Reformation. Not only did Christian bishops serve their Germanic conquerors, they made sure that Christianity served the Germanic people. Christian liturgy accommodated images from Germanic mythic lore rather than rejecting and dismissing them. The attitude and skill of Christian leaders during the early part of the Dark Ages cannot be underestimated as crucial to the Christianization of the West.

The Church's Contribution to Germanic Rulers

Eventually the role of clerics expanded from placating Germanic leaders to teaching and providing administrative skills. The education of church *leaders* during the Dark Ages should not be exaggerated, but they could read and write and possessed organizational skills through the inherited influence of Rome. As Germanic rule took form, the warrior kings needed someone to provide and read written records and help with organizational problems. Church leaders were glad to help, and thereby established the church's foothold into political power in the medieval world. The educational and administrative services provided by clerics laid the foundation for the close ties of church and state that would dominate Western political institutions for well over a thousand years.

In addition, Christian teachings that the authority of both religious and political leaders flows from God provided Germanic tribal leaders with a far more stable and extensive authority than a warrior king could ever imagine. For that stature, Germanic kings and chiefs accepted Christianity and happily stamped out minor heresies. One of the earliest examples of this relationship developed between French bishops and Clovis, King of the Franks.

Around 480, church leaders began to cultivate their relationship with the young warrior in order to manipulate, for their purposes, his opposition to the Arian[5] form of Christianity that won a following among nearly all of the major Germanic tribes. In 481, Clovis became King of the Franks and began to build a disciplined army. Bit by bit he conquered territories that extended east to the Rhine and west to the Atlantic until he was faced by the Arian Visigoths in the south, along the Lorie river.

In 493, Clovis married a Burgundian princess who was Christian. She converted him. In 496, his army defeated the Germans near Cologne, which established his power on both sides of the Rhine. On Christmas day of that year he and 3000 of his followers were baptized in Rheims. When Clovis finally crossed the Lorie, he enjoyed the support of Christian bishops living in the territories controlled by the Visigoths.

We notice that prior to 500, the modern boundaries of France were largely defined. Its ancient peoples (the Gauls) and their descendants, Gallo-Romans, and the Germanic invaders (the Franks) were united in a common culture that was based on Christianity and which established an alliance between bishops and the rulers.

---

[5]Arianism taught that God-the-Son and God-the-Father were separate beings distinct from one another, which of course violated the monotheistic tradition. It derived its named from its founder Arius (c. 280-336), a priest from Alexandria, Egypt, and was refuted by St. Athanasius (c. 293-373), a theologian whose *Athanasian Creed* defined the authoritative Christian view of the Trinity.

These, however, are the stories of politics. If the people not been converted to Christianity, Christian bishops and kings would not have enjoyed their tremendous power and influence. Even more important to our interests, Christianity provided psychological and sociological assurances that formed communal foundations for Western culture. Christian faith and values could never have been imposed on the people by religious or political leaders. During both the first invasion that ended in the sixth century (known generally as the Germanic tribal migrations) and the second invasion (the Viking invasion) that ended in the tenth century, every tribe adopted either Arian or orthodox Christianity in the midst of their military conquests. We must be curious about how the religion of conquered peoples continuously defeated the religion of the conquerors. It seems that Christianity offered special attractions to everyone.

The Christianization of the Heroic Myth

We have already seen the attraction that Christianity presented to Germanic kings. It vested their authority in the authority of God and built an alliance with church leaders. In addition, Germanic myth and Christianity shared considerable similarities. The Christianization of the Germanic myth consisted largely of translating Germanic imagery and rituals into Christian symbols and liturgy. Both Christian and Germanic myths were interested in heroes who were real historical figures. The stories of warrior heroes told around the fire at night were easily translated into stories of the lives of Jesus and the saints. Germanic religious rituals followed the sequence and rhythms of the agricultural year. They were easily translated into Christian liturgy which also was based on the agricultural cycle.

The conversion of the warrior class to Christianity is especially impressive for it was they who received the greatest esteem and benefit from the ancient myths. But they found even greater meaning in Christianity. As I have mentioned, death raises troubling questions. Life is filled with pain, suffering, and loss, especially in periods such as the Dark Ages. Conscious of pain and dreading death, we ask, How can a life that we did not choose, that causes us pain and suffering and ultimately ends in death, how can this life be meaningful?

The Germanic people answered these questions by immortalizing the heroic acts of their warriors. Warrior heroes who endured the most extreme forms of life's pain, ennobled suffering by accepting, facing, and in some ways defeating it through courage. They were not helpless victims of death. They killed and were killed by each other. They were the masters of each others death. They may not have been able to choose their birth or alter the inevitability of their death, but they could choose how to die. And they could deliver the death blow. Everyone participated in their valor and saw their lives ennobled and empowered by their heroes. But let's face it. Who knew better than living heroes the depth of fear, the longing to live, and in the dark of night before the battle how little solace came from the notion that they might be remembered or that they had killed others. Each warrior knew many brave men who died and were forgotten. Each dreaded his disappearance in death. Christianity provided profound comfort to these men.

A Christian is not alone. There is a God who lives outside the world, outside of time and space, who is free from death and suffering, and who created us and all that is. This God knows and loves each one of us. But more than that, God understands that we fear death and resent pain. Therefore God sent the Son, Jesus, to live as we live, to suffer and die as we do, but most of all to tell us that our suffering is not futile because we never truly die. The Son has told us that death is but a passage to a new and better life, with God in eternity. In Jesus, God gave us a new answer to the death question, and a new hero, the Son of God, a man of uncommon courage and generosity. Jesus was a real living human who brought the message of love. He comforted and healed his brothers and sisters, was betrayed by a friend, and was scourged and mocked and crucified with thieves. The son of God shared all of our suffering and showed us "how a brave man dies on a tree."[6] And then he rose from the dead and joined his Father in heaven for eternity. That is how Christians can live and what they can look forward to.

Even 20th century non-believers can understand how Christianity was able to convert Germanic warriors as it had the Romans, Greeks and Ethiopians: The hero who died that his people might live translated the ultimate heroic act of Germanic lore into an eternal heroic act.

Importantly, the changes accepted by the Germanic warriors were eschatological in nature. They still were warriors. The transformation of their personal ethics into the idealized ethics of Christian knights, to the extent that it happened at all, took centuries and constitutes the

---

[6] Ezra Pound, "The Ballad of the Goodly Fere."

enchanting lore of chivalry. But the Germanic warriors clearly adopted the new eschatology, and the people followed, but not blindly.

Church Respect for Folk Ways

As mentioned earlier, during the Dark Ages, church leaders respected the people just as they were clever with the rulers. Bishops did not reject the peoples' myths or crush their symbols. Christopher Dawson provides an emblematic incident:

> In many cases the local pagan cult was displaced only by the deliberate substitution of the cult of a local saint . . . the Bishop of Javols put an end to the annual pagan festival of the peasants at Lake Helanus by building a church to St. Hilary of Poitiers . . . to which they could bring the offerings which had formerly been thrown into the sacred lake.[7]

Rather than insisting that the people stop treating the lake as sacred, the bishop built a church that became as compelling an attraction as the lake, and as psychologists might say, the people transferred their sense of the sacred from the lake to the church. Very clever, very accommodating.

It is also notable that the saint who was honored in this story was a woman. Similarly, the role of Mary the mother of Jesus and the lives of the many women saints offered a special attraction to German women. The heroines in Germanic lore were matched by the stature of Mary; Ann, Mary's mother; Mary Magdalene; Elizabeth, the mother of John the Baptist; Anastasia, the 4th century martyr, and many others.

Christian Respect for Labor

Christianity's unique impact upon peasants resulted from the spread of monasteries. The Benedictine rule, which eventually dominated all European monasteries, defined in precise detail the daily lives of the monks. It defined specific schedules for prayer, study, *and work*. Treating work as equal in importance to prayer and study provided a shift in social values of revolutionary proportions. The Germanic warrior culture, like Rome, treated peasants and laborers with no regard. But monks did peasants' work and invested it with sacramental respect. They made labor an essential part of their service to God, a form of prayer. The Germanic peasants were impressed. They formed a bond with the church

[7]*Religion and the Rise of Western Culture*, (p. 34).

unique in the history of their class. Throughout its history, Europe's peasants have maintained a deep, personal attachment to Christianity.

Early Christianity created an unprecedented kind of cultural unity in Europe: the warrior kings and nobles, swept up in the new religion, identified with Christ and the saints. The daily administration and emerging educational programs for the ruling class were provided by bishops and monks; and the peasants' lives were ennobled by the monastic value of labor. The spirituality, usefulness, and humanism of Christianity during a time of enormous personal suffering accounts for its dominance. The dignity and worth of every human, the dignity of labor, the responsibility of the leader to the people, and the ultimate meaning and purpose of life were defined by Christianity in terms that persisted in the West for over a thousand years. Some of these shared values were rooted in Germanic lore, but even those were enhanced by Christianity.

Western civilization was constructed on psychological and sociological foundations that were profoundly dependent upon Christianity. From Christianity, individuals received motivation to work, build society, and conduct their lives with regard for both God and each other. Christianity's impact on the conscious and unconscious psyche of Westerners has persisted into the late 20th century. As the second millennium ends and the third begins, we must notice that each generation seems to base its faith less and less on a personal relationship to a personal God, and more and more on vague, impersonal assurances that something nice follows death. We must wonder if such assurances are as sustainable as a personal relationship to a loving God. If not, we must wonder if Western societies can retain their most essential characteristics when these religious foundations disappear from our individual and collective psyches.

Importantly, that problem is new. The continuing significance of Christianity in the daily lives of all social classes provided psychological and cultural stability during the High Middle Ages and Renaissance when intellectual issues began to divide theology and the university. We turn now to the story of intellectual life in the Middle Ages.

3

Intellectual Life in the Middle Ages

Before turning to specific intellectual issues and achievements of the Middle Ages, it is important to set the stage. We must recognize the extent and cause of the church's dominance of learning during this period. The unique cultural place of the church has already been described in terms of religion and secular governance. When we recall the chaos that dominated life during the Dark Ages, we are not inclined to inquire about who competed for control of intellectual life. Rather we ask, How was it possible to have any intellectual life at all? Who had the time or the place or the security to conduct intellectual activity? Not surprisingly, the answer to that question is found in the major institutional achievement of the Dark Ages: the monastery. But once again it is important to distinguish the Dark Ages from the High Middle Ages because early in the High Middle Ages, universities replaced monasteries as centers of learning.

Monasteries and convents provided the most stable and productive settings existent during the Dark Ages. Monks and nuns could grow enough food for their community and still permit others to work on construction, black smithing, food preparation, crafts, and study. During the Dark Ages, there was virtually no intellectual activity outside of monasteries and, therefore, no secular intellectual activity for the church to suppress. The Dark Ages were not dark because the church suppressed the light of reason. The Dark Ages were dark because civil chaos destroyed productivity and thereby prevented the advancement of learning.

Importantly, monastic study during the Dark Ages was only marginally informed by Greek and Roman thought because only fragments[1] of Greek

---

[1]MacIntyre, *After Virtue*, p. 1. The major source for this chapter is MacIntyre's *Three Rival Versions of Moral Inquiry*. My original writing of material contained in this chapter developed study guides in which I was careful not to translate MacIntyre's language into mine and unconsciously lose his meaning. A close examination of the two texts would likely reveal that I have failed to identify quotations from his text. MacIntyre has generously permitted this use of his work.

and Roman texts survived the Germanic conquests. As civil society deteriorated cities were abandoned. Rome for instance was reduced from a population of half a million to 50,000. Those who stayed suffered hunger and lawlessness. Mobs formed, sometimes comprised of Christians, and one of the atrocities they committed was the destruction of libraries. However, popes, bishops, and monasteries preserved scripture, scriptural commentaries, and the texts of the Doctors of the church all of whom but one were born between 329 (Basil) and 354 (Augustine).[2]

From Origen (185-254) to Augustine, early Christianity's great scholars were educated in the classics. It is probably more accurate to say that they developed rather than studied early Christian theology. Furthermore they acknowledge that scriptural study was impossible without secular learning especially history, geography, rhetoric, grammar (including diction and syntax), and various methods of textual analysis. Origen even considered mathematics, astrology, and music essential to the study of scripture. But that kind of scholarship could not be conducted during the Dark Ages except in isolated instances such as Isidore enjoyed in Spain. Monastic scholarship is better understood in terms of the location of study in monasteries, the scriptorium and library.

The major intellectual achievements of monks in the Dark Ages was to copy and preserve scriptural texts and the commentaries and other works of the fathers of the church. Beyond that, they read scripture using what might be called literal interpretation. When forced to speak on theological questions, some monks and bishops could quote the Doctors of the Church, but there was little of what one would call formal study of theology and speculative theology was nonexistent. In order to study medieval intellectual activities, we must leave the Dark Ages and enter the High Middle Ages.

The Dark Ages ended shortly after the turn of the first millennium. When we say that one cultural era has ended and another begun, we claim that the foundations, goals, and structure of society have changed. That is precisely what began to happen in the late 900's and to accelerate after 1050. Widening political stability permitted substantial economic growth outside the monestary. With stable economic growth came the rebirth of what most of us think of as culture: cities were formed, crafts grew,

---

[2]The lone exception was Gregory the Great (540-604).

technology expanded, trading fleets were launched to bring goods from the East, and universities were founded. The growth of cities provided a new challenge to the authority of kings, and the growing influence of both cities and states threatened the authority and stature of bishops and the pope. Not surprisingly, the history of this period typically focuses on politics, war, economics, and travel. However none of those topics count quite so much to our investigation as the growth of universities and the intellectual events that took place in them.

Early medieval universities worked off of the body of knowledge, mostly theology, that had been preserved in monasteries. Although compared to the libraries in the Byzantine and Moslem worlds, these collections were sparse, but they provided a significant starting point for early Western scholars. The great interest of these scholars was in theology, and texts by the Doctors of the Church had to be mastered and taught. Recalling that the Doctors were educated in the classics, the first medieval scholars must have been out of their depth trying to interpret these erudite early Christian works. But every year brought more help, for while Western monks groped through the Dark Ages, intellectuals in the Byzantine world and Islam thrived. In the East, nearly the entire body of Greek and Roman learning was kept alive and enhanced by Eastern European, Arabic,[3] and Hebrew scholars. As Europe made its way out of the Dark Ages and established more and more contact with the East and Spain, European scholars gained access to classical texts that helped them engage the Doctors' texts.

Attempts to engage the writings of the Doctors of the church required classical learning, especially Plato and Aristotle. And the Doctors' texts along with Isidore's *Etymologaie* provided links to the ancient world. Not surprisingly, Augustine of Hippo, the most prolific of the Doctors, had enormous influence on early medieval scholars. But as the writings of Plato, Aristotle, and later Averroës became better known, they began to exert independent influence. Because Plato had so much influence on Augustine, his work was almost automatically reinterpreted in Augustinian terms. But the views of Aristotle and Averroës contradicted Augustine. In the 13th century the conflict among proponents of Augustine, Aristotle,

---

[3] Averroës (1126-98) was a major Arabian philosopher whose commentaries on Aristotle helped precipitate the conflict between theology and the arts at the University of Paris. Aquinas was called to Paris to help resolve that dispute.

and Averroës came to a head. We give special attention to Augustine whose work set the stage for the conflict and St. Thomas Aquinas who solved it and in doing so charted a whole new course for Western scholarship.

Augustine's Complex Influence on Western Knowledge

Augustine lived during Rome's decline, not after its collapse. He was educated in the Greek and Roman classics and made great use of Platonic thought. He was the most influential Christian theologian prior to St. Thomas Aquinas, and his influence has extended into the present. He is also the most controversial of the Doctors of the Church. His intellectual life constituted a complex journey during which he rejected his mother's Christianity; adopted the Manichaean religion; became enamored of the Greeks, *especially Plato*; converted to Christianity and developed the Christian views for which he is famous; and then let himself wander into extreme speculation for which he is infamous. Plato influenced his famous work, the Manichees his infamous.

Our interest is with the epistemology of his sound work. However, we must acknowledge his excesses for, to the misfortune of his reputation, they inspired Duns Scotus to reject the achievements of Aquinas and polarize Christian theology in the 14th century. They have also inspired some contemporary conservative Christians activists whose conduct in the public square polarizes ethical discourse and threatens civil society. In addition, late 20th century feminist theologians have exposed this strand of Augustine's work as providing the theological basis for a Christian anthropology that has been destructive to the spiritual development and ethical stature of women throughout the history of Christianity.[4] Augustine is a theologian worth studying. First we look at his famous work, then his infamous.

Platonic-Augustinian Idealism

Plato believed that ultimate being and good are located outside the physical world. He called this place the realm of ideas. If the ultimate reality of physical objects and events exists in a transcendent realm of ideas, then the direct study of physical objects and events can only provide a secondary kind of knowledge. For example, consider the reality of

---

[4]See, for example, I. Gebara and M. Bingemer, *Mary Mother of God, Mother of the Poor.*

chair. We can look at individual chairs and notice significant and incompatible differences. Individual, physical chairs are either rocking chairs or straight back wooden chairs, or typing chairs, etc. Each physical chair can manifest only a single type of chair or a small portion of the reality of *chair*. Only the *idea chair*, as Plato would say, contains all of the possibilities of all individual chairs and *therefore the idea of any object is more real than any single example or expression of it.* This epistemology is called idealism. In idealism, the singular, physical object is set in contradistinction to the universal, abstract idea. It is helpful to remember those terms and their opposition: singular, physical vs. universal, abstract.

When idealism is thought of in these terms, the physical world takes on a fairly neutral, benign place in our lives, as it did in Plato's philosophy. The physical world is not evil, but it is inferior or insignificant in comparison to the ideal. Paying attention to the physical world can be interesting, but it can never lead to the fulness of human life which is to establish some form of communion with the ideal.

Augustine made two significant changes to the work of Plato. First, he moved the location of the good from the realm of ideas to the mind of God. According to Augustine, the fullness of being, the good, resides in the divine mind. Second, whereas Plato identified philosophy as the link between humans and the realm of ideas, Augustine taught that humans find truth in their relationship with God through: 1) faith, the acceptance of Jesus as the son of God and the savior, 2) God's revelations that have been provided through the teachings of Jesus which are contained in scripture, and 3) the flow of grace from the Holy Spirit.

In this part of Augustine's work and throughout the Dark Ages, grace and faith were treated as rather beyond human capacity to understand and therefore were not given tremendous attention in intellectual inquiry. Both were essential to the life of every Christian, but each operated at the personal level in humans with the mysterious participation by God. However, after publishing these views, Augustine seems to have become conflicted, either directly with his old friends the Manichees or within himself.

The Augustinian/Manichaean Controversy

Pressed by his conflict with Manichaean views (whether in actual or reflective dialog), Augustine advanced some extreme arguments that have survived as deeply problematic in Christian theology. Aquinas and other supporters of Augustine ignored these lines of his work which benefitted his reputation. Others such as Duns Scotus expanded these arguments to the detriment of Augustine and Christianity. Of course, none of these discussions would have troubled Christianity if they had been confined to speculative theology where they belong. Instead, they have been incorporated into dogmatic theology and ethical instruction. In any event, we need to know about the Manichaean influence on Augustine's extreme views because these topics remain unresolved in Christianity, continue to haunt ethical discourse, and provide essential background to the conflict between Thomists and Duns Scotus that destroyed medieval theology.

The Manichees were interested in the presence of good and evil in nature and human lives. They faced the question, How do we understand God when we cannot help but notice that evil often seems to be more present and powerful than good? If God is all powerful and all good, why does he tolerate so much evil? The question seems to demand that we acknowledge that either God is not all that good or that he is indifferent and remote (not present, loving, and caring) or that he is not all powerful. Considering the characteristics of God that seem to be compromised by this question, it makes sense that they would give up his power. We certainly would not want to give up his goodness, presence, and care. And that is what the Manichees did. They gave up God's power claiming that evil is coexistent with God. In other words, just as God exists, so does evil. Each exists as separate beings; each possesses its own essence.

Augustine had accepted this view early in his intellectual life, before he knew the Greeks, but he rejected it when he adopted the Platonic position that being and good by definition exist as one. (Recall that Augustine placed *being and good* in the mind of God.) While influenced by Plato, he argued that *evil does not exist in itself.* Evil occurs when humans turn away from God and the good and perform evil acts. *Humans must will evil for evil to exist.* These arguments make great sense in themselves, but they are incompatible with the concept of original sin advanced by St. Paul.[5]

Paul taught that the sin of Adam caused all humans to be *born in sin* which means that every person requires redemption. But that means that sin exists in each of us independent of our will or deeds. The Manichees were particularly interested in the problem of good and evil. When

[5] See Paul's Letter to the Romans, Chapter 5.

Augustine tried to resolve the differences between Paul's personal notion of original sin with the Manichees' questions about the nature of God as understood in the context of the prevalence of evil, he abandoned the Platonic notion that evil is entirely dependent upon individual acts committed by humans and has no necessary and separate existence of its own. Augustine rejected the teachings of Pelagius (c. 350-425) who claimed that infants are innocence at birth, *before* baptism.

The combined views of St. Paul, Pelagians, and the Manichees brought three major theological problems to the center of debate: 1)How was the sin of Adam transmitted to all other humans? 2) How does original sin manifest itself in and impact the ethical life of the person? and 3) How is the activation of this sinfulness reconciled with free will? Fortunately, we only have to notice these problems; we do not have to solve them. Even modern moral theology, so long as it allows St Paul's view of original sin to shape the debate, handles these questions poorly. When Augustine allowed Paul's text to shape the issues for him, he gave some very problematic answers to these questions: 1) Sin is transmitted through the sex act which is the source of each person's life. This answer has created huge problems with the inherent nature (goodness) of sex and of course the sexuality and nature of women. 2) Original sin makes each of us incapable of redemption without faith in Jesus and incapable of moral conduct without grace. 3) The necessity of grace precludes free will, Augustine actually admitted to a form of predestination.

Importantly, speculative theology did not occupy the attention of monks in the monasteries of the Dark Ages or scholars in the early medieval universities that drew from Augustine's more moderate period. These issues resurfaced in speculative theology during the 14th century and were part of church dogma by the Protestant Reformation. They continue to be problematic.

The Epistemology of the Early Medieval University

Early medieval scholars did not encounter the epistemological problems that interest us. They worked confidently within powerful epistemological assumptions. Their *source of knowledge* was the divine mind. Their method of inquiry employed techniques that permit scholars to read, interpret, discuss, and explain sacred texts: history, geography, grammar, logic, rhetoric, dialectic, hermeneutics, and so on. These methods are important to note and some require later discussion, but the major point to be noticed here is that their source of knowledge was located in the universal exemplars of the divine mind.

Because theology is the discipline that studies these ultimate truths, early medieval scholars (c. 1050-1250)[6] grounded their work in two important claims: 1) Because all truth exists *and is unified* in the mind of God, all human knowledge must be integrated or unified in order even to make any claim to truth. 2) The final integration of knowledge is a task that only theology can achieve. The negative expression of these assumptions is that any claims that contradict each other or that cannot be accommodated in theology's great summary must be wrong or in some manner flawed.

It is important to note that in Augustine's epistemology, all truth exists in and comes from one God. There is only one truth and it does not depend upon individuals for its nature or content. It does not matter if you or I hear a tree fall in the woods, what matters is what God hears and knows. Truth does not depend upon what individuals perceive or do not perceive, know or do not know. What humans claim to know is only correct if those claims are consistent with the universal, unalterable truths that exist in the mind of God.

We could call the Christian epistemology that identified the source of truth with God *Christian idealism*, but we must be careful not to confuse it with Platonic or other forms of secular idealism. So we call it *revelation* and note its similarities to idealism. Revelation is the epistemology that locates the source of knowledge in the universal exemplars of the divine mind and gains access to that knowledge through God's revealed truths that are contained in sacred texts. Knowledge not touched upon in sacred texts has little hope of achieving truth, but demonstrates its inadequacy by being contradictory with other such knowledge or, even more fatally, by contradicting the truths of theology.

---

[6]Early medieval scholars worked in universities and monasteries. I distinguish them from the monks of the Dark Ages who worked only in monasteries and predated the founding of universities. Recall that universities were not founded until the High Middle Ages. So when I talk about medieval scholars we are out of the Dark Ages. I also distinguish the Augustinian scholars who used *revelation* as their epistemology and dominated the university from its inception to until around 1250 from Thomistic scholars who used *rationalism* and dominated the university from around 1250 until the 17th century. Thomistic scholars are also called *scholastic philosophers*.

Revelation is the first great epistemology in the Western intellectual tradition. No other epistemology matched its clarity and authority until the invention of modern science. For early Christians, *the source of truth is God*, just as for modern scientists, *the source of truth is nature*. Revelation's limits did not become evident until it was contrasted with later views. We turn to that discussion now.

St. Thomas, Rationalism, and the Scholastic Tradition

By the time Thomas Aquinas (1225-1276) began his career at the University of Paris in the middle of the 13th century, Greek and Arabic scholarship already dominated the attention of Western universities. Ironically, the isolation of Western Christianity from competing views, the classical training of the Doctors of the Church, and the authority of the Augustinian tradition within the church supported an eager acceptance of new knowledge. Six hundred years of being removed from legitimate secular challenges to Christian intellectual authority precluded paranoia. Only after ancient, Eastern, and Moslem texts entered the university and were studied in depth did their incompatibility with Christianity become known.

Once Christian scholars recognized the incompatibility of Eastern views with Christian teachings, they faced a profound dilemma. If they admitted that theology could not accommodate and enhance the new knowledge, they would in fact admit the inadequacy of the entire Augustinian system, the concept of the unity of knowledge in the universal exemplars of the divine mind, and the assumption that theology can integrate all knowledge. On the other hand, if they merely accepted Eastern (especially Aristotelian) views, they would create unresolvable contradictions in their body of knowledge. For these scholars, contradiction and incompatibility were a sure indication of error. Medieval scholars lived with a profound commitment to the unity of knowledge, a commitment that could not tolerate unresolvable contradictions. What ever they did, it seemed, they would dramatically undermine their deepest intellectual assumptions.

Aquinas Makes the West Safe for Reason

Thomas Aquinas's great achievement was that he constructed a philosophical accommodation between Aristotelian and Augustinian views and thereby secured the place of *reason* in the Western university. What Aquinas did is among the greatest achievements in the history of Western philosophy. But let me leave that judgement to the reader. I'll just tell the story and clarify the issues that are critical to our discussion. And it is a pretty good story.

Aristotle thought that the physical world was eternal, a concept quite unfriendly to biblical accounts of creation as the origin of life. Even more important, Aristotle's beliefs were based on reason. When reason enters the picture, it acts like a mirror in which theologians using revelation were able to see their methods for the first time. During the early period of the medieval university, few scholars suggested that Christian teachings were unreasonable or logically flawed.[7] But when Aristotle's teachings and the structure of his arguments were set side by side with Christian teachings, it became clear that revelation involves a deep, fundamental commitment to scripture as the primary source of knowledge and truth. As Western scholars studied Aristotle, they realized that their theology was based on a very different kind of logic than the reasoned arguments of Aristotle. Early medieval theology contained an internal logic, but that logic began with the revealed truths of scripture and the developing body of official church teachings. There were no questions regarding the rational defensibility of theology's *a priori* assumptions, for they were grounded in scripture. The ultimate or first intellectual or logical act of the early medieval scholar was an *act of faith*.

We have just identified an important distinction that even today impacts ethical inquiry and discourse, the difference and inevitable tensions between moral theology and religious moral philosophy. Moral theology grounds inquiry and discourse in sacred texts and uses reason as a tool. Religious moral philosophy grounds inquiry in reason and relies on sacred texts for *a priori* assumptions. When sacred texts defy reason, religious moral philosophers sometimes develop rational alternatives. That is what Augustine did in his famous work and failed to do in his infamous work. Moral theology and religious moral philosophy are sufficiently important distinctions to require different departments in the university, but from the perspective of the public square or other departments in the university, they seem almost indistinguishable. Moral

---

[7]Peter Abelard (1079-1142) was a major exception. Abelard was a brilliant logician who studied Aristotle and noted logical inconsistencies in Christian theology. He was silenced which points out an enduring problem in Christianity and the vital role that Aquinas played in the Western intellectual tradition.

philosophy simply cannot extricate itself from the theological traditions in which it is embedded. As a result, when religious moral philosophers attempt to engage theologians or philosophers from other religious traditions or secular moral philosophers, they encounter irreconcilable differences. But that problem did not become evident until the Protestant Reformation. During the High Middle Ages, Europe was still united in one form of Christianity. The challenge that threatened the university at this time was to accommodate Christianity with the very un-Christian teachings of the ancient world. Modern intellectuals must be interested in the fact that medieval scholars were more successful accommodating Christian knowledge with ancient knowledge than modern intellectuals have been accommodating diverse Christian views with each other or with secular inquiry.

When the deep contradictions between the teachings of the church and the teachings of the ancient world were discovered, all theological assumptions were threatened as was the logic of revelation. Because Christians were in power, these threats placed all classical knowledge in jeopardy. But again that dilemma: the Augustinian claim that theology is the queen of the sciences because it integrates all knowledge would be put at risk if Christians exercised some brutish authority and suppressed the vast body of Eastern knowledge. Everyone needed a solution. Aquinas provided it.

Aquinas demonstrated that there could be no difference between the conclusions of rational thought and the conclusions of revelation. God, he argued, would not create humans and give them a mode of thinking that at its best would not lead to God. To reveal the end of this drama before we tell the story, Aquinas developed a way of doing theology that used Aristotle's rational method to prove Christian truths. He resolved the incompatibility between Augustine and Aristotle and *made the West safe for reason.* In order to understand the immensity of this achievement, we must understand a bit about the method of inquiry used by Aristotle and Aquinas which is called rationalism.

Aristotelian/Thomistic Rationalism

Rationalism is much more clear regarding its logical method, which is called deductive reason, than it is regarding its source of knowledge. Deductive reason proceeds from the general to the specific through structured arguments, the classic form of which is called a syllogism. An example of a syllogism is:

> A. In the far north where there is snow year round, the bears are white.
> B. Novaya Zemlya is in the far north.
> C. The bears of Novaya Zemlya are white.[8]

The premises, the general statements that are given *prior* to the conclusion and upon which the conclusion is based, are sometimes referred to as *a priori* assumptions. The method that moves from *a priori* assumptions through logically ruled steps to what become incontestable conclusions is sometimes referred to as *a priori reasoning*, but the name we use is deductive reasoning. Importantly, if the premises of a deductive argument are accepted as true, then the conclusion must be accepted as true–so long as all of the rules of logic are followed. Thus:

> *If:* All bears in the far north where it snows year round are white,
> *And:* Novaya Zemlya is in the far north,
> *Then:* All of the bears in Novaya Zemlya *must be* white.

An important point to notice about deductive reason is that the premises are more general than the conclusion. Deductive reason moves from the general to the specific. Inductive reason, which provides the logical structure of empiricism, proceeds from the concrete to the abstract. This is no small matter; for, as we have seen, there is a fundamental conflict in philosophy between the universal/abstract and the singular/concrete. It would appear that at least at their starting points, deductive reasoning commits to the universal/abstract and that inductive reasoning commits to the singular/concrete. And in the context of the High Middle Ages, arguments that begin with the universal/abstract must compete with the intellectual authority of the universal exemplars of the divine mind that provide the source of knowledge in revelation. Whether moral philosophy can successfully replace the authority of the universal

---

[8] This syllogism was among those used by Lev Vygotsky and A.R. Luria in studying the impact of literacy on the logical habits and cognitive development of preliterate Soviet citizens. See A.R. Luria; *The Making of Mind: A Personal Account of Soviet Psychology*, p. 77.

exemplars of the divine mind is a questions that has not been answered to this day.

It is also important to notice that in rationalism, the focus of discourse is either on the premises or the structure of the conclusion. If one can prove that not all of the bears in the far north are white, or that Novaya Zemlya is not so far north that it snows year round, then the conclusion can be rejected. On the other hand, even if the premises are true, if the conclusion is not logically coherent with the premises, then the conclusion can be rejected. Had the conclusion been, "All white bears live in Novaya Zemlya," it could have been rejected, because that conclusion violates a rule of logic. Both the logical and linguistic structure of these arguments are such that if the first two are agreed upon, and the conclusion follows the rules of logic, then there is no rational basis for contesting the conclusion, with one exception. If a conclusion is reprehensible or simply not acceptable, then one is forced to revisit the assumptions, which is exactly the problem that deductive reasoning encountered in secular moral philosophy and the social sciences, but we are getting ahead of ourselves. For now we must look at Thomistic rationalism in theology and how it impacted inquiry throughout the medieval university.

The enormous change that Aquinas brought to Christian theology was that he used rationalism rather than revelation to argue the fundamental truths of Christianity. This new method is evident in Aquinas's five proofs of the existence of God. It is not necessary to look at each, for his method becomes clear with slight repetition. The *first* and *third* proofs are fairly easily understood in isolation.

1. A. Whatever is in motion is put in motion by another. It is impossible for a thing to be at once mover and moved. It is impossible for a thing at rest to move itself.

   B. And it is irrational or impossible to retrace a series of the moved and mover to infinity.

   C. Therefore: there must be a first mover, the unmoved mover which "everyone understands to be God."[9]

---

[9] *Summa Theologica*, Part I; Question II, The Existence of God; Article 3, Whether God Exists, (p. 12).

3. A. That which does not exist only begins to exist by something already existing.

   B. There must exist something which never came to exist and can never cease to exist, whose existence is necessary.

   C. Therefore we must admit the existence of some being having of itself its own necessity, and not receiving it from another, but rather causing in others their necessity. This "all men speak of as God," (ibid., p. 13).

Now it is important to remember that the point of this discussion is not to argue Aquinas's conclusions. This story is not about proving the existence of God. Rather it is about understanding rationalism, being able to describe how it differed from revelation, and explaining the enormous role that Aquinas played in the development of the Western intellectual tradition.

What we must notice in these two proofs is that none of Aquinas's arguments for the existence of God relies on scripture; rather, they employ an Aristotelian structure of knowing. And still they confirm the most fundamental assertions of Christian faith and Augustinian teachings regarding the existence of God and the belief that all things flow from and to God. By the time Aquinas is done with his five little arguments, aspects of Aristotelian teachings that are incompatible with Christianity (such as the infinity of physical existence) have been rationally refuted through rational proofs, *not by the imposition of scripture*. Just as important, Aristotle's rational method has been incorporated into Christian methods of inquiry. The impact of that achievement was not limited to theology. It profoundly and permanently transformed the Western intellectual tradition.

When Aquinas demonstrated the compatibility of the Aristotelian method with Christian teachings, he also proved that it was possible to bring the whole body of Greek and Arabic thought into reasonable coexistence with Christian teachings. He secured the place of Eastern thought and knowledge in the medieval university. This achievement made the West safe for reason, which is why I suggest that his might have been the single greatest achievement in Western philosophy. Had he failed, one can at least argue (and current events in countries dominated by religious fundamentalism support this point) Isaac Newton might never have risen above the considerable mechanical cleverness he showed as a child.

"But wait a minute!" you exclaim. "If Aquinas achieved a reasonable coexistence between the decidedly secular scholarship of the ancient world and Christianity, what happened? Why are Christianity and secular philosophy so much at odds seven hundred years later?" And I say, "Take it easy. I told you that this is a pretty good story." Three things happened: 1) The medieval university and the nature of inquiry underwent deep restructuring; 2) Theology took some positions that isolated it from the rest of the university; and 3) *Secular* philosophy encountered problems that plague it today–700 years later. First we turn to the restructuring of the university.

The Restructuring of the Medieval University

As we have noted, early medieval universities had very little knowledge to study, and all knowledge was organized under the queen of the sciences, theology. The whole surviving body of ancient Egyptian, Persian, Hebrew, and Greek scholarship as well as Byzantine, Arabic, and Jewish commentary arrived in Europe from the East in a relatively short period of time. Once arrived, it had to be accommodated without obliterating or vitiating a comparatively meager body of Western knowledge. Theology remained a permanent department, but out of necessity, students and teachers organized themselves around various areas of interest. The point is not that theology could no longer organize and direct all knowledge, for that conclusion had not yet been reached, and some theologians might argue even today that it is not true. What did become evident early on was that there was just too much knowledge to organize and study in one department. Knowledge was re-defined in terms of categories of content, and these categories formed the basis of departments that were created along side theology. Both teachers and students chose where to focus their attention.

Theologians continued to study scripture and to claim that theology could provide the ultimate meaning of all knowledge. Philosophers[10]

---

[10]For the purposes of this discussion, I use the term *theologians* to refer to all scholars working in theology and *philosophers* to refer to all scholars working in all other departments. Conventionally, they are *all* known as scholastic philosophers, but that term does not facilitate the distinctions I am trying to make.

formed other departments *secure in their Christianity and safe in their use of reason*. The task that these philosophers faced was so great, the content of Eastern knowledge so vast, that they had little time even to be curious about what was going on in theology. Importantly, the division of the medieval university into departments did not constitute a schism. The problems that developed rather soon after the death of Aquinas had nothing to do with these early, secular scholars. It had everything to do with theologians. The great theological crisis in the 14th century university did not involve theologians and philosophers. It involved theologians arguing incompatible theological views.

The Polarization of Medieval Theology

Soon after the death of Aquinas, Duns Scotus and his followers[11] reasserted the Augustinian view that humans are incapable of salvation without grace. The intellectualization of grace dramatically altered its role in theology and created a split between views that emphasized human dependence on grace as opposed to views that emphasized human freedom and responsibility. Duns Scotus and his followers defined salvation in terms of grace and dependence on God. Thomists defined salvation in terms of freedom and responsibility. A brief description of the two positions is adequate for our purposes.

The purpose of moral philosophy is to build consensus in the university and the public square regarding what is meant by ethical conduct. According to Aquinas, in order to achieve that consensus, moral philosophers must do two things: 1) Establish a system of ethical reasoning and use it to develop an ethical canon, and 2) Teach that system of ethical reasoning and its canon. The Thomistic tradition developed around the assumption that reason informs moral theology and moral philosophy. When philosophers identify and describe the nature and purpose of humanity, they describe humanity's ultimate good. Knowing the ultimate good allows philosophers to distinguish virtues (acts that lead to the good) from vices (acts that lead away from the good). This schematic: 1) The *good,* 2) *Virtues* that lead to the good, and 3) *Vices* that lead away from the good, describes the fundamental structure of both Aristotelian and Thomistic moral reasoning. We find it much more helpful to inquiry in education and the social sciences than one might imagine, for

---

[11]The followers of *Duns* Scotus were called *Dunces*. I have declined to use that term in reference to these scholars, an act that has required both reason and will.

it describes a structure of ethical inquiry that could contribute to the social sciences.

The application of this schematic in medieval moral theology and moral philosophy produced fairly predictable results. The ultimate purpose (good) of humanity is to gain salvation and live with God for eternity in heaven. The virtues that lead to eternal salvation are contained in the Ten Commandments; the Christian virtues of faith, hope, and charity; and the Greek virtues of justice, prudence, temperance, and courage. Vices include violations of the Ten Commandments and anything that leads the individual away from God or undermines the Christian life or community. Christian moral theology from the Dark Ages to the 20th century has placed more emphasis on defining sin and levels of sin than in explicating virtues, levels of virtues, and most important, the system of ethical reasoning that is capable of making these distinctions. This aberration of ethical inquiry has produced a substantial problem in ethical discourse.

Central to Aquinas's view is his belief that if people know what is best or right, they need no additional motivation or direction to act accordingly.[12] Nothing else makes sense, and to act otherwise, although possible, is to act irrationally and against one's nature. Not only is it God's command that we tell the truth, for instance; it is impossible to conduct relationships, business, or any aspect of society unless we tell the truth. To tell the truth is both a rational and an ethical imperative. MacIntyre is quite clear on this point:

> On Aristotle's account, as on Plato's, the human being who has acquired the necessary education in the intellectual and moral virtues and who thereby apprehends what his or her true good is acts so as to achieve that good. For Aristotle and Plato, as for other ancient writers, reason is an active goal-setting, goal-achieving power. Aquinas follows them . . . Aquinas, like Aristotle, can find no room for any question as to why, given that

---

[12]As we noted earlier, the psychological and sociological motivation to do what is good *as an individual and as a member of society* is a major issue in secular ethics. It may be impossible to separate Thomas's belief in eternal salvation from his assumptions regarding the motivation to do what is right. Aristotle and Plato may be more helpful to secular moral philosophers.

one recognizes that something is one's true good, one should act so as to achieve it. Neither further reason, nor (for the morally educated, virtue-informed person whose will is rightly ordered by the intellect) further motive, are either necessary or possible.[13]

We cannot help but notice that all of the rigor, inquiry, and education ascribed to the development of the ethical person has to do with discovering what is the right thing to do. The motivation that drives the will to act rightly seems to be contained in the energy of the reason which is activated by being educated to recognize the good. If that is the case, distinguishing virtues from vices constitutes an important part of educating the reason so that it can identify the good. By treating ethics as exclusively about avoiding vices, by developing and teaching prohibitive ethics, we ignore the role of reason and inhibit the development of its energy to seek what is good. However, there seems to be such a consistent focus of ethics on prohibitive rules rather than on educating the reason to identify and seek the good, that there must be some rather serious flaw in both religious and secular ethics. We gain some understanding of this issue in chapter seven.

Another ongoing controversy that became intractable and destructive in the 14th century has to do with free will. Fundamental to Thomistic ethics is the assumption that humans are free. This freedom is grounded in the understanding that reason allows humans to figure out right from wrong. These terms recur throughout this text. All humans are *capable* of reason and all humans are *free* to choose to do the right thing or to do the wrong thing; therefore, all humans are *responsible* for their conduct and salvation. For Duns Scotus and his followers, that conclusion placed reason in conflict with faith and especially grace.

Rather than admit that humans can know what is right and good from reason, Duns Scotus, stressed that humans can never know the truth of the divine mind by themselves. According to Duns Scotus, not reason but revelation, faith, and, most important, grace permit humans to distinguish good from evil. Part of Duns Scotus' argument is familiar to Western students of Platonic idealism. Plato emphasized that the body and senses rely solely on experiences in the physical world for the information used by reason to form knowledge. But physical objects are mere shadows,

---

[13]*Three Rival Versions*, (p. 154).

imitations, or *singular* examples of the full reality that exists in universal ideas. Since reason relies on the senses, its source of knowledge is physical objects. For idealists such as Plato, Augustine, and Duns Scotus, the universal and abstract must be given primacy over the singular and concrete. Plato did not consider the physical world evil, just uninteresting.

Duns Scotus, supported by the extreme views in Augustine, taught that the body is not only the source of error; it is also the source of evil. According to Duns Scotus, the soul must be filled with grace to distinguish good from evil and to fight the influence of the body. That fight is conducted by the soul's great asset, its will, which explains how humans earn salvation. Informed by grace and made resolute by the will, we perform the meritorious acts that *earn* salvation. Even today, the concrete simplicity of this view attracts many adults. It provides an ethical content that is easy to teach in a community of believers. It is especially effective in the ethical instruction of young children. However, it makes rational ethical discourse impossible in a faith community or the public square. The fundamental irrationality of the concrete orthodox ethics taught in conservative religious communities (whether Moslem, Jewish, Mormon, or Christian) explains the disruption and dangers presented by orthodox religious activism.

We can begin to appreciate the importance of Thomistic ethics. By asserting the efficacy of reason, Aquinas advanced the notion that humans can learn to act morally from the core of their physical nature. We must know our nature, not overcome it. To act naturally means to act morally, but we must pay considerable intellectual attention to understanding and describing what is natural and truly good. The driving force for the good is reason, not the will, but the reason must be informed by inquiry and teaching.[14]

The problem with the teachings of Duns Scotus and similar theologians is that they inevitably make humans dependent upon grace, *a*

[14]The Thomistic view that natural law dictates Christian moral truths has suffered a bit since the emergence of modern anthropology and the evidence that primitive peoples, living in nature, do not always develop Christian morality. At least arguably, as we see in chapter seven, this problem is better understood as the lack of cognitive development that persists in preliterate societies (see Vygotsky and Luria) which precludes the development of mature moral reasoning.

form of divine intervention, in order to be saved. It is very difficult to reconcile grace and divine intervention with freedom and responsibility. Although the act of will, informed by grace, may constitute meritorious behavior, the absence of will, due to the absence of grace (which is the state of all humans who are not chosen by God to be recipients of grace) is virtually impossible to reconcile with responsibility. And since eternal salvation and eternal damnation are in the balance, either God is a monster or reason plays a parallel role to grace. These arguments are particularly troubling to believers whose understanding relies on the exclusive study of scripture with no access to religious moral philosophy. Moral theology, important in faith communities, can have virtually no voice in the public square other that to file an *amicus* brief, noting interest in issues, but always remaining outside the actual arguments.

But, let us remember our task. We are not here to argue for or against the views of Aquinas or Duns Scotus. We are here to notice that this argument arose in the 14th century, and that it divided theology. Because of that division, theology lost its capacity to communicate with other departments in the university. The views of salvation held by Duns Scotus and Thomists deeply contradicted one another. Unable to integrate knowledge within their own discipline, they destroyed the claim that theology can integrate all knowledge. Overtime, this failure led to the complete marginalization of theology in the university.

Importantly, any attempt to qualify the place of reason in other departments was eliminated by the marginalization of theology which contained the only view interested in challenging reason. In spite of theology's intellectual schism having occurred soon after Aquinas's death, it did not reverse his greatest achievement. Aquinas made the West safe for reason. The schism in theology did not impact the university in general nearly so much as it might have it if had preceded Aquinas. Scholars in other departments were generally free to investigate the newly discovered subjects of their inquiry. The amount of subject matter with which they were working left them far too busy to worry about the arguments that academic theologians conducted. These *pre-secular* philosophers studied their new worlds at the university, went home to their families, and among other events in their lives, practiced their Christian faith in a manner that had not substantially changed in a thousand years.

Throughout most of the intervening history of Western intellectual development, the separation of theology from other areas of inquiry has been celebrated as a necessary liberation without which we would have been a different and diminished culture. The university became a place where intellectual inquiry could be conducted without interference from theology.

That view misses a significant point: the shared values and religious beliefs that existed *outside* the university provided the foundation of civil order and stability. Civil order depended upon the universal ethical principles that were unchallenged in civil society. It did not matter that Thomistic philosophers and Duns Scotus could not agree on the source of moral values, everyone inside and outside the university agreed on their *content*. No one argued about the existence of God, the Ten Commandments and so on. Civil society enjoyed strong moral leadership and clear teaching that was grounded in a thousand year old religious moral tradition and its universal ethical principles. The intellectual habit of thinking in terms of universal principles that dated in the West back to Augustine coupled with the Thomistic victory for reason enabled intellectuals to declare the place of reason and intellectual freedom in the university. As we are beginning to realize in the last years of the 20th century, when a culture loses its capacity to articulate and commit to shared universal values, civil society is threatened and so is intellectual freedom. When scholars complain that lawyers and accountants have taken over the university, they acknowledge that they have lost their freedom. But they do not seem to notice that their inability to identify and commit to universal intellectual values has created the vacuum that lawyers and accountants have filled. Very few realize that the problem was born in a 14th century conflict between Thomists and Duns Scotus.

Moral Philosophy vs. Moral Theology

Rather than experiencing crisis during the High Middle Ages, the secular side of the university enjoyed considerable freedom. For reasons that become evident when we discuss Kant, these liberated scholars inevitably encountered intellectual questions that were grounded in ethics. To assist themselves in answering ethical questions without having to bother with those confused, bickering folks over in the theology department, they created a whole new discipline: moral philosophy. Philosophers outside theology used their method of knowing, rationalism, to conduct independent inquiry—even into ethics.

54

Theologians studied theology, natural philosophers studied what today we call natural science (physics, chemistry, and biology), and moral philosophers studied ethics and what today we call psychology, law, and the social sciences. Other great collections of knowledge received from the East dealt with medicine and literature. The great intellectual achievement of the High Middle Ages was more along the lines of library development (organizing, categorizing, and cataloguing knowledge) rather than advancing knowledge. It was no mean achievement to have brought ancient and Eastern knowledge into the core of the Western university. However, what interests us is that these philosophers, called scholastic philosophers, failed to build on their new base and further advance knowledge.

From their origins in the Western intellectual tradition, natural philosophy (natural science) and moral philosophy had the opportunity to function independent of theology. As we establish in chapters five and six, natural philosophy achieved both independence and competence during the 17th century. Secular moral philosophy has successfully distanced itself from theology, but it has not achieved competence. Secular moral philosophy has not been able to build an intellectual or public consensus regarding the structure of ethical reasoning or its ethical content. Secular moral philosophy has never resolved its problems regarding the source of knowledge. For the same reasons that scholastic philosophers were not able to achieve real, productive independence from theology in any area of inquiry, secular moral philosophy has not achieved competence. The same fundamental problems that plagued scholastic philosophy plague secular moral philosophy and the social sciences today. These problems date from the 14th century.

Again, we begin to see helpful distinctions among the disciplines that develop and teach ethics. Moral theology uses revelation and relies on sacred texts. It has high degrees of intellectual authority within its faith community and is capable of developing concrete rules that are easy to teach. It also supports the authority of its faith community and the central role of religious teachers. But moral theology is not amenable to discourse in the public square where it disrupts rather than builds ethical consensus.

Religious moral philosophy uses rationalism as its method of inquiry. It is influenced by sacred texts but (at least theoretically) does not allow these texts to impose positions that cannot be resolved rationally.

Religious moral philosophers develop ethical content that is compatible with their religious community's moral theology. But they also have the capacity to participate in discourse aimed at building ethical consensus in the public square. However, the content of secular public ethics is bound, inevitably, to conflict with the ethical canon of faith communities. Depending on the role of moral theologians in a faith community and their relationship to the group of leaders that wields ultimate executive authority over the community, these differences can be tolerated or prohibited. The intellectual downfall of Islam came about largely because the ulama (Islam's intellectual elite scholar-jurists who interpreted the Koran) began to assert their authority in all areas of Islamic religious, political, and intellectual life.

This problem is evident in contemporary Iran where the *mojtaheds* interpret and translate holy law into principles that govern modern life. But modern life, even in Moslem Iran, must connect with the rest of the world. Iran faces the same problems when it attempts to build bridges with the rest of the world that the West faces in attempting to articulate the values of civil society in the face of diverse religious views. Both societies must permit public discourse that is independent of the strict interpretation of religious texts. Otherwise, the public must be defined by membership in only one religious community. Even Iran, which may appear to be uniformly Moslem, contains different sects and could benefit from mature secular moral reasoning. And Iran simply cannot connect effectively with the rest of the world unless it can base discourse on mature secular moral reasoning. What troubles religious countries such as Iran is that they are not in fact asked to accept mature moral reasoning when engaging the rest of the world. They are asked to accept ethical nihilism and gross materialism.

The same problem seems to be emerging in contemporary Catholicism where powerful orthodox religious leaders in Rome are beginning to assert their authority in Catholic universities throughout the world and encouraging Catholic religious activism in political life. It is also evident in the political activism of conservative Christian communities in the United States. Although it is evident that these leaders cannot build consensus in the university or the public square, they are reluctant to accept the nihilism and materialism that dominate discourse in the university and public square.

Because Aquinas's achievement was so great, and because the development of independent departments in the university represented such dramatic and important intellectual achievements, it is hard to understand how orthodox religious activists have reasserted themselves in Catholic and conservative Christian universities and in the public square. The devastating consequences of these errors in Islam would seem to have precluded such developments. The opening for these quite dangerous views came from the failure of rationalism, which takes us back to our more central point. We turn now to a closer look at the achievements and limits of rationalism and our deepening understanding of the problems that plague contemporary secular moral philosophy and the social sciences.

Rationalism's Achievements, Rationalism's Failure

Rationalism enjoyed a sweeping victory in the university. It was the epistemology that guided inquiry in all disciplines including much of theology from the early 14th century until the 17th century. And yet, the intellectual *achievements* of these liberated scholars were minimal. Rationalism's problem is the same problem that secular philosophers and educational philosophers face today: how to answer the question, What is our source of knowledge? This question is similar to asking, How can one develop authoritative, universal *a priori* assumptions independent of the universal exemplars of the divine mind, sacred texts, or the revealed truths of a religious tradition?

As we have seen, one cannot rationally argue the merits of a conclusion unless one knows the arguments that support it. Once identified, these arguments must withstand rational scrutiny. *A priori* assumptions that can withstand rational scrutiny are said to have authority. So the obvious question about rationalism is, What is the source of authority that supports the *a priori* assumptions of a particular view or discipline?

Aquinas did not have a problem with that question because scripture provides that authority. This observation brings us to a very important point about the work of Aquinas. He was actually doing religious moral philosophy and theology, working within the authority of scripture, and within the absolute authority of the universal exemplars of the divine mind. He used deductive reason with secular sounding premises, but the authority of his premises came from God. Therefore it is not quite accurate to call Aquinas's method rationalism. Or it is necessary to distinguish theological rationalism from secular rationalism, *which is the distinction that must be noted today among moral theologians and religious moral philosophers on the one hand and secular moral philosophers and social scientists on the other*.

In defining rationalism, then, we must be able to distinguish two traditions that have developed within it. Religious rationalism is a rational system that derives the authority of its *a priori* assumptions from scripture or sacred texts. Secular rationalism is the method used by Aristotle. Some scholastic philosophers attempted to use it to conduct inquiry in disciplines outside of theology. Indeed, that is what the scholastic philosophers of the High Middle Ages were so excited about: the opportunity to develop knowledge free of theology. But what happened?

Secular rationalism did not produce useful new knowledge. As we noted earlier, the great achievements of philosophers during this period had more to do with cataloguing, integrating, and teaching Eastern knowledge than in generating original knowledge. Aquinas freed scholastic philosophers from theology, but he did not show them how to conduct inquiry free of theology's impressive authority. He did not define or describe an *authoritative secular* source of knowledge. He was, after all, a theologian, so that was not his job. But it is interesting to note that both natural philosophers (natural scientists) and moral philosophers (social scientists) suffered enormously from their inability to identify a secular source of knowledge. Natural philosophers (Newton et al) solved this problem in the 17th century, but secular moral philosophers and social scientists still struggle with it.

The failure of *scholastic philosophers* to replace God and sacred texts as their source of knowledge accounts for their continuing to rely on these religious sources of knowledge when attempting to do natural philosophy and moral philosophy. This failure also explains why none of the content of natural philosophy or moral philosophy survived in the content of modern natural science and social science. Astonishingly, the inadequacy of modern secular moral philosophy and the social sciences when compared to the natural sciences results from their inability to resolve an epistemological problem that first surfaced early in the 14th century.

The need to free inquiry from theology did not become obvious in the medieval university. There was no great intellectual breakthrough during that time that clarified the problem scholastic philosophers were having with the source of knowledge. They worked in an inadequate paradigm, but could not characterize its inadequacy. Its inadequacy became obvious in part by advancements in science. Most clearly and dramatically, its inadequacy resulted from the collapse of the unified church following the Protestant Reformation and the impact of that collapse on political order. We conclude our review of the medieval period with the story of its collapse, for in that collapse we see clearly the inadequacy of scholastic philosophy and the 700 year old problem that plagues inquiry in education and the social sciences today.

4

The Collapse of the Medieval World

During the 300 years following the end of the first millennium, political stability, economic growth, and trade with the East contributed to a staggering improvement in the quality of European life. Scholars became interested in the humanities, or in humans as humans not merely as beings whose ultimate meaning resides in the next life. Similarly, peasants, crafts persons, and the emerging merchant class became increasingly interested in the possibilities of *the* good life *here on earth*. Heaven no longer offered the only possible explanation for one's enduring life. Life was increasingly something attractive in its own right. Precisely because *the good life* began to be associated with *this life* rather than *eternal life*, the church found itself in competition with secular definitions of the meaning of life and other core moral and spiritual issues. Ironically, the church fell victim to temporal terms in this competition.

At the same time, the church encountered competition for political influence from increasingly rich and powerful kings, cities, and families. These events only exacerbated the competition for intellectual leadership from independent[1] universities seeking to be secular even if they had not quite figured out how to do so. Over time, the church lost contact with the people due to its competition with monarchies and cities. It became preoccupied with wealth and power which led to internal corruption. The *city of man* overwhelmed the *city of God* within the church.

Neither historical accuracy nor insight into our own times is served by portraying the history of Christianity as unceasing corruption and betrayal. It is both more accurate and interesting to focus this criticism on when it truly applied. There is probably no time in the history of Christianity during which the church can be so clearly singled out for corruption and

[1]Very early in their development, Western universities were formed as corporate entities and funded by endowments. This structure allowed them to survive through good economic times and bad. Each university was independent from other universities as well as from the state and church. This enormously important development in the Western intellectual tradition continues to justify the support of independent, private universities.

betrayal as the 14th and 15th centuries. Corruption turned to tragedy when, in the middle of the 14th century, life began to worsen in significant ways.

Human Suffering in the 14th & 15th Centuries

In 1337 France and England commenced hostilities known as the Hundred Years War. In addition, a plague (the Black Death) hit Europe in 1347 and lasted 50 years. The Hundred Years War ended mainly because a civil war in England made it impossible for it to continue fighting France. Those hostilities, known as the War of the Roses, lasted from 1455 to 1485.

England was at war either with France or itself from 1337 to 1485, 152 years of war! From 1337 to 1455 France was at war with England during the middle of which it suffered from the Black Death in which over half of a town could die within a few months. In the past, such devastating events in the physical world had affirmed the importance of the church with its clear, unwavering reminder of humanity's ultimate fate: eternal joy with God in heaven. But these devastating events were presided over by corrupt church leaders who turned their backs on the suffering and agony of the people.

Church Corruption

Pope Boniface VIII may not be recognized by name, but two of his decisions are among the most recognizable in Western religious history. Around 1300 he invented the *indulgence*: a mechanism believers could use in this life to reduce the punishment for sins in the next. Although it is clearly absurd to argue that one can purchase forgiveness for sins, indulgences were often granted in association with monetary donations or material sacrifices. This practice came on the heels of the institution of taxes called *annates* which required a newly appointed bishop to send the first year's revenues to Rome. At the same time, it was not unusual for lucrative church offices to be purchased (a forbidden practice known as *simony*) or given to the children of bishops and abbots (forbidden *nepotism*). Combined, these unholy practices made it increasingly clear that church leaders had institutionalized greed.

This is not to say that there was no corruption during earlier periods in church history. Abuse of power, ignorance, and all of the vices that vex humanity occurred among the clergy. But that corruption was the corruption of individuals. The distinction that is so important to notice is that during the 14th and 15th centuries, the church created corrupt laws and doctrines.

Back to Boniface. Not satisfied by greed, in 1302 he made the most extreme claim to papal authority in church history by declaring that there is no salvation outside the Roman church and that every human is subject to the authority of the Roman pontiff. Boniface's claims to power responded to attempts by the kings of England and France to tax church property. In return, the French king, Philip the Fair, sent an army to Rome to arrest Boniface who died shortly thereafter. The successor to Boniface, subservient to Philip, moved the papal residence to Avignon, France. The rest of Europe distrusted the French popes of Avignon throughout the century.

Pro-French and anti-French sentiment grew throughout Europe and entered the College of Cardinals. In 1378 the cardinals elected *two* popes: one took up residence in Rome, the other in Avignon. Europe, which was still a Christian community that was organized in one church and derived its sense of spiritual and eternal meaning from that church, was now asked to endure unending war and plague, misery and death, and an increasingly greedy church preoccupied by power which it exercised through divided leadership. The results were predictable at least from an historical perspective. In the most personal way, at the level of the individual, Europe became alarmingly un-Christian and from the perspective of modern psychology, one might say psychotic.

Black masses made a mockery of Christianity's most sacred rite in an attempt to appease the devil. The Order of Flagellants formed in which members marched through the streets beating each other with whips and chains. Witches, who had always been a part of folk lore but were ignored for lack of power against Christian protection, now became an obsession. They were feared, sought out, and burned alive.

All the while, the papal courts at Rome and Avignon grew more opulent than any king's court. While the people suffered what must be one of the longest sustained spiritual crises in the history of Christianity, the leadership of the church was divided on political issues and occupied by greed. Abandoned, the people danced with the devil and killed each other. Lacking clerical leadership, some laymen attempted to help.

Laymen Strive to Save the Church

Around 1380, John Wycliff began to preach in England (and to teach at Oxford) a doctrine that was as logical a conclusion from current events as one can imagine. The doctrine espoused that no visible church was needed to gain salvation because ordinary people can find redemption in reading the Bible. That *individuals* are capable of a valid interpretation of scripture, independent of church and priest, is widely recognized today as the *individual interpretation of the Bible*. Clearly, this principle undermines the authority of any church community, but it provides a significant spiritual safety net for individuals who find themselves at cross purposes with the local pastor. In any event, Wycliff's teachings were branded as heresy, but they endured and spread. And somehow, Wycliff avoided the church's prosecution and died of old age.

In Bohemia, John Hus (1369-1415) took up Wycliff's ideas; but anticipating the dynamics of the Reformation more than a century later, this politically innocent doctrine was transformed into a national political movement. Czech and Slavic people made the Hussite party a forum for protesting the excessive influence of Germans living in Bohemia, and the Hussite wars ravaged Central Europe for decades during the early 15th century. Hus was also declared a heretic but did not escape the church's wrath. He was ordered before the Council of Constance and burned at the stake.

Around 1400, the Conciliar movement was started by university professors, ministers to kings, concerned bishops, and thoughtful burghers who formed a European wide council of laymen that set out to bring order to the church. They doubted the ability of cardinals to reform from within, especially with a divided papacy. Although they had to work through a discouraging set back when the impossibility of two popes was extended to three, in 1414 the council garnered enough influence to compel all three popes to resign and Martin V became the new, sole Pope, with residence in Rome.

The council intended to continue to meet and even to expand throughout Europe. They called for a general council to meet every ten years or as needed, asserted the supremacy of the council over the pope thus refuting Boniface's claim to papal power, and insisted that the selling of indulgences, simony, and nepotism be abandoned. However, Martin V reasserted papal authority, disbanded the council, and set off a thirty year struggle for church authority, this time against laymen rather than kings and emperors.

The Conciliar movement was weakened when European fears regarding the church and the French were substantiated. The Pope made a special arrangement with the French and gained their support. In 1438 the Pope, Eugenius IV, agreed to the Pragmatic Sanction of Bourges that permitted the French church to establish the primacy of its council over the pope and to declare its administrative independence from and cease paying annates to Rome. It also prohibited the pope from interfering in the appointment of French bishops. These concessions to France divided and conquered the Conciliar movement. It also extended the stage upon which the church of France exerted extraordinary influence on French policy and culture that lasted into the 20th century and upon which Cardinal Richelieu[2] wielded his tragic influence during the 17th century.

In 1450, the church held a jubilee celebrating the full return of papal independence. Coincidentally, around this same time peace returned to Europe. And as should be increasingly predictable, with peace, agricultural productivity increased, commerce became more vigorous, and a general sense of well being prevailed. Replacing war with peace made many things look improved. And the church, which had revealed deep problems during this time, ceased to experience conflict and settled into self-destructive practices that went largely unnoticed. The papacy passed into the hands of a series of refined, educated gentlemen. Ironically, the decisive victory over laymen who would have reformed and preserved the unified Christian church lead to the alliance between theologians and laymen that became known as the Protestant Reformation. The Reformation succeeded in institutionalizing diverse Christian views and freed the followers of Luther, Calvin, and the Church of England from the authority of Rome. It also destroyed Christian unity. But before we turn to the Reformation, we must notice what had been going on in Germany, for that part of the story is essential to understanding the forces that drove the Reformation, the Thirty Years War, the pluralization of Christianity, and ultimately the end of the Middle Ages.

---

[2]Chief minister to Louis XIII, Richelieu is credited with halting attempts by Louis mother (Marie de Medici) to build French alliances with Austria and Spain. The conflicts that arose in place of those alliances encouraged the Thirty Years War. He solidified the French monarchy's power over the aristocracy which at least arguably contributed to the violent character of the French Revolution. Neither the nobles nor the people of France were able to spend a hundred years reforming the monarchy and devising new forms of governance. But he also advanced learning and culture in France. He is one of the more complex figures in European history. I lean toward the unsympathetic.

The High Middle Ages in Germany

The German states have been left virtually ignored during this discussion. Other than suffering from the plague, they experienced a very different history during the 14th and 15th centuries than did France, England and the rest of Europe. One might even refer to the 14th and 15th centuries as the High Middle Ages in the German states.

During the 14th century, a great European trade route extended from Italy through Switzerland and north through the Rhineland of western Germany. Towns along the way prospered as did other German communities. German commerce was further advanced by the prosperity of the famous Fugger and other great German banking families who provided their services to, among others, the extraordinarily wealthy popes.

During this period, enrollments at other European universities were in decline, and no new universities were founded in Italy and only a few in France, Spain, Scotland, and Scandinavia. In Germany, however, fourteen universities were founded between 1386 and 1506. Technology in the form of what we today would call mechanical engineering also made significant progress, with the greatest cultural impact coming from Gutenberg's invention of the moveable type printing press at Mainz in 1450.

Other significant achievements by Germans of this time often go unnoticed because of the fad of adopting Latin names. Thus Copernicus who was of Polish decent and spent most of his life in East Prussia is known for his work in astronomy, but is usually not recognized as Nikolaus Koppernigk. Similarly, Johann Muller of Konigsburg who laid the foundation for a mathematical conception of the universe has been obscured by his use of the name Regiomontanus. The frequently noticed Paracelsus who re-conceptualized medicine at the University of Basel is virtually unknown by his family name, Hohenheim.

By 1500, western and southern Germany were prosperous and were emerging as centers of European intellectual and cultural life. They also loomed as a political, military, and economic rival of Spain and France. If the German people could find some way to unite their numerous, ill-defined, and disorganized political parts, they could become the major economic, cultural, and military power of Europe. The growing influence of the independent German states and the threat to France and Spain presented by the prospect of a united, dominant Germany cannot be separated from the religious issues that drove the Protestant Reformation.

The important conditions in Europe that ushered in the Reformation were: 1) The division of intellectual leadership in the universities that isolated theology and separated secular rationalism from that department. 2) A widespread distrust of church leadership and the emergence of secular independence in civil society. 3) Impending domination by the German states.

The Protestant Reformation

As we have seen, the unity of Christianity was not as clear in academic theology as it was in the daily lives of Christian people. What made the Protestant Reformation so important was that it brought theological controversies into the daily and civil lives of Christians. Below we will discuss some of the theological controversies that developed, not to make an argument for or against the Protestant Reformation, but to highlight those differences and to note the complete collapse of anything resembling a united Christian community.

Europe had been a Christian community for a thousand years when the Reformation began. Furthermore, the authority of the church had increasingly been expressed through the pope and the clerical bureaucracy (the Curia) that surrounded him. As we have seen, church corruption had tested the patience of monarchs and laymen. The growing disenchantment, distrust, and disregard for the teachings and authority of Rome came to a head when Martin Luther, a German priest educated in a German university, posted his 95 theses to a door in the castle church in Wittenberg. The date was October 31, 1517.

Martin Luther

Luther challenged the validity of indulgences as having any role in the forgiveness of sins and asserted that only faith could lead to redemption. His insistence upon the validity of his claims and suggestion that *secular* leaders must reform the church represented a profound and familiar challenge to the authority of the pope. Whereas the recondite arguments of theologians typically bored the people, Luther's arguments awakened great interest. The most visible change came in Luther's rejection of five of the seven sacraments: confirmation (adult baptism), holy orders (ordination of priests), confession, matrimony, and the last rites. He acknowledge only the two sacraments for which he could find evidence in the New Testament, baptism and communion. Throughout the German states, the practice of Luther's reformed Christianity spread with astonishing quickness.

Isolated and arrogant, Rome did not listen. Luther's teachings were outlawed and the formal division of Christianity was begun, for Rome did not limit its reaction to the excommunication of Luther. Once again, Rome called upon secular leaders in an attempt to coerce compliance. The Holy Roman Emperor immediately joined the Pope, but because this strategy had so often been used to the benefit of France (with its long history of a single monarchy and close ties to Rome), the numerous German states[3] known for their commitment to local control and deep distrust of Rome threw their support to Luther.

In February, 1531, six German princes and the leaders of ten cities responded to attempts at papal coercion by forming a military alliance. It is somewhat startling to realize that in just over 14 years from Luther's posting his theological questions, a military alliance was formed to oppose both Rome and the Emperor. Additional princes and towns of like interest sought to join this league, and most of the Protestant states of the Holy Roman Empire joined the alliance, solidifying the hold of Protestantism in Germany.

By 1555 the Lutherans were so strong and numerous that they had to be recognized. In that year, the Emperor crafted the Peace of Augsburg which granted each prince or city the right to decide whether the people would be Catholic or Lutheran. This arrangement provided some resolution regarding religion at least for a time but had the immediate effect of contributing to the disunity of the German States, which as we shall see shortly, exposed the German people to a disaster unmatched in their history until the twentieth century. While other monarchies were being strengthened all around them, the German States were becoming

---

[3]The Holy Roman Empire stretched from France in the west to Poland and Hungary in the east. Included were Bohemia (largely Czech, though Germans exerted controversial influence) and French speaking countries of Belgium, Lorraine, eastern Burgundy, and western Switzerland. With these exceptions, the Empire consisted of German speaking people organized in small principalities and cities. The Emperor governed through the Reichstag forming something akin to a constitutional, parliamentarian monarchy. Of the 300 units represented in the Reichstag, eight could vote in the election of the Emperor.

less unified and more vulnerable. As disruptive as these events were to prove to be, they were not the only major reforms.

John Calvin

In 1534 John Calvin settled in Basel, Switzerland, and began to write *The Institutes of the Christian Religion.* Calvin shared Luther's demand for reform but differed greatly in theology. Rather than focusing on God's mercy which required only faith for forgiveness, Calvin relied on the authority of the Old Testament and taught of a mighty and forbidding God. He shared with Rome and Luther such basics as the doctrine of the Trinity, the divinity of Christ, and redemption after death. He differed from Rome and agreed with Luther on the scriptural basis for only two sacraments, baptism and communion. And he differed with both Rome and Luther on the source of salvation. Rome placed great significance on the role of *good works* and *earning* salvation. Luther taught that faith alone could win salvation. Calvin taught the *doctrine of the elect* (predestination) which made salvation dependent upon one's being a member of God's chosen.

If the reader will step out of context with me for a moment, we can notice in this discussion a defining dimension of American culture. The Puritans who settled the northeastern states were Calvinists, and the Puritan ethic that demands hard work and delayed gratification is grounded in an interesting twist of Calvin's view. If during this life, some of us are already part of *the elect* and some are not, we all must wonder how we might distinguish one from the other. The Puritans believed that material success in this life provides evidence of one's being part of the elect. Since hard work and financial prudence are essential to material success, these behaviors came to have eternal significance. Material success and the accumulation of material possessions became an expression of spiritual accomplishment and righteousness. The American character that is defined by hard work, delayed gratification, and materialism grew out of this tradition. We are getting ahead of ourselves in these observations, but it is helpful to note that understanding Calvin provides useful insights into American culture.

Finally, Calvin asserted the unity of church and state. He taught that civil government fulfills the will of God by providing peace and tranquility; therefore, to reject the civil law is to reject God. On the other hand, a tyrannical government that fails to provide such care faces the vengeance of God. Recalling that the university had lost virtually all capacity for resolving fundamental differences regarding theological and ethical issues more than two hundred years earlier, one can anticipate that applying the concept of God's vengeance to both civil and religious life put peace and tranquility at great risk.

Henry VIII and The Church of England

Meanwhile in England, the teachings of Luther had become well known but had not aroused the same interest among the English people as had occurred among the Germans. The English were occupied by the task of recovering from 152 years of war and were not interested in more conflict with Europe. However, when Henry VIII encountered difficulty securing a male heir, he sought a series of divorces that Rome rejected. He split with Rome and the people followed.[4] The English church remained the closest to Rome in doctrine and liturgy of all the Protestant denominations, but the English monarch became the head of both church and state. Although somewhat tolerant of other Protestant groups, the English became increasingly concerned regarding the authoritarian role of the Roman pontiff. The English monarch and people feared what seemed to be the inevitable divided loyalties of English Catholics. Throughout Europe, the loss of religious unity had that same effect in the relationship between rulers and their subjects. Questions of loyalty abounded as did acts of treachery which were justified on religious grounds.

The Unavoidable Mix of Religious and Political Conflict

The co-mingling of the Reformation's theological controversies with politics is of great importance in explaining the evolution of the secular philosophical tradition which in part defines the modern world. In a united Christian world, the authority of the ruler flowed from God, albeit as moderated by the church. However, with Christianity divided, the logic of the authority of the ruler flowing from God lost its clarity. As long as all rulers, all people, and all political theories were united in the same religion; a theological explanation of the ruler's authority contributed

---

[4]The War of the Roses was fought over the rights of succession to the English throne. That war ended because the marriage of Henry VIII's parents united the houses of Lancaster and York, not because the English had developed adequate rules of succession. Henry's failure to secure an heir, therefore, was no small matter to the English people. They were recovering from 150 years of war, and the failure to stabilize succession posed the threat of seemingly endless conflict. Looking back on those events, one can imagine siding with the king.

stability to political life. But when the ruler and the people were divided by religion, theological explanations ceased to serve political tranquility. By the 17th century, religious diversity had become the major source of conflict in civil life. The table below lists the major Protestant denominations that existed in addition to the Catholic Church. Importantly, conflicts could arise wherever competing denominations confronted each other in civil life. In 16th century England, for instance, Catholicism had been suppressed, but civil conflicts between members of the Church of England were waged against Puritans and Presbyterians.

16TH CENTURY PROTESTANT DENOMINATIONS		
CALVIN	**LUTHER**	**HENRY VIII**
Reformed Churches:	Lutheran	Church of England
Dutch, German, Swiss		Anglican
French Huguenots		Episcopal
Puritans		
American		
Congregationalists		
Scottish Presbyterians		

During these early conflicts, opponents were not viewed as merely different, they were viewed as unforgivably wrong. They betrayed God. It was impossible for citizens to accept the authority invested in rulers by God if the ruler had betrayed God. It did not matter which new or old form of Christianity the people followed. If the ruler's religious beliefs were different from the peoples', the ruler had no authority.

Having lost the theological basis for the authority of sovereigns that had prevailed since the Dark Ages, rulers and their people had to discover a new basis for authority and loyalty. The details of the attempts to redefine the source and nature of political authority must wait for our discussion of the modern era. Before we turn to that saga, we must conclude our story of the collapse of the medieval world. The Middle Ages culminated in the ultimate religious/political war, the Thirty Years War.

The Thirty Years War

In *Cosmopolis: The Hidden Agenda of Modernity*, Stephen Toulmin argues convincingly that the beginning of the modern era can be identified with the assassination of Henry IV of France, for with him died any hope of

Europe's avoiding the hostilities that we know as the Thirty Year's War. That war so altered the role and stature of Europe's institutions, as well as the fundamental assumptions of the intellectual community, that what followed constituted a complete cultural break with the past. Before considering its impact, we must take note of the war itself.

The Thirty Years War was fought from 1618 to 1648, almost entirely on German soil. It was a religious war because religion was the issue that allowed it to reach its depth and breadth, and its outcome permanently altered the status and structure of religion in Europe. But much more was at work.

Entangled Interests that Drove the War

I   The Civil War in Germany in Which Various Groups Were Alternatingly Allies and Enemies:

Catholic and Lutheran cities and principalities vied over religious domination as set up by the Peace of Augsburg. The ability of the local ruler (prince, bishop, or abbot) to name the religion of a civil entity became disruptive when the leader died and Catholic and Lutherans strove to install one of their own as the new leader and thus secure the territory to their religious view.

Both Catholic and Lutheran cities and principalities, when they were not at war with each other over succession issues as described above, vied with the Catholic Emperor (Ferdinand II) over his efforts to strengthen the central government. So much for a religious war.

II Economic Issues

Europe's major trade route had run from Italy and Switzerland through the Rhineland. It shifted to the Atlantic, from land to sea. The Dutch controlled the mouth of the Rhine and used that control to advance their interests. Baltic trade was on the rise, but the king of Denmark controlled the mouth of the Baltic, a geologic phenomenon as striking as the Dardanelles. In addition, the king of Sweden controlled most of its shores. These two kings opened the Baltic to the Dutch and English, and German trade suffered.

The decline in German wealth during the 16th century was so severe that the Fugger and other German bankers became insignificant as wealth shifted to the west.

III International Conflicts

The Spanish were about to renew longstanding hostilities with the Dutch, but even more importantly, sought to unify the Rhine valley under their control. This interest aroused tremendous concern among the French.

The French feared and vigorously opposed the threat of Spanish control of the Rhine and, continuing its opposition to German power and influence that dates back to Clovis, undermined attempts by the Emperor to strengthen central control and build a modern nation state of the vast Holy Roman Empire.

IV Participants in the Conflict

Mercenaries did much of the fighting, and their personal ambitions grew with their success. Hired by one side or the other, they often pursued their own more lucrative agendas.

To capture the bizarre nature of things is to build a religious, economic, political, and military montage in which actors often move against themselves. A notable example was Catholic France, led by the powerful Cardinal Richelieu whose interests were in France the state rather than in the French church. Thus Catholic France acted as the great defender of Protestantism by opposing the economic and political interests of Catholic Spain and the Catholic Emperor of the increasingly Protestant Holy Roman Empire. At this level of analysis, the war nearly achieves farce. But analyzed at the level of the lives of the people impacted by these conflicts (especially the Germans, for it was on their land that virtually the entire war was waged) it constituted a horror.

The Peace of Westphalia

By 1644 the German states were exhausted and devastated. Leaders from all over Europe met at Westphalia finally to resolve religious issues and such state issues as boundaries and the structure of governance. Importantly, the representative of the pope was ignored. Peace was reached in 1648, although France and Spain refused to sign the treaties and continued to fight each other until 1659.

Known as the Peace of Westphalia, the treaties signed in 1648 not only ended hostilities in Germany but established the Constitution of Germany. The German constitution, then, was not written by Germans for Germans, nor was it secured by popular assent. It was written into international agreements secured by foreign powers, Sweden and France. Protestant rights were confirmed, and much of the western part of the Empire was lost including control of the great rivers.

Spain and France achieved their greatest goal, the weakening of the central authority of the Emperor, via the terms of the constitution they imposed. It guaranteed the numerous German States virtual sovereignty, each was permitted to conduct its own diplomacy. The Emperor was prohibited from making laws, collecting taxes, recruiting soldiers, declaring war, or confirming peace except with the consent of the 300 plus states assembled in the Reichstag. Because it would be virtually impossible for such an assembly to agree on anything, the Empire was eliminated as a viable entity. Indeed, when Enlightenment intellectuals of the eighteenth century shook their heads at the backwardness of German governance, they paid homage to the success of Spain and France, and especially Cardinal Richelieu.

The Impact of the Thirty Years War On Western Culture

None of this account gets at the destruction or the immensity of the human suffering experienced by the German people during the war. At the time, it was estimated that nearly half of the German population had perished. Modern estimates place it at closer to one third of extensive parts of Germany. Entire towns were wiped out. Even the Second World War did not depopulate Germany to the extent of the Thirty Years War. In addition, farmers were tortured in order to discover their few possessions. As with the Germanic tribal migrations of the Dark Ages, agriculture virtually ceased and economic life was ravaged. But unlike the Germanic tribal migrations which represented the invasion of one part of Europe by people from the outside pursuing a better life, the Thirty Years War was inflicted upon the people of Europe by the pope, kings, emperor, a Cardinal who was first minister to a king, and so on. It was a war inflicted upon the people of Europe by their own political and religious leaders.

From 1300 to 1500, the people of France had experienced the spiritual abandonment of the church while suffering through the Black Death and the

Hundred Years War with England. Now, the people of Germany suffered utter devastation from internal religious and political conflicts and external political exploitation. Christianity, which had unified the medieval world, divided into Catholicism and various Protestant sects. Christianity could no longer inform and integrate political theory. The 14th century division in theology caused it to lose its voice, its capacity to integrate and guide inquiry in the university. The division of Christianity in the 16th and 17th centuries caused it to lose its capacity to integrate and guide political and civil life. Most devastating for religion and society, Christianity's capacity to explain the meaning of human life and suffering was permanently diminished. United Western Christendom, which had begun to crack in the 14th century university, ended, and the modern world had to be invented.

This of course is especially interesting to the contemporary reader because some current commentators claim that the modern period has ended. Intellectual, spiritual, political, and economic leaders of the new age, whatever it will eventually be called, are struggling mightily to figure out what will provide us with a workable foundation of our culture. But when one recalls in some detail the devastation and the complete failure of the prevailing culture that defined the end of the Middle Ages and the beginning of the modern era, it is difficult to identify any similarity today. Certainly there are a lot of people who are angry and upset, but it is not the same as a continent devastated by three hundred years of self inflicted tragedy, chaos, and death.

And so we turn to the modern era, not nearly so convinced that it is ending as we are that it was needed. Furthermore, we should not allow the decisive collapse of the medieval period to blind us to its achievements and lasting influence. Christianity, deeply grounded in humanistic principles, asserted the dignity and worth of every individual, of every soul. Because Christianity reigned as the single, unifying foundation of Western culture for over a thousand years, Western civilization retains a deep commitment to values that protect the rights and dignity of every individual. Indeed, we may have lost our sense of the historical significance of Christianity, but we cannot overlook its contributions to the universally held principles that made 18th century economic and political theory possible. Nor can we ignore it as the source of the incontestable claims made by the United States' Declaration of Independence and Constitution regarding the equality of all humans.

Furthermore, we merely need to look at the intellectual and political confusion that exists in modern theocracies to appreciate the contribution Aquinas made to the medieval university and the Western intellectual tradition. His achievement secured reason's independence from faith and continues to provide the foundation of intellectual freedom in Western civilization. Intellectuals and educators must consider that rejecting reason does not constitute an unarguable intellectual achievement. It threatens a fall into chaos or a return to attempts by religious leaders to exert religious authority on civil society.

Religious pluralism is a product of unresolved conflicts among religious leaders and places enormous demands on secular philosophers to answer fundamental moral questions necessary to construct and sustain civil society. Religious leaders have not universally accepted that point and somewhat disingenuously complain about the deterioration of civic virtues. Yet they continue to wage their bitter disputes and refuse to participate in the articulation of mature secular moral reasoning or to develop secular ethical content. The Catholic Counter Reformation, which began at the Council of Trent (1545-1563), has been waged, almost continuously, since the late 16th century. Its purpose has been to advance arguments for the superiority of the Catholic view. Similarly, the Protestant Reformation has never ended. Protestant theologians argue for the superiority of their view. These arguments are all well and good within Catholic and Protestant faith communities. But moral theologians and religious moral philosophers have not seemed to notice that they have an enormous stake in contributing to the development of ethical consensus in the public square which requires mature, *secular* moral reasoning and a canon of secular ethics.

Unfortunately, the importance of secular moral philosophy is not an obvious conclusion. As we will see, social scientists have distanced themselves from *all* moral philosophy which has contributed to ethical schizophrenia in Western societies. Western culture is grounded in Jewish and Christian ethical teaching, but modern intellectuals have increasingly attempted to distance the social sciences from religious and secular moral philosophy. Christian and Jewish moral philosophers while competing for the supremacy of their views have largely turned their backs on civil society's need for mature secular moral reasoning. A religiously pluralistic society needs shared ethical values, but they must be secular. That point has been clear since the end of the Thirty Years War. By competing with rather than participating in the development of secular ethics, religious moral philosophers have perpetuated one of the most enduring and damaging conflicts in the modern period, the conflict between religion and the social sciences. They have thereby contributed, far more than they seem willing to admit, to the diminishment of virtue in public life. We turn now to a discussion of the attempts made by secular moral philosophers to develop secular ethical principles for civil society.

5

The Birth of the Modern Era

While the medieval period of Western history was being catastrophically concluded on the European continent during the 17th century, the modern era was being born in a less troubled but certainly not strife-free England. By the 17th century, Europe faced such devastating political-religious conflicts that it was forced to separate church and state. But separating the church and state required a major redefinition of religion's place in civil life. It required the invention of a whole new, secular political philosophy. As we see when we discuss Hobbes and Locke, philosophers and politicians had to articulate entirely new political principles, translate them into laws, and invent the institutions that could implement them. At the beginning of the century, the only epistemology that could guide their inquiry was rationalism with its 300 year record of inadequacy.

The medieval period may have just been ending in the 17th century, and the modern era may have been struggling to break that shell, but one thing was already in place that is familiar to the reader in the late twentieth century. Knowledge was controlled in an existing bureaucracy that did not want to give up its hold. Universities provided major opposition to change. Scholastic philosophers had conducted inquiry using rationalism for 300 years. It had not been productive, but it commanded the loyalty of most intellectuals.

Early in the 17th century, Frances Bacon complained about the lack of productivity in the natural sciences, challenging the way science was conducted during the Middle Ages:

> We have seen now for twice a thousand years . . . that the sciences stand where they did and remain almost in the same condition, receiving no noticeable increase . . . Whereas in the mechanical arts, which are founded on nature and the light of experience, we see the contrary happen, for these . . . are continually thriving and growing, . . . and at all times advancing.[1]

---

[1] *Magna Instauratio* (The Great Renewal), LXXIV, (p. 299-300).

Bacon insisted that theoretical science must base its knowledge on nature and experience. In other words, science had to abandon *rationalism* for *empiricism*. But his plea for the recognition and use of empiricism attracted little support in universities. Rather, the success of scientists who used the empirical method won the argument. Of course, rationalism's long history of producing papers, arguments, and intellectual claims that had no relationship to or impact upon the mechanical arts contributed to its downfall. Early on, however, philosophers claimed that empiricism would not work. Steeped in the lofty notions of Platonic/Augustinian idealism and the abstract principles of Aristotelian/Thomistic rationalism, university dons scoffed at the very notion of originating inquiry in the dirt and grime of nature and experience. "Impossible!" they shouted, while implying, "Insulting, undignified!" But it worked. Scientists adopted and demonstrated the wonders of empiricism. For the first time in 2000 years, natural science produced theories that guided, predicted, and explained developments in the mechanical arts.

Recall, however, that the issues that troubled civil society at the beginning of the 17th century had nothing to do with science. The pressure was on moral philosophy and political science to secure domestic tranquility. As scientists were able increasingly to celebrate their astonishing new successes, moral philosophers looked to the epistemology of science for help.

The order of events is impossible to duplicate in a readable manner because everything was happening at once. In order to conduct a coherent discussion, I have developed a few themes which I describe below:

1. By the beginning of the 17th century, the Protestant Reformation was a *fait accompli*. Western religious pluralism was an unalterable historical fact that had resulted from the conduct and decisions of religious leaders.

2. Violence stemming from religious conflicts established with compelling clarity and increasing urgency the need to work out secular principles capable of guiding the development of legal and institutional solutions to questions regarding the authority and structure of government. The assassination of Henry IV, the

Protestant King of France, by Catholics; the ongoing tragedies of the Thirty Year's War; and the execution of Charles I, the Catholic King of England, by Protestants are the most notable but certainly not the only examples of such violence. Unable to agree on religious principles of human conduct, leaders had to discover secular principles that could guide the development of laws and public institutions.

3. Major scientific discoveries were made early in the century and only increased with time. But most important for this discussion, early in the century *empiricism* won its place as the promising new epistemology of natural philosophy, i.e., science.

4. Political philosophers adopted empiricism as their epistemology, some even began to call themselves scientists, and all claimed to have brought enlightenment to the West.

Rather all at once, the need for secular moral philosophy in political life became an urgent issue, science adopted empiricism, and secular moral philosophy adopted empiricism as its epistemology.

This chapter first discusses empiricism as the new epistemology of science and then empiricism as the claimed epistemology of secular moral philosophy. The discussion highlights the real success of empiricism in science and the enormous problems it has faced in moral philosophy, political philosophy, and the social sciences.

Independent Authority of the Scientific Community

To begin this discussion, we must make sure we know what we mean by the term empiricism, especially as it is used in the natural sciences. Empiricism is grounded in inductive reasoning. It uses concrete, physical evidence to establish general conclusions. As we noted earlier, inductive and deductive reason proceed in opposite directions: inductive from the concrete to the general, deductive from the general to concrete. As the two fundamental structures of logic, inductive and deductive reason have ancient roots.

Like other epistemologies we have seen, empiricism's essential characteristics are revealed when comparing it to other epistemologies. Platonic/Augustinian idealism identified the realm of ideas and the universal exemplars of the divine mind as the source of knowledge. Aristotelian/ Thomistic rationalism identified the source of knowledge as located in the mind (reason). Both relied, for the most part, on deductive reason.

No useful distinction can be made between *realism* and *idealism* (after all, idealists claim to have identified what is most real), but it is useful to make a distinction between *materialism* and *idealism*. Both materialism and one form of idealism identify the *mind* as the source of knowledge. If one considers the mind as indistinguishable from the brain and therefore as part of the physical world, one's view is considered a kind of materialism. If one considers the mind as something profoundly different from the brain, and the mind's constructs as profoundly different from nature's constructs, then one's view is considered a form of idealism. Kant, as we will see, believed that the source of knowledge is in the mind and that the products of the mind are *not* part of the physical world. His was a form of immanent idealism: the mind and its ideas are in but not part of the physical world. *Supersensible* was the term Kant used to distinguish the world of the mind from the physical world. That is quite different from Plato and Augustine who believed that the source of knowledge exists completely outside the physical world. Theirs was a form of transcendent idealism.

As we see when we begin to construct an epistemology in Part II, the confusion imposed on epistemological discourse by such terms as materialism, immanent idealism, and transcendent idealism result from attempting to solve epistemological problems from an ontological view. Ontology attempts to answer questions about what is real, what *exists*, and tends to get caught up in arguments about what is or is not material. In dealing with the nature of knowledge and inquiry, ontological arguments tend to result in false dichotomies. We know that there is a world of things, and we know that ideas about things are not material. We need to understand the relationship between ideas and their objects, but ontological views have frustrated that understanding. This discussion will make more sense when we stop discussing philosophy and attempt to do it, when we attempt to solve philosophical problems. In the meantime, it is helpful to notice the problem during our historical review. Empiricism and the scientific method have confounded general epistemology by successfully *locating* the source of knowledge in the material world. The epistemology of science has been so successful that it seems to have required philosophers attempting to do epistemology in disciplines other than natural science to provide a *material* answer to questions regarding the source of knowledge in their disciplines. It is almost as if we must answer the loaded question, Where is our source of knowledge located? rather than more open questions such as, What is our source of knowledge? or How do we account for our source of knowledge?

Empiricism and the scientific method locate the source of truth in nature, the physical world, and rely on inductive reasoning. Both are appropriately considered materialist philosophies. The reader probably learned the essentials of the scientific method in high school: observe some phenomenon, identify a problem or question, form an hypothesis, test the hypothesis, analyze the results of the tests, and form a conclusion. Hypotheses are grounded in reflections upon *observations of physical phenomena* which is what scientists mean by experience. Physical phenomena can be purely natural such as the movement of planets, weather, or geological events; or they can be man made such as bridges, clocks, or medicine.

Now, let us stop and check our focus. We are interested in the intellectual barriers that prevent educators from integrating research, integrating research and practice, and conducting rational discourse that leads to agreement, commitment, and action. We are discussing the epistemology of science because of its influential place in the history of Western knowledge and because it provides such a striking example of intellectual conduct that produces powerful knowledge, knowledge that predicts and explains physical phenomena. We are also interested in the epistemology of science because it integrates research, integrates research and practice, and permits discourse that leads to agreement, commitment, and action. Crucial to this discussion is the fact that empiricism alone cannot account for the intellectual achievements that have been made in science. We must ask, How did the epistemology of science evolve from a slightly elaborated expression of inductive reason to an enormously successful, institutionalized, and authoritative epistemology?

Restructuring Empiricism as The Scientific Method

I have referred to three intellectual tasks that confronted philosophers in the 17th century: 1) articulate philosophical principles, 2) translate those principles into laws, and 3) invent the institutions that implement the laws. Scientists achieved all of these tasks during the 17th century, although not in the order indicated. Almost all at once: scientists, especially Galileo, made startling discoveries; Bacon described empiricism; scientists in England and France formed academic societies;[2] and Newton published *Mathematical Principles of Natural Philosophy* (1687) that contained the "Rules of Reasoning in Philosophy."

Clearly, the ongoing ability of science to produce successful theories and guide practice has won prestige and influence outside science. But the *intellectual authority* that guided science grew out of the institutional authority of the Royal Society and French and German Academies which based their authority on Newton' principles. Since we have started our discussion of epistemology, we continue by reviewing Newton's rules of reasoning, and then we turn to the institutional developments. But again, the logic of the text violates historical sequence. For historical clarity we must recall that The Royal Society was founded in 1662, and Newton's *Mathematical Principles of Natural Philosophy* was published in 1687. We discuss the two out of historical sequence.

The Contributions of Isaac Newton

Not only did Newton articulate the rules of the scientific method, he also made two significant advances in mathematics. He (and Leibnitz) invented calculus, and he invented the mathematically structured scientific statement. Calculus was essential as a tool to describe and manipulate an array of functions such as measuring an area bounded by curves and the properties of the limits of such areas (fundamental to integral calculus) as well as the limits of the instantaneous rate of change or derivatives (fundamental to differential calculus). His and others' scientific work could not have been conducted without these and the other mathematical tools invented at that time.

In *Mathematical Principles of Natural Philosophy,* Newton demonstrated the use of higher mathematics in solving scientific problems. Of more lasting impact, he introduced the scientific process that proceeds from identifying a question or problem to *translating the question or*

---

[2]In France, the Academy of Sciences was founded in 1666. In 1700, Leibnitz convinced Frederick I of Prussia to found the Academy of Science at Berlin. Leibnitz became the Academy's first president. In addition, it became clear early on that it did not pay to be modest and hide one's work. Newton delayed publishing his findings on calculus and has had to share credit for that important discovery with Leibnitz.

problem into a mathematical statement or hypothesis. This step is followed by experiments which are described in mathematical terms (data) that can be analyzed (quantitative analysis) to confirm or reject the (mathematical) hypothesis. One of the major differences between inductive reasoning or empiricism and the scientific method is that the former can be conducted independent of mathematics; the latter cannot. Newton built the intellectual principles that necessitated that development. The contributions that quantitative analysis has made to intellectual authority cannot be underestimated. In fact, it is much more likely to be blamed by non-scientists for being too restraining than ignored as an unessential source of authority.

Newton also established methodological rules that have had a continuing impact on the way science is conducted. In "Book III" of *The Mathematical Principles of Natural Philosophy*, Newton established four rules of reasoning in natural science.

RULE I   *We are to admit no more causes of natural things than such as are both true and sufficient to explain their appearances.*[3]

By *true* (as we see in Rules III and IV), he means that claims have been demonstrated by empirical evidence. By *sufficient* he means that once a cause has been demonstrated by experimental and mathematical evidence, no other cause can be admitted. Scientists do not tolerate such statements as, That's all well and good, but more significantly, the truth of the matter is that the ultimate purpose of the universe is to please man, and the ultimate purpose of man is to please God, so the real cause of the planetary motions is secondarily the pleasure of man and primarily the pleasure of God, or some such final cause talk that filled the texts of scholastic natural philosophers. Students of management may recognize the influence of this rule in the law of parsimony which requires that when given a choice between a simple (inexpensive) solution and a complex (expensive) solution, one always selects the simple. "More is in vain where less will serve," as Newton said.

---

[3]*Mathematical Principals of Natural Philosophy*; Book Three: System of the World; Rules of Reasoning in Philosophy, (p. 270).

RULE II   *Therefore to the same natural effects we must, as far as possible, assign the same causes,* (ibid.) .

This rule refers to the generalizability of causes. If gravity explains the falling of an apple in Europe, it explains the falling of an apple in America or Asia. Generalizing causes is important because by doing so we limit the number of causes wherever possible. The ability to discern and act upon the conclusion that the cause of a falling apple is the same as the cause of any other falling object helps us bring order to our understanding of natural phenomena. Nature is sufficiently complex without humans imposing fanciful multiplications of causes.   The ability to perceive consistency and to form general interpretations of nature has profoundly enhanced inquiry in natural science.   It has provided the intellectual discipline that permits imagination to thrive without slipping into fancy.

RULE III   *The   qualities   of   bodies,   which   admit   neither intensification nor remission of degrees, and which are found to belong to all bodies within the reach of our experiments, are to be esteemed the universal qualities of all bodies whatsoever,* (ibid.).

In this rule, Newton essentially states the requirement of empiricism over rationalism. Now that conclusion is not immediately evident in the language of the rule, but is clear in his supporting comments:

> We are certainly not to relinquish the evidence of experiments for the sake of dreams and vain fictions of our own devising . . .   We no other way know the extension of bodies than by our senses. That abundance of bodies are hard, we learn by experience, and because the hardness of the whole arises from the hardness of the parts, we therefore justly infer the hardness of the undivided particles not only of the bodies we feel but of all others... That all bodies are impenetrable, we gather not from reason, but from sensations, (ibid.).[4]

---

[4] That Newton was wrong about the hardness of matter, as modern physics makes evident, does not alter his point about the preference of evidence over dreams. The instruments that assist the senses and allow contemporary physicists

We learn about the physical world from our senses, and the most precise use of our senses is rigorous experimentation. Only rigorous experimentation justifies generalized conclusions about the natural world, not lofty reason operating independent of the senses.

RULE IV *In experimental philosophy we are to look upon propositions inferred by general induction from phenomena as accurately or very nearly true,* *notwithstanding any contrary hypotheses that may be imagined, till such time as the other phenomena occur, by which they may either be made more accurate, or liable to exceptions,* (p. 271).

This rule supports Rule II by emphasizing the authority of induction and adds to it the authority of conclusions reached by the observation of phenomena in the experimental setting. Inductive reason must be guided by empirical evidence and the conclusions reached by such reasoning must not be changed by any other method (deductive reason, feelings, meditation, or just thinking about it). However, if new phenomena are observed, Newton points out, they must be included in experiments which must be repeated to confirm, alter, or reject earlier conclusions.

Calculus allowed Newton to describe the theory of gravity, and the application of these four rules allowed him to expand that theory into what he called *The System of the World.* He expanded or generalized the evidence and mathematical descriptions he developed about gravity to the entire universe. This achievement provided what Kuhn called the *paradigm* in which the study of physics and astronomy was conducted until Einstein.

The achievements of 17th century scientists could have been lost if the principles of empiricism and the scientific method had not been articulated as laws and institutionalized. We have seen that Newton established the principles of natural philosophy and translated them into laws. We now turn to the institutionalization of those laws.

The Institutionalization of Scientific Inquiry

In 1645, Robert Boyle, Bishop John Wilkins, and others founded a loosely organized group they called the Philosophical College. They met

to observe what Newton could not have dreamed explain the different conclusions.

regularly and discussed the work being done in natural philosophy, with special interest in experimental inquiry grounded in empiricism. In 1662, this group was incorporated as The Royal Society of London for Improving Natural Knowledge, and in 1669, it received a royal charter. From 1669, England and France had institutions with royal charters that provided the authority that validated scientific conclusions using the new scientific method. The nature of that authority is significant. It did not rest in a board of directors who accepted or rejected others' work based simply on their expert opinion. Rather, a validation process was established and quickly advanced along with the development of the scientific method as described above. The process is quite recognizable today. It consisted of:

1. Use of the scientific method when conducting scientific research.

2. Publication of findings (including hypotheses, experimental and statistical methods, data, and conclusions) with sufficient details so that the work can be replicated.

3. Wide distribution of published findings and calls for replication with the understanding that claims are not accepted until replicated.

The three societies provided a clearing house for the diffusion of scientific findings and responses based on replication, thus assuring the flow of information throughout the entire scientific community. In addition to Newton's philosophy of science, Latin made a huge contribution to the formation of a unified scientific community in Europe.

Latin, which had been the European language of intellectual discourse since the Dark Ages, continued to form a common language among scientists of all nationalities. The Royal Society of London, The French Academy, and the soon to be formed German Academy published scientific treatises in Latin, and these works were read throughout the continent. Scientists who wished to be taken seriously had to publish their work in Latin through one of these societies and then had to withstand the professional scrutiny that was expected via replication and comment. Had these scientists not shared a common language, the early unification of the scientific community might have been slowed significantly. In more recent times, German served the same purpose. Today, virtually all scientists publish in English.

Scientific Achievements

Of course there is nothing that contributes to independence, authority, and prestige like success. And scientists enjoyed unprecedented success in the 17th century. Their work may seem quite primitive when compared to modern science, but when compared to what had been achieved during the previous 2000 years, it was astonishing.

In addition to the achievements of Newton whom we have already discussed, William Harvey (1578-1657) an English physician, defined biology as its own discipline. Robert Boyle (1627-91) described the difference between elements, compounds, and mixtures and advanced his law regarding the conduct of gases under compression. Although the contributions of Lavoisier (1743-94) and Dalton (1766-1844) were required to set chemistry on its way, Boyle began the quest into the fundamental theories of chemistry. The great Dutch scientist Christiaan Huygens (1629-95) and Isaac Newton commenced a scientific argument regarding the nature of light that was waged into the 20th century.

In addition, the scientific method brought new importance and focus to mathematics and stimulated its growth. We have already noted Newton's contributions, but there were more. Blaise Pascal (1623-62), in one of the most notable human interest stories ever to touch theoretical mathematics, invented the mathematical principles of probability that form the foundation of statistics. The original descriptions of mathematical probability are contained in letters from Pascal to a friend who was a failed gambler. In addition, Rene DesCartes (a.k.a., Cartesius, 1596-1650) is credited as the founder of analytical geometry.

Two Major Challenges to the Independence of Science

The point of all this discussion is that science has not enjoyed its success, independence, authority, and prestige merely because it identified its source of knowledge, adopted empiricism, and learned to use mathematics. Scientists as individuals and as a group have committed to the language, intellectual rules, and institutional authority that have guided scientific inquiry since the late 17th century. Importantly, the scientific community has not endured merely because it was never challenged. The threat to science that erupted after Darwin published his findings on evolution was real and continues to be asserted. Its endurance seems unimpressive if we underestimate the nature of that revolution.

Evolution's enduring shock has very little to do with its suggesting that humans are related to primates. Evolution's enduring shock results from its shattering our sense of time. Prior to evolution, humans could easily grasp the time frame of human and physical existence. Physical and biological evolution have created a sense of time so vast that it makes it seem that we really might exist by chance. It is truly astounding that a scientific view that carries such dramatic religious and existential consequences has not been more vigorously opposed. One explanation for the stability and security in the scientific community is that its intellectual authority was born during a time when science had delivered an intellectual revolution nearly the equal to evolution's.

Just as the source of Darwin's controversy is often misplaced in the role of primates in human development rather than in the shattering of our sense of time, the source of the Copernican revolution's controversy is often misplaced with its undermining the theological and sociological images inherent in the Ptolemaic system of the universe that had permeated Western Christendom since the Dark Ages. That change was indeed traumatic at the time. But the devastating and lasting existential crisis created by the Copernican revolutions results from its shattering our sense of space.

Not only did Copernicus remove the earth and humans from the center of the universe and render the hierarchical images of medieval theology and art obsolete, he also destroyed any sense of the closeness of God. The Copernican view of the universe required the educated European to think of the universe as 23,000 times bigger than it had been thought of under the Ptolemaic theory.

Prior to Copernicus, Europeans believed that the earth was the center of the universe and that it rotated on a *fixed axis*. Since it was known that the diameter of the earth is 8,000 miles, the fixed circle the earth made as it rotated was understood to have an 8,000 mile diameter. Medieval Europeans stood on the earth and looked up at the heavens and perceived the universe as some multiple of their 8,000 mile point of view. When Copernicus explained that the sun is the center of the earth's rotation, and described the circle the earth makes around the sun, that point of view and understanding of the universe changed. Because the earth is 93,000,000 miles from the sun which is the center of its circular movement, the circle the earth makes as it rotates around the sun has a 93,000,000 mile radius and therefore a 186,000,000 mile diameter. From Copernicus on, as

Europeans gazed at the heavens, they did so from a rotating perspective that had increased from 8,000 miles to 186,000,000 miles. The view of the universe increased from some multiple of 8,000 miles to some multiple of 186,000,000 miles or by a factor of 23,000. Because Copernicus's assumptions lacked definitive evidence, one cannot blame his contemporaries for responding with some variation of, As if! However, when Galileo spoke, people listened, not because he changed the language of Copernicus's argument but because he changed the evidence.

Galileo Galilei (1564-1642) was an Italian scientist born in Pisa. Galileo benefitted from the Dutch invention of the telescope which he used to collect visible, irrefutable evidence that proved the Copernican theory. His findings were not so easily dismissed, and the revolutionary implications of the Copernican theory could no longer be ignored. Galileo shattered the educated European's sense of space. And that was no small matter. Not only did this revolution remove humans and the earth from the center of the universe, it also placed us in some undefined spot in an infinitely vast expanse. The earth appeared lost in chaos, and God seemed distant and indifferent. Newton's contribution to theology was that his system of the world restored order to the universe. But he could not minimize the vastness of space.

When we understand the compounded existential crises science has created by destroying our sense of time and space, by placing us on a speck in the universe and giving our lives and nations a mere blink in time, we can appreciate the enduring independence, authority, and prestige of the scientific community as an astounding achievement. We cannot underestimate the importance of the scientific community's success in institutionalizing the scientific method in England, France, and Germany. Educators who feel reluctant to form an intellectual community and establish and support intellectual authority might consider the enormous contributions that institutionalized intellectual authority has made to the scientific community's independence, authority, and prestige, and to the stature and security of individual scientists.

Significantly, the victory of empiricism over rationalism was complete and lasting only in natural science. Science solved the great questions that natural philosophers had struggled with since becoming independent of theology in the 14th century: 1) What is our source of knowledge? The answer, of course, is nature. 2) How do we organize, conduct, and govern inquiry in natural science? The answer is the scientific method and the royal societies. In addition, although science sometimes upsets theological imagery, it has enjoyed a longstanding intellectual compatibility with theology.

The Compatibility of Theology and Science

Scientific empiricism did not conflict with revelation; it conflicted with and replaced rationalism. As we have seen, since the 14th century natural scientists had been liberated from revelation and theology, but the inadequacy of their new method, rationalism, prevented them from advancing scientific inquiry. Bacon did not attack theology; he attacked rationalism. Indeed, in the 17th century, scientists were treated quite well in such Protestant countries as England, Holland, and Germany, and they were generally left alone in such Catholic countries as France.[5] Moreover, even in the 17th century it was becoming clear that the scientific method studies nature, or what classical philosophy has called intermediate formal and efficient causes.

A long standing philosophical description of the place of science in the whole of knowledge relies on familiarity with different kinds of causes. An efficient cause is the agent that works upon a thing; it alters, changes, influences, or modifies a thing. One easily understands God as the first efficient cause, and the big bang as the first intermediate efficient cause. Forces within nature, such as gravity, also work on other things and can be understood as intermediate efficient causes. None of this conceptualization of science threatens theology or revelation.

Formal cause refers to the design of a thing, the internal logic that holds it together. Thus God created not just the universe, but the design of the universe. Scientists study that design (formal cause) as well as the forces (efficient causes) that pertain in nature. Without a doubt, the Copernican design of the universe startled theologians as did Darwin's design of biology. But neither necessarily excluded God as the first formal or first efficient cause in order to describe the design of the

---

[5]The Spanish Inquisition was used by Ferdinand and Isabella to identify and expel Moores and Jews. It left Spain so intellectually impoverished that they had few scientific discoveries to suppress. The Roman Inquisition which began in 1542 exacerbated the conflicts between theology and science, but those conflicts are better understood in the study of ecclesiastical authority than in the epistemologies of theology and science.

universe or life.[6] Copernicus and Darwin forced theologians to reconsider some imagery and language, but they did not challenge the core teachings of the Jewish and Christian traditions, the Ten Commandments, the divinity of Christ, the promise of eternal salvation, and the imperative of charity.

On the other hand, the more we study moral philosophy and the social sciences, the more we encounter unresolvable conflicts with religion. The relationships among moral theology, religious moral philosophy, and secular moral philosophy require far more intellectual attention than they have received. We turn now to the birth of the social sciences and notice that from the outset, social scientists have, by necessity, distanced themselves from moral theology and religious moral philosophy. But they have also distanced themselves from secular moral philosophy.

Achievements of 17th Century Secular Philosophy

Although science made important discoveries during the 17th century, science did not preoccupy 17th century discourse. When Christianity divided into violent opposing camps, political principles lost their under pinnings. As Montaigne pointed out, regicide, the killing of a king, which had been forbidden since ancient times, became the subject of debate with Catholics defending the execution of Protestant kings while forbidding the execution of Catholics. Protestants took the opposite view.

> See the horrible impudence with which we toss back and forth arguments concerning God's will, and how irreligiously we have both rejected them and re-adopted them as fortune has changed sides is these public storms. This most solemn proposition: "Whether it is permissible for the subject to rebel and take up arms against his prince for the defense of religion," remember in what mouths this past year the affirmative was the buttress of one party, the negative the buttress of what other party? . . . And we burn people who say that one must subject truth to the yoke of our

---

[6]This explanation of the *compatibility* of religion and science must tolerate a dualism that produces inadequate theology (God is detached from both nature and human lives) and inadequate science (its metaphysics, which it cannot help but assert, is materialistic and fatalistic). This dualism is humiliating for theologians and debilitating for scientists, but it is not a topic this book can address.

expediency. And how much worse is France in doing it rather than merely saying it? [7]

Moral philosophy had begun to deliver absurdly contradictory, expedient arguments to the public square. Clearly, European societies had to replace the theological foundations of political theory. But the intellectual challenge that confronted moral philosophers was not new. Questions such as, Leaving out God, what can we identify as the source of the monarch's authority and the peoples' loyalty? had been asked since the 14th century when scholastic philosophers began attempts to develop secular *a priori* assumptions in moral philosophy. But they had failed to replace theology's answers to these questions. What changed in the 17th century were not the questions but their urgency. These questions ceased being a matter of intellectual curiosity and became pressing social issues which philosophers had to answer. However, urgency alone rarely provides clarity, motivation to work harder, but not clarity. Pressed by the crisis, philosophers found assistance in the new epistemology of the natural sciences.

There is no mystery in why moral philosophers turned to empiricism. What other choices did they have? They had been stumped for three hundred years, but their colleagues in natural science had developed a new epistemology and it worked. The question is not, Why did moral philosophers turn to empiricism? but Did empiricism work in moral philosophy?

The main characters in this story are two English philosophers Thomas Hobbes and John Locke. What Francis Bacon and Isaac Newton did for natural science, they attempted for political science. But to what extent were their efforts successful? To answer that question, we must review the political history of the 17th century in England, and in particular the *timing* of philosophical *discoveries* and the political events they *influenced*. For if Hobbes and Locke were the equal of Bacon and Newton, *their political philosophies were able to guide, predict, and explain political practice*.

Major Political Events in 17th Century England

Clearly, the English made tremendous advances in political practice during the 17th century. The enormity of the change, the need to govern

---

[7] *In Defense of Raymond Sebond*, (p. 8).

while reconstituting the government, and the lack of political precedent explain why it took virtually the entire 17th century. Again, events and intellectual insight did not develop in a tidy sequence. Everything seemed to happen at once. Rather than attempting a sequential approach, I have identified major topics and described each briefly.

The Redefinition of the Monarchy

Shortly after the beginning of the century, Queen Elizabeth I died. The daughter of Henry VIII, she was one of the greatest, most powerful, and most beloved monarchs in the history of England. However, Henry and Elizabeth had been so dominant that by the end of Elizabeth's reign, nobles and parliament were looking for ways to reduce the power of the monarchy.

Elizabeth was followed by James I, the first of the *Catholic* Stuart kings, who was brilliant but distant and extraordinarily unlucky. James I argued for the divine right of kings, the most extreme claim to power in the history of the English monarchy. Not surprisingly, a Catholic king with a distant personality who made such extraordinary claims to power at precisely the time nobles and parliament were committed to reducing the power of the monarchy, met resistance. Parliament dis-empowered him by impoverishing him. But in order to establish and sustain a limited monarchy, Parliament had to redefine English governmental principles, laws, and institutions. Those tasks occupied most of the century. James I was followed by his son Charles I who lacked his father's intellect and caution. Charles eliminated the issue of luck by being flagrantly duplicitous and inept. Charles was overthrown, executed, and replaced by Oliver Cromwell in 1649, the year after the Thirty Years War ended.

Oliver Cromwell can best be described as a religious military dictator, and his reign can be described as a period of religious war with nearly as many factions as had participated in the war in Europe. Although the damage done in England cannot be compared to what occurred in the German states, it was a traumatic period for the English people. By the time Cromwell died, parliament realized that the solution to their governance problems would not be found through such simple methods as just getting rid of the monarchy.

Following Cromwell, the monarchy was restored with Charles II who had James I's caution if not intellect. During his reign considerable progress was made. But he was followed by James II who had most of Charles I's ineptitude and recklessness. Still feeling the dreadful guilt of having executed a king, the English ran James II out of the country and then declared that he had abandoned the throne. The Stuart kings were gone forever. By the end of the century, the English people, through Parliament, virtually hired William and Mary to serve as monarchs under considerable limits.

The selection or recruitment of William and Mary to the throne enjoyed wide spread support in England, but was not one of those dream like investitures of hope and confidence in anyone new. The arrangement was notably practical and the limits placed on William and Mary expressed in the Declaration of Rights to which they agreed before being crowned are easily recognized as precursors to the United States' Bill of Rights. Indeed, when enacted into law on December 16, 1689, the *Declaration of Rights* became the English *Bill of Rights*.[8]

The English Bill of Rights

Thirteen rights were declared by the Lords Spiritual and Temporal and Commons assembled at Westminster. Some of these laws had already been enacted, but the issue of stability caused by not having a constitution had never been resolved. By requiring the candidates for the crown to swear that they would uphold these rights, Parliament created a kind of constitutional authority for the Bill of Rights.

The bill prohibited the crown from suspending laws or executing its own laws without the consent of Parliament, thus limiting the power of the crown. It made it illegal for the king to convene royal and ecclesiastical courts in which the monarch's appointees acted as prosecutor, judge, and jury. Familiar to all Americans and somewhat ironically, it prohibited the crown from levying taxes without the consent of Parliament (or without representation).

It gave citizens the right to petition the king and made any retribution for such petitions illegal. It gave citizens (but only Protestants) the right to bear arms, and assured the freedom of speech, (but only to debates in

---

[8] During the century, various laws were passed that greatly influenced the United States Constitution. However, the English never adopted a constitution *per se*, which even today provides campaign issues in English national elections. But in the 17th century it presented a huge problem, for it meant that the *rights* won throughout the civil war were very difficult to sustain. In one of history's harmless quirks, the English get credit for inventing the *constitutional monarchy* in spite of never having agreed upon a constitution.

Parliament). And it forbad excessive bail, fines, or cruel and unusual punishment, and required trial by jury.

The separation of church and state was not accomplished, for the monarch remained the head of the Church of England and university professors were required to take religious loyalty oaths late into the 19th century. For most of the 17th century, the church/state struggle was waged to determine which Protestant sect would be the state's church rather than to separate church and state. Nonetheless, by the end of the century, religious freedom had been pretty well assured, at least for Protestants.

Habeas Corpus

From the point of view of the individual citizen relating to the government, no law passed during this century was more important than the right of *habeas corpus*. The *Habeas Corpus* Act of 1679 established the right of citizens to seek protection by the courts against those who arrested them and their jailers. If so requested, judges were obligated to issue to the prisoner a writ of *habeas corpus* which required the jailer to produce the body of the prisoner and also to show cause for the imprisonment. This act extended the judicial laws developed between 1640-1642 by requiring that *judges act in behalf of the prisoner*. It set time limits within which trials had to be conducted so that persons could not be jailed indefinitely without a trial, and prohibited the arrest and trial of persons for crimes of which they had already been accused if they had been set free by the court.

What made this law extraordinary was that it helped articulate a principle by which one branch of government was charged with protecting individual citizens from another branch of government. That was new, and it is one of the most significant concepts advanced in all of political science. Indeed, if one is a citizen in an emerging nation, this kind of protection provides far greater security than is afforded by the right to vote for leaders who when elected rule without restraint. The right of *habeas corpus* established the principle of the division of powers and invented the mechanism for implementing and institutionalizing it. It established the fundamental character of the Bill of Rights in English and American law.

There is no question about the political achievements made in England during the 17th century. They rival the achievements made in America a century later, and were accomplished with really very little bloodshed, a fact that the English will forever point out to the French. English historians give credit to the special character of the English people and the achievements of their two great political philosophers, Hobbes and Locke. Their achievements seem significant because each view is represented well by the claims made by political leaders in their time. Hobbes was active during the first half of the century, Locke during the second. It is easy to conclude that the work of these philosophers *guided, predicted, and explained* the political events of their times. But whether or not that was so remains the question we are asking.

Thomas Hobbes (1588-1679)

Thomas Hobbes was born thirty years before and died thirty one years after the Thirty Years War. He provides a stark philosophical reflection of the state of mind that initiated the quest for a new basis of government. In his most influential work,[9] Hobbes reflects three major attitudes critical to understanding his work: 1) The need to develop a political philosophy that is based on secular, rational principles and not religion. 2) The need to develop a political system that secures life and property. 3) A willingness to forsake significant levels of liberty in order to gain security.

Hobbes began his consideration with a rational analysis of natural man.[10] Both of these terms, *rational* and *natural man*, require special attention lest we assume we know today what they meant then.

Hobbes' Source of Knowledge: Natural Man

Hobbes and other 17th century philosophers sought to explain the fundamental basis of the power and authority of the state (monarch) and the duty owed by the citizen to the ruler without employing Christian assumptions. So his *natural law* was a departure from that of Aquinas. Hobbes sought an explanation for the source of the ruler's authority that did not flow from God. Hobbes asked, if we are *not* going to start with scripture or church teachings, where do we start? His answer was: natural man, man in nature not only before Christianity, but before humans

---

[9]*Leviathan: Or the Matter, Forme, and Power of a Commonwealth Ecclesiastical and Civil.*

[10] Hobbes and Locke used the term *man* to denote humans of both genders. I use their language when quoting them or summarizing their views and use more inclusive language when expressing my own views.

organized themselves into civil societies. Hobbes' question about the condition of man in nature was an anthropological question not a religious or even philosophical one. But he lacked the research tools modern anthropologists use to study *natural* or pre-civilized humans. Admittedly, European thinking about natural man was beginning to change because of their contact with the people and cultures of Africa, America, Asia, and the Pacific islands, but Hobbes predated legitimate anthropological methodology.

Although Hobbes' description of natural man clearly was not scientific, it provides a very accurate depiction of what he and many of his contemporaries concluded from their experiences to be the nature of man. And that was not a pretty picture. Hobbes claimed that in the state of nature, human lives are solitary, poor, nasty, brutish, and short. That sets a mood, I think. This was Hobbes' view of human life without government regardless of race. European as well as non-European humans need government because naturally, or without government, they find themselves in the *state of war* and kill each other. According to Hobbes, humans are naturally inclined to war because of three principle causes:

> First, competition; secondly, diffidence; thirdly, glory. The first, maketh men invade for gain; the second, for safety; and the third, for reputation.[11]

Hobbes concluded that humans are so naturally inclined to thwart their own happiness, to start fights and wars, and to lie and cheat, that they need a strong government to assure their well being. *The justification for the power of the state* derives from the ability of the state to provide humans with what they cannot provide themselves: security and prosperity. Hobbes believed that since power of the state can protect, absolute power can protect absolutely.

The Social Contract, Its Purpose and Terms

But what forms the bond between the citizen and the ruler? Hobbes' answer to that question was his greatest achievement, one that endures today. His answer is known as the social contract. The contract is a legal arrangement with ancient traditions in England. So the concept enjoyed

---

[11] *Leviathan*, Part 1, Chapter 13, (p. 99).

an immediate resonance with the people and government. Two questions must be answered about the social contract: 1) How does a citizen come under the terms of a social contract? and 2) What ought those terms be? Hobbes' answers to those questions did not survive in his life time, but are important to note. How does a citizen come under the terms of the social contract with the ruler? Hobbes provided three conditions: 1) Be a member of a society when it originally forms the compact. 2) Live in a state that is conquered and therefore comes under the rule or contractual commitment with a new leader. 3) Return to and reside within a conquered state.

According to Hobbes, Citizens are bound to a contract through a process in which they have had only passive or no involvement. Shocking to the modern reader, it did not matter to Hobbes that an individual may not have been heard or may not have been included in making the contract or in the debate that lead to it. Indeed, Hobbes invested such complete and stable authority in the ruler that he termed the only solution to a bad and unjust ruler to be tyrannicide, the murder of a tyrant.

This rather extreme political theory is neither irrational nor unprecedented. After all, as we have seen, the fundamental conflict waged between the followers of Aquinas and Duns Scotus at the beginning of the 14th century centered on questions of whether humans are naturally good or bad, whether the physical world is naturally good or bad. According to Duns Scotus, humans cannot even know what is right without the help of God. Humans living in the state of nature would live in a state of war. Duns Scotus claimed that humans cannot survive without God; Hobbes said humans cannot survive without government. Each placed little value on freedom.

Because Hobbes believed that humans needed government in order to have any chance of security and prosperity, the terms he suggested for the social contract gave the ruler absolute power and the citizen virtually no liberty. We see this view more clearly in our discussion of John Locke.

John Locke (1632-1704)

When John Locke was born, Henry VIII had been dead 85 years and Elizabeth I, 29. Charles I was king. Although the reign of Henry probably seemed somewhat remote to Locke, the reign of Elizabeth must have been quite present. It is hard to imagine that he did not hear first hand accounts of her reign from parents and grandparents. But none of these second hand experiences are likely to have matched the intensity of what he experienced in his early teens: the execution of Charles I and the rise to power of Oliver Cromwell. When Cromwell took office, Locke was seventeen and attending Westminster School which he had entered at age fourteen, and where he remained until he was twenty. In 1652, he won a scholarship to Christ Church College, Oxford. Lock continued at Oxford for a number of years completing both his bachelors and masters degrees, becoming a lecturer and even *censor of moral philosophy* in 1664.

During the course of Locke's intellectually formative years, he witnessed the beheading of Charles I, the reign of a military religious dictator, a year with no head of state, and the restoration of the monarchy under Charles II. However, the monarchy that was restored in no way resembled the *divine rights* monarchy sought by James I and Charles I. It was a monarchy to be conducted in conjunction with parliament, giving neither king nor parliament absolute power.

Locke stood side by side with Hobbes contemplating natural man with virtually no evidence regarding how humans conducted their affairs before they formed civilized societies and drawing *a priori* assumptions regarding the nature of government that flowed from his personal opinion regarding the nature of man. To the benefit of his reputation, Locke worked within the context of a political establishment that enjoyed some success in redefining government.

Locke published his *Two Treatises of Government* in 1690. Recall that Hobbes had focused on securing the safety of person and property at virtually any cost to individual liberty at about the time when the English people were compelled to cut that exact deal with their government, Cromwell's military religious dictatorship. But Locke witnessed Cromwell's failure. It was clear to him that the goal of securing safety of person and property cannot be achieved by a government that dissolves or violates individual liberties. He also observed the quasi-constitutional achievements which had been invented during the century and were contained in the English Bill of Rights as well as the contract that William and Mary signed with parliament in order to gain the crown.

Locke Redefines the State of Natural Man

Like Hobbes, Locke concluded that the basis for the authority of a ruler is contained in the social contract the people enter into with the government. But in contemplating human nature, Locke drew very different conclusions from those of Hobbes:

> To understand political power aright, and derive it from its original, we must consider what estate all men are naturally in, and that is a state of perfect freedom to order their actions, and dispose of their possessions and persons as they think fit, within the bounds of the law of Nature, without asking leave, or depending upon the will of any other man.
>
> A state also of equality, wherein all the power and the jurisdiction is reciprocal . . .[12]

Clearly, man in the state of nature did not present to 17th century philosophers a clear, unequivocal definition of the nature of humanity. Rather than studying humans in nature as modern anthropologists have attempted, 17th century philosophers studied the history of the ancient world and Christendom and the events of their time. From those observations, they drew their conclusions. In the case of Hobbes and Locke, those conclusions were significantly different. What Hobbes called the state of nature, Locke called the state of war.

> And here we have the plain difference between the state of Nature and the state of war, which however some men have confounded, are as far distant as a state of peace, goodwill, mutual assistance, and preservation; and a state of enmity, malice, violence and mutual destruction are one from another.[13]

Hobbes contemplated the nature of man and concluded that man is naturally in a state of war. Locke contemplated the nature of man and concluded that man is naturally in a state of peace. Obviously, the two would draw very different notions regarding the extent of a ruler's authority and what might be called the size of government. Hobbes concluded that man requires extensive government at virtually any cost to personal liberty. Locke concluded that man needs very little from government and even that not so desperately as to justify forgoing anything but a minimum loss of liberty. Thus the contractual agreements the two suggested contained very different terms.

---

[12] The Second Treatise on Civil Government, Chapter 2, Paragraph 4, (p. 404).

[13] Ibid., Chapter 3, Paragraph 19, (p. 410-411).

Locke Redefines the Terms of the Social Contract

Hobbes insisted that in securing peace, the people must forsake vast personal liberty and subject themselves to the sovereign's absolute power. Locke insisted that the people retain vast liberties and that the government be structured such that the potential abuses by both the ruler and the legislature be minimized. Locke attributed supreme power to the people:

> Thus the community perpetually retains a supreme power of saving themselves from the attempts and designs of anybody, even of their legislators, whenever they shall be so foolish or so wicked as to lay and carry on designs against the liberties and properties of the subject.[14]

Locke stressed the right of the people to turn out any government that would abridge their rights, but, interestingly, he saw no way for citizens to impose their will on the standing government, but only to overthrow it. Citizens have the right:

> To rid themselves of those who invade this fundamental, sacred, and unalterable law of self-preservation for which they entered into society. And thus the community may be said in this respect to be always the supreme power, but not as considered under any form of government, because this power of the people can never take place till the government be dissolved, (ibid., p. 464).

Similar to Hobbes, Locke's solution to a bad government was revolution.[15]

---

[14] Ibid., Chapter 13, Paragraph 149 (p. 463-464).

[15] I do not discuss the American phase of the English-American political revolution, but we should note that democracy provides a solution to the ancient problem of succession, a peaceful means of removing a legislator or ruler who would abridge the peoples' rights, and, most importantly, a mechanism for the ongoing review and affirmation of the terms of the social contract. Democratic elections select legislators and rulers based on campaigns that articulate competing terms of the social contract. Both elections and campaigns are quite serious matters.

Evaluating the Achievements of Locke and Hobbes

What then were the real and phantom achievements of Hobbes and Locke? If one merely lists Hobbes philosophical statements, it appears that he was enormously influential. But what were his achievements? His method? He claimed to have been influenced by Galileo and to have developed a version of Galileo's *resoluto-compositive* method. However, his method was little different from that of scholastic philosophers. It began with absolute but *unproven* principles that functioned as nothing other than the *a priori* assumptions of deductive reasoning. Call it whatever he would, he had no source for his premises. Hobbes announced *a priori* assumptions and treated them with the weight of geometric principles without supplying proofs. It is impossible to enter into rational discourse regarding assumptions that are derived without rational support. One can reject his assumptions as wrong or accept them as correct, but one cannot argue rationally about them.

The whole question of influence requires some attention to timing. Hobbes' work most directly supported the views of the Stuart kings and Cromwell. Since *Leviathan* was not published until 1651, he could not have influenced either James I who died in 1625 or Charles I who established his views in the 1620's. Although Cromwell's reign began in 1649, he did not become the dictator for which he is famous until 1653. One might argue, then, that Hobbes influenced Cromwell, but even that is a stretch. Indeed, if any philosopher were to be given credit for identifying the principles that guided the first half of the century it would have to be James I whose *The True Law of Free Monarchy* was published before he began his reign. But James I was a medieval scholastic philosopher who made no claim to being an empiricist.

Furthermore the absolute and unpopular power of Cromwell represented a failed experiment, and therefore, if anything, proved Hobbes wrong. To the extent that Hobbes influenced that experiment, he too must bear responsibility for the failure. He cannot be counted as a successful philosopher whose work indicates the enormous promise of secular philosophy or empirical methods in moral philosophy.

Most importantly, the great political achievements of the first half of the 17th century limited the power of the monarch, increased the authority of Parliament, and granted and protected the rights of individual citizens. By the time Hobbes published, political reality had already firmly established the rejection of his views. Not only did his philosophy fail to explain or predict what worked in practice, what worked in practice rejected his philosophy.

However, he did invent the social contract which provides a secular source of the government's authority and the citizen's loyalty. Although the terms of the contract he described were not such that any well adjusted citizen would accept them, he must be given one high mark for inventing the structure of the social contract.

Clearly, neither Hobbes nor his use of empiricism can be called a success. He did not discover lasting political theory and he did not guide successful practice. In fact, it was not even empirical. Which means that secular philosophy, outside of science, still did not have its first victory over rationalism, which had been failing for over 300 years. Maybe John Locke was the true father of empiricism and modern secular philosophy.

Locke's achievements are quite different from Hobbes'. First, he backed a winner. All of the lasting achievements of 17th century political theory are supported in Locke's work. However, he published his work in 1690, one year after William and Mary ascended to the throne. Virtually everything that he pronounced as philosophical principles had been worked out by Parliament during the reigns of Charles I and Charles II, and between the Glorious Revolution and the hiring of William and Mary. Locke's achievement was as an historian of political philosophy, not as an inventive thinker. I do not mean to underestimate the enormous contribution that Locke's historical record made to Western political theory, especially to the authors of the United States Constitution. But what we are interested in is philosophical method and its ability to guide inquiry and predict developments in the social sciences.

From the point of view of secular philosophy, one must view this century with great ambivalence. The one great invention that can be attributed to a philosopher is the *social contract. B*ut that invention was based on an ancient English tradition of contract law, was advanced by the philosopher who in virtually all other matters was wrong, and contained terms that were rejected by the English following their experience with Cromwell. Indeed the great achievement of the social contract had to wait until the 18th century when the American constitution combined it with democracy and effectively shifted the source of the ruler's authority from God to the people. All other major political achievements of the 17th century must be credited to practical politicians who used that time honored but very informal and limited method, trial and error. They succeeded through effort and perseverance rather than intellectual achievements that guided, predicted, and explained practical political activity.

At a time when natural science began to inform practical science as never before, philosophy became historical and descriptive, informed by practitioners rather than informing them. But that distinction was not recognized. Both Hobbes and Locke claimed to be empiricists. Hobbes claimed to use methods similar to Galileo's mathematics. Locke claimed to be a scientist. But Hobbes offered no proofs for his theorems, and Locke no evidence for his science. Their notoriety is based upon the extraordinary changes that marked their century, the importance of their intellectual claims, and the accomplishments of parliament. If natural scientists had accepted such weak methodology, we might still be doing science in terms of earth, air, fire, and water. By deriving their success from historical events but claiming to be accomplished empiricists, Hobbes and Locke continued the inadequacy of secular philosophy that had begun 300 years earlier.

Secular philosophy was not destined to continue its errors. Hobbes and Locke and the general optimism known as the Enlightenment was countered by skeptics such as David Hume. Interestingly, none of the views we have studied explains how modern moral philosophy devolved into individualism. For that discussion we must look to a particular strand of Immanuel Kant's work and two under examined 19th century views. We turn now to that discussion.

6

The Devolution of Secular Philosophy

Let us make sure we know where we are in our project. We know that public education must educate all children well, and we know that in order to do so we must change and change rather quickly. We are interested in the intellectual barriers that prevent educators from integrating research, integrating research and practice, and conducting discourse that leads to agreement, commitment, and action. We have agreed that these intellectual barriers create major challenges to change and that they require intellectual solutions. We have chosen to focus on epistemology as the best source of solutions to these intellectual problems.

We have reviewed the history of Christianity and witnessed the transformation of a unified Christian community into a religiously pluralistic society that required secular solutions to principles of governance and public life. We have, therefore, a deeper understanding of why the philosophy of public education must be grounded in secular principles. We have recognized that in a pluralistic society, we cannot employ moral theology or its epistemology, which we have called revelation, to guide inquiry. And we have seen that religious pluralism resulted from the conduct of religious leaders not the conduct of secular philosophers. We are disinclined to endure criticism from religious leaders or activists who despise anything secular.

We have acknowledged that science has been enormously successful in developing an epistemology that is an expanded version of empiricism. Science has been both clear and successful in identifying its source of knowledge and method of inquiry. In addition, science is conducted within an intellectual community that has secured its independence, stability, and prestige by institutionalizing its intellectual authority.

On the other hand, we have noted that secular moral philosophy has never quite figured out how to conduct inquiry. Since the 14th century, philosophers have failed to solve the problems regarding the source of knowledge encountered in rationalism, the epistemology of Aristotle, Aquinas, and the scholastic philosophers. Beginning with Hobbes and Locke, a tradition developed among modern secular philosophers that attempted to replace rationalism with empiricism. These philosophers have also failed to identify their source of knowledge. Although there are some pretty good stories contained in our study, this is not a novel. So let me add some clarity to the discussion by revealing where we are going.

In the introduction, I claimed that education is currently guided by individualism which I call an anti-epistemology. What may not be obvious is that the roots of individualism do not lie in any of the schools of thought we have studied. Understanding revelation, rationalism, and empiricism gives no insight into how moral philosophy and epistemology could have degenerated into individualism. Attempts to understand the current epistemology in education are not aided by understanding revelation, rationalism and empiricism. We need to know about those epistemologies in order to understand epistemology as a formal structure and to avoid misusing them. But for now we must set all of that aside and consider how education could have adopted individualism as its epistemology. Importantly, ancient, medieval, and 17th century philosophers called individualism *solipsism*. All of them rejected it.

I trace the failure of modern philosophy to Kant which is not a universally held conclusion. Toulmin traces it to DesCartes and MacIntyre to Duns Scotus. I have selected Kant because he developed two important strands of thought regarding the source of knowledge. One seems to have set in motion, whether intentionally or not, the direction of modern philosophy that ended in individualism. The other strand provides what I argue is the most compelling answer to the question of the source of knowledge that exists in secular philosophy. Both Toulmin and MacIntyre provide very important insights into the disservice their culprits dispensed on Western intellectual development. However, one can understand both DesCartes and Duns Scotus and not understand how Western philosophy devolved into individualism. Within a study of Kant, we can discover the derivation of modern philosophy's devolution into individualism and a solution to the problem of the source of knowledge in moral philosophy and the social sciences. The study of Kant's work unveils the source of the major contemporary problems in moral philosophy and the solution to the 700 year old problem. In this chapter, we look at the strand of Kant's work that began the devolution of modern philosophy and the increasingly problematic developments that followed it. In chapter seven we use another strand of his work to solve the problem of the source of knowledge in the epistemology of education and the social sciences.

In tracing the devolution of modern philosophy, we do not attempt to discuss every major philosopher since Hobbes and Locke. Rather, we look at Kant, who was an 18th century philosopher, and two major 19th century views that are virtually unknown to contemporary educators but dramatically influence the way we think. The first is encyclopaedia, the second, genealogy. These two views are important because they are influential without being known or understood. They account for *habits of thinking*[1] in moral philosophy, the social sciences, the public square, and even our private lives. We also discuss the two major 20th century philosophical views that currently claim to explain how inquiry must be conducted in education: analytical philosophy (in which I include positivism) and post-modernism.

An historian of philosophy might wonder why I left out Hume's skepticism, Mill's utilitarianism, James's pragmatism, Maritain's neo-Thomism, or Dewey's progressivism. The answer is that I do not believe that they help explain how we arrived at individualism nor do I believe that they are used today to guide inquiry in education. I tried to omit analytical philosophy and post modernism, but colleagues pointed out the necessity of including those views. No one has suggested that I must include a discussion of Hume, Mill, James, Maritain, or even Dewey in order to frame current intellectual habits or arguments in education.

The Problematic Strand of Kant's Work

By now it is fair to expect that the reader is developing some comfort with questions regarding the source of knowledge. We know that in theology the source of knowledge is God, in science it is nature, and in secular philosophy it is a huge, 700 year old problem, although in Kant's day, it was only a 450 to 500 year old problem. Kant's *problematic* answer to the source of knowledge question was not as problematic in itself as in the way it has been elaborated by subsequent scholars. First we discuss Kant's view, then we look at its problematic development.

Kant claimed that the source of knowledge is in the mind. As he wrote in *The Critique of Pure Reason,* Preface to the First Edition:

---

[1]Not all habits of thinking are grounded in the unknown, but some are. When I use the term, I refer to manners of thinking that are unexamined and routine.

> I confine myself to the examination of reason alone and its pure thought; and I do not need to seek far for the sum-total of its cognition, because it has its seat in my own mind, (p. 2).

By confining inquiry to reason alone, Kant severed inquiry from all other sources of knowledge. He established the independence of the secular scholar from God and sacred texts, thus rejecting revelation, and he liberated secular moral philosophy from the domination of nature and the scientific method as well as from empirical aberrations such as Hobbes' and Locke's *man in the state of nature*. Kant insisted that the mind provides the sensible or physical world with the mind's order without interfering with the physical world's mechanisms, which are its own. If one recalls the mechanical view of the universe that Newton advanced, it is easy to notice the profound use Kant made of that view.

Copernicus and Galileo destroyed Ptolemy's geocentric order of the universe–the notion that the earth is the center of the universe, and the planets, sun, and stars rotate, machine like, around that center. Their discoveries created a psychological crisis in the West because the Ptolemaic order seemed to have been shattered *and left in chaos*. Newton's system of the world employed the law of gravity and mathematical precision to re-establish a machine like order to the universe. Kant's point is that the universe may operate like a machine, but it does not know and is unable to describe that order. When the mind perceives, reflects upon, and describes the principles by which the universe operates, it creates a world (a *super-sensible* system, a system above the senses) that is superior to the mechanical, *unconscious* operations of nature.

There is indeed the mechanistic relationship among planets that Newton described, but the human understanding of those relationships is more complex and of a higher order than the mechanistic relationships. One particular sentence in Kant's discussion of this point in *Critique of Practical Reason* requires special attention:

> The supersensible nature of the same beings, on the other hand, is their existence according to laws which are independent of every empirical condition and, therefore, belong to the *autonomy* of pure reason, (p. 308).

Kant described two worlds: the physical, empirical world of nature and the senses; and the supersensible world that is parallel to but clearly different from and superior to the physical world. The fact that there is a world of the mind that is different from but related to the physical world is unarguable. But the precise nature of that relationship is not so clear and arguments regarding it define the competing views that are often described as materialism and idealism.

Without giving way to that digression, we can notice that the contemporary reader is familiar with many examples of the supersensible world although we may never have thought of them in that way. Gravity may indeed describe an aspect of the physical world that was observed before it was understood, but the *concept* of gravity, *its mathematical properties, and its logical exclusion of what is not gravity* are clearly intellectual achievements that do not exist in nature. Similarly, language is a product of the mind, not nature. *Grass* refers to various forms of plant life, but there is no single thing that is grass, and nature is unaltered by the presence or absence of the name. Such insights regarding a concept or the word not being the thing are quite familiar to the modern reader, so we might ask, What's the big deal?

The big deal is that Kant appeared to resolve the problem of the source of knowledge in a manner that increased the self esteem of philosophers and provided relief to citizens of the West who feared that science was beginning to dominate their lives with its mathematical and mechanical limits. The apparent rising above science and mathematics explains why Kant became a major cult hero in his day and a minor hero in the 1960's.

This strand of his work becomes even more interesting when we notice that the elaboration of Kant's views by 19th and 20th century philosophers has produced major problems in Western philosophy and the social sciences. Three particular problems seem rooted in this strand of Kant's work: 1) Inquiry has been severed from tradition. 2) Inquiry has been severed from community. 3) The authority of the individual has been elevated to the absolute. Again, Kant did not reach these conclusions, but they seem to be the inevitable if not the intended consequences of this strand of his work.

Classical vs. Post-Kantian Realism

MacIntyre's distinction between what he called classical realism and post-Kantian realism helps us understand the importance of Kant's influence on current thinking. According to MacIntyre, classical realism requires that we: 1) Know external objects and events in and of themselves so that the knowledge of the external transforms the internal, making it an embodiment or intellectual replication of the external. 2) Interpret the external in terms of the values, judgments, and purpose of the particular community or tradition of which we are members. 3) Make competent judgments as a mature member or master of the community.[2]

Classical realism acknowledges that a reality exists outside the mind, and stresses that the mind's task is to develop an adequate internal representation of the external world. Notice that MacIntyre uses a very interesting phrase to describe the role of the mind in classical realism: the mind "must become adequate to" the external world. In addition, classical realism acknowledges the difficulty that each of us would have if left alone to develop an adequate understanding of the external world. Each of us would have to invent all of the disciplines and crafts that define the accumulated knowledge of our society. The solution to this difficulty is education, whether housed in schools and universities or apprenticeship programs. Classical realism has a clear understanding of the role of the teacher: we must have mastered our craft or discipline to the highest standards of our community and teach it to our students in a way that assures that if they learn well, their knowledge and skill will be accepted in the larger community. It is impossible, according to classical realism, to develop knowledge, teach, or learn independent of the community of scholars that composes a discipline or craft. Classical realism is very different from the *autonomy* of post-Kantian realism. Admittedly, post-Kantian realism is not identical to Kant's views, but one cannot explain what developed after Kant without understanding Kant's influence upon it.

Kant claimed that the world of the mind is different from and superior to the physical world. Physical reality is inferior to the world of the mind. As MacIntyre explains, when post-Kantian philosophers read statements in Kant such as, "The *supersensible* nature of the same beings, on the other hand, is their existence according to laws which are independent of every empirical condition and, therefore, belong to the *autonomy* of pure reason;"[3] they concluded that reason must be independent of (autonomous

---

[2]*Three Rival Versions*, (p. 68).

[3]*The Critique of Practical Reason*, (p.308).

from) the "bonds of any particular moral and religious tradition,"[4] and ultimately from any community or any tradition. Autonomy, isolation from community and tradition, was the ultimate eventuality of this view, quite possibly the unintended consequence of Kant's having placed so much emphasis on pure, independent, superior reason. MacIntyre gives considerable attention to two groups of 19th century intellectuals. The first, encyclopaedists, invited their followers to form an allegiance, "To reason as such, impersonal, impartial, disinterested, uniting, and universal," (ibid.). The second MacIntyre called genealogists. We discuss them in some detail below.

I have listed three problems that MacIntyre identified with post-Kantian realism: the severing of inquiry from tradition, the severing of inquiry from community, and the assigning of absolute intellectual authority to the individual. We can begin to discuss the seriousness of these problems. If the source of truth is in the mind, then one must look only to the mind for truth. As Kant said, "I confine myself to the examination of reason alone and its pure thought; and I do not need to seek far for the sum-total of its cognition, because it has its seat in my own mind."[5] In Kant's historical context, not seeking far for the *sum-total of cognition* most obviously excluded revelation, the scientific method, and empiricism. Those were the well established views that Kant rejected. But his exclusive use of reason also excluded tradition and community. Once intellectuals sever inquiry from their community, it is rationally impossible to sustain claims that any one view is superior to any other view about anything. No individual can sustain a claim that his or her work is superior to that of everyone else. Only a community, through some agreed upon process, can assert and sustain such claims. As we have seen, reason plays a fundamental role in science, but reason alone cannot explain the intellectual authority enjoyed by scientists. Rather, the scientific method, the use of mathematics, and the demand that all claims be published, reviewed, and replicated in order for *the community* to acknowledge their validity explains authority in science. It is impossible for individual scientists to establish the authority of their findings. Only the community can establish authority. Kant's claim that only reason is

---

[4]*Three Rival Versions,* (p. 59).

[5]*Preface to the Critique of Pure Reason*, (p. 2).

required for the establishment of truth permitted individuals to claim intellectual authority. Nietzsche followed this strand of thinking when he claimed that the source of truth resides within each individual, which is a fundamental assertion of what MacIntyre called genealogy[6] and what is more popularly known as individualism.

It is important to stress that post-Kantian realism is different from Kant's view or it is difficult to engage the other strand of Kant's work. Not only did Kant reject individualism, he was guarded even regarding the timing and place of popular discussions of ethics:

> This descending to popular notions is certainly very commendable, if the ascent to the principles of pure reason has first taken place and been satisfactorily accomplished. This implies that we first *found* ethics on metaphysics, and then, when it is firmly established, procure a hearing for it by giving it a popular character. But it is quite absurd to try to be popular in the first inquiry, on which the soundness of the principles depend.[7]

Clearly, Kant did not support the individualist's view that the mind is the unique reservoir of knowledge and that every mind must be considered the equal to every other mind. He would never have conceded that any opinion must be considered the equal to any other opinion regardless of the quality or rigor of inquiry brought to a topic. To the contrary, he

[6]If we think of genealogy as simply identifying the names of ancestors, this term makes no sense in this context. But if we think of studying our family's genealogy as an anthropological attempt to discover the root causes and historical development of our family's culture, it makes sense. In *The Genealogy of Morals*, Nietzsche set out to discover the root causes of moral judgements, to answer the question, "Under what conditions did man construct the value judgements *good* and *evil?*" (p. 151). Importantly, he disdained the conclusions about good and evil reached by Western scholars and rejected the traditions that supported those conclusions, i.e., Christianity and the emerging liberal tradition. He considered both to be fatally weak, that they destroyed valor and the dignity of man that can only be expressed in heroic acts.

[7]*The Metaphysic of Morals*, Second Section, "Transition from Popular Moral Philosophy to the Metaphysic of Morals," (p. 263).

distinguished the supersensible realm of pure reason from both the physical world and *popular opinions*. Notice, he refers to this *descending* to popular opinions, which emphasizes the superiority, the higher, elevated status that he assigned to pure reason. And yet there is that troubling quality to this stand of his work that suggests that the truth somehow resides in the mind, autonomous from God, nature, community, and tradition.

We turn now to the discussion of the two major 19th century versions of post-Kantian realism. First we discuss encyclopaedia, then genealogy.

Encyclopaedia

We face a new problem as we begin to study the encyclopaedists, a personal challenge. Up until now we have discussed the history of philosophy, notable achievements and intractable problems. Now, we begin to talk about ourselves, how we think. We may even find ourselves saying, I do that. We may be inclined toward defensiveness and denial which of course impede inquiry. Therefore it is important to notice at the outset of this discussion that encyclopaedia and all its errors occur throughout society in a thoroughly bi-partisan, multi-cultural, multi-ethnic, ecumenical, inter-disciplinary, and cross-class manner. The encyclopaedic view has been universally implemented. All of us tend to hate it in our opponents and yet remain blind to it in ourselves. So one of our goals must be, eventually, to get everyone to stand up and say, Hello, my name is _____, and I am a recovering encyclopaedist.

Before I get into the formal definitions of encyclopaedia, let me provide some of the sociological characteristics of encyclopaedists: 1) They exist only in groups, 2) The group has a shared sense of superiority over all other groups, and 3) The group has power at least in its own frame of reference. Brief reflection on these traits reveals serious social consequences of such groups. They hold views as a group that have not been rationally argued and therefore have no rational support. Consequently, it is impossible for encyclopaedic groups that hold conflicting views to engage each other rationally. But they also have power. Encyclopaedists are the modern intellectuals who have given *shared universal values* a bad name because they exercised power over their immediate surroundings, imposing their values on weaker individuals and groups without establishing a rational basis of or persuasive argument for their positions. In order to understand encyclopaedia, we must pay attention to the sociological consequences of encyclopaedia, but first we turn to their epistemology.

MacIntyre identifies four elements of the encyclopaedists' theory of knowledge: data, unifying synthetic conceptions, deductive and inductive methodology, and the continuous progress of history.[8] The first three elements describe the encyclopaedists' method of knowing. The fourth reveals their source of knowledge. We begin with the source.

Encyclopaedia's Source of Knowledge

The continuous progress of history assumes that human events evolve such that there is inevitable, ongoing, qualitative improvement in knowledge and culture. The encyclopaedists noted that if history produces ongoing development and one participates in the *current, prevailing view,* then one is not only correct, one is more correct than anyone has ever been before. For the encyclopaedists, then, *the source of knowledge is inevitably located in the views of the current prevailing group.* Not surprisingly, encyclopaedia originated in 19th Century England, Scotland, and Germany where the British and German empires vied for intellectual, technological, economic, and military domination.[9]

As we noted earlier, it is helpful to understand the encyclopaedists as post-Kantian realists. They believed that there is an absolute and uniform rationality that is available to normally competent minds. This rationality assures that individuals will reach the same conclusions, but the sameness is due to the nature of rationality not to truths located in the external world. It does not depend on past traditions or any rational process that works out agreement among a community of scholars. The task of encyclopaedists was simply to be rational. Because they believed that the nature of rationality is singular, they assumed that rationality, wherever practiced, must eventually lead to the same conclusions. Because of different levels of rational development, they explained patiently, the world contains different views. However, the truth, the most correct conclusions possible, must be the conclusions held by the most enlightened people on earth, or the current prevailing group.

[8]*Three Rival Versions*, (p. 20).

[9]The French encyclopaedists are a different group whose lasting influence had more to do with opposing religious influence in French civil society than in advancing a world view.

The encyclopaedists expressed their humanity by stressing that the lack of development in rude, rudimentary, and backward societies is not a hopeless condition. Backward people are not hopelessly backward, but they do need to work harder to catch up. Recognizing that the task was difficult, encyclopaedists noted that life for backward people would be made ever so much easier if they just had the opportunity to share the light of the most advanced society in the world. In order to provide that opportunity among their own people and the people of backward societies, the English and Scottish encyclopaedists developed the Ninth Edition of the *Encyclopaedia Britannica*. This view is astoundingly arrogant, but in the 19th century it enjoyed wide support.

Intellectual Affirmation of the Continuous Progress of History

Three factors in 19th Century Europe provided intellectual support to the encyclopaedists' confidence in the inevitable progress of history: the benign circumstances of 19th century Europe, Hegel's historical dialectic, and Darwin's theory of evolution, especially the survival of the fittest.

The encyclopaedists lived during the longest period of uninterrupted peace and economic growth in the history of Europe. Great Britain, which contained both England and Scotland, was the dominant economic and military power on earth. Germany had finally overcome the restraints of decentralization that had been imposed on it at the end of the Thirty Years War. Germany was emerging politically, economically, and militarily so much so as to threaten the interests of England, France, and Russia as colonial powers. One might forgive the intellectual leaders in England and Germany for feeling that, at the very least, they were historically blessed if not superior.

Hegel (1770-1831) developed a view of history that also contributed to their confidence. An idealist, Hegel (like Kant) made ideas superior to the physical world. A rationalist, he asserted that everything is rational, and that everything rational is real. But he was also a spiritualist, and his most famous achievement, the Hegelian dialectic, demonstrated how the spirit works within and to the inevitable benefit of human history. Hegel's dialectic process begins with a *thesis* (the current view) which is inevitably confronted by an *anti-thesis* (a competing view). The conflict between the thesis and anti-thesis must, inevitably, be resolved in what he called the *synthesis*. According to Hegel, rationality and spirit demand that the synthesis be the best solution that is inherent in the competition between the thesis and antithesis. "The truth lies somewhere in between . . ." is a familiar, common sense expression of the assumption that the best answer is inevitably contained in the terms of a dispute. Adding the assumption that the spirit guides this process deepens the necessity of the synthesis' being the best possible solution.

To make the historical dialectic their own, the encyclopaedists dropped the influence of the spirit and replaced it with the concept of *absolute and uniform rationality*. Thus adapted, the historical dialectic provided a rational explanation for why the continuous progress of history demands that the current view is not only the best possible view at this time but the best view of all time.

The third argument for the inevitable progress of history was found in the *progress* of the natural sciences. Mysteries had been explained, medicine was advancing with astonishing consistency, and wealth was increasing at unprecedented rates. Scientific and economic progress contributed a complex intellectual and visceral confidence in progress in general. When Charles Darwin (1809-82) published his theory of evolution, and in particular the principle of the survival of the fittest, he provided a scientific explanation for the continuous progress of history. Hegel claimed the spirit drove the dialectic, the encyclopaedists preferred absolute and uniform rationality, but scientists topped both by providing an underlying force of nature that wipes out the inferior and assures the ascendance of the superior.

Religious Support for Encyclopaedia

Although 19th century encyclopaedists in general and social scientists in particular were decidedly secular, religious groups were not immune to encyclopaedic influences. Indeed, encyclopaedia provides a fascinating insight into the emergence of what some theologians consider the most troubling dogma in Catholicism, the infallibility of the pope. During the pontificate of Pope Pius IX (1846-1878), the First Vatican Council defined papal infallibility. The Catholic magisterium was very fond of Hegel, and they did not drop his reference to the spirit. Rather the church added *holy* to spirit and developed a Catholic form of encyclopaedia. The doctrine of the infallibility of the pope insists that because of the influence of the Holy Spirit, the pope cannot make errors when speaking officially. The elite classes of Europe claimed to be the reservoirs of truth, and the pope would not be outdone. We should also note the susceptibility of the Puritan tradition to elitism.

As noted earlier, the Puritans were followers of Calvin. His *doctrine of the elect* described a kind of predestination. Only the elect could look forward to eternal life. However, not knowing if one is a part of the elect creates significant existential angst. The Puritans had to answer the question, How do we tell who is part of the elect? Their answer is that those who are God's blessed are blessed in this life as well as the next. We can tell who is blessed by paying attention to the most obvious manifestations of temporal well being: cleanliness, self-control, and wealth. Ignoring the notion that one's destiny is predetermined, the Puritans developed a moral code that permitted one to work very hard and exert tremendous self control so as to establish material success and *demonstrate* one's being elect.

The Puritan view has had an enormous impact on the American character. Hard work and self control are deeply imbedded virtues. But there is more to it than that. Materialism has been unusually powerful in America. Rather than defining virtues in the Christian and classic terms (faith, hope, and charity and justice, prudence, temperance, and courage respectively[10]), American culture, more than others, has treated material prosperity as a *fundamental virtue*. But more to the point, American culture has tended to assign a special kind of righteousness and intellectual and spiritual authority to those who achieve material success. The wealth of financiers and the power of corporate leaders have invested them with a unique brand of American righteousness.

Immigrant Catholics and Jews from Europe constituted an American counter culture in the late 19th and early 20th century. These groups spawned many activists for social justice, especially in the labor movement. But aristocratic bishops have supported the principle of the unquestioned authority of religious and political leaders from the core of Catholic theology. And Puritanism has long supported the righteousness of the elite. Encyclopaedists enjoyed multiple sources of support among the elite which helps predict which segments of society are typically served well by it.

The people who are served well by encyclopaedia are the people who select the intellectual premises of society. Those decisions are made in the university, corporate board rooms, among lobbyists and politicians, and of course in the media. If we imagine ourselves in any of those settings

[10]MacIntyre, *After Virtue*, (p. 167).

during the 19th century we would have quite an array of arguments from which to choose that would lead us to affirm encyclopaedia. Since we would be people living in the most benign times in the history of the human race, we might indeed believe that we represent the pinnacle of human development. Not only had we survived, which demonstrated our being the fittest, we had created the most affluent, safest, most dominant culture on earth. Indeed, one is a bit pressed to believe that he or she might have avoided being caught in the prevailing hubris.

After a far less benign political and economic period that started with World War I and has not subsided, we do not feel so blessed, nor do we celebrate our genius as an absolute given. However, intellectual habits that developed during the 19th century have endured, mainly because no serious philosophical view has confronted them. As we discuss below, the genealogists attacked encyclopaedia and won important victories for the status of the individual, but theirs is an anti-epistemological view that rejects all tradition and confounds any attempt to build community.

Genealogists rejected encyclopaedia but by also rejecting tradition they were unable or disinclined to articulate the tradition in which encyclopaedia had been developed. As a result, genealogists did not expose the collapse of encyclopaedia's foundations and thereby failed to assure the final defeat of that view in the university and the public square. Rather, genealogy created an ethical vacuum in the public square that was filled by encyclopaedic habits of thinking. Below we talk about the transformation of encyclopaedia in the 20th century that has made it virtually invisible, but before we turn to that topic, we must complete our discussion of its epistemological claims.

Encyclopaedia's Methodological Claims

It is important to recall that natural scientists established their epistemology in the 17th century. By the 19th century, they were merely improving their intellectual skills and experimental instruments. They did not claim to have improved inquiry in science by hammering out the insights of encyclopaedia. The epistemology of natural science and the conduct of inquiry in the natural sciences were unaffected by encyclopaedia. We return to this point.

The original encyclopaedists are best understood as 19th century moral philosophers, social scientists, and cultural historians. As noted earlier, MacIntyre identifies four elements of the encyclopaedists' theory of knowledge, the first three of which (data, unifying synthetic conceptions, and deductive and inductive reason) define the encyclopaedists' method of inquiry. From our earlier discussions, it should be quite clear that data are meaningless outside of inductive reasoning. Furthermore, deductive and inductive reasoning are helpless without an authoritative source of knowledge. By being wrong about their source of knowledge (the continuous progress of history) they debilitated their rational methods. There is no need to repeat those discussions. But what about *unifying synthetic concepts*? Before we answer that question we must understand the encyclopaedic view of rationality.

Encyclopaedists claimed that the rules of rationality are the rules of rationality as such. But as our historical review has revealed, that is wrong. The rules of rationality in the sciences are the rules that derive their truth by being demonstrably consistent with nature. As we have seen, the scientific community plays a major role in passing final judgement on rational claims by requiring that they be published and replicated. The more important the claim, the greater the scrutiny that it receives. Thus the rules of rationality in science are far better understood as the rules of the scientific community's rationality than the rules of rationality as such.

Since we are attempting to point to different rules of rationality, it is helpful to notice the rules of rationality in mathematics. Mathematical proofs are not established in nature but in logic. Mathematicians use a highly developed form of deductive reasoning. But again, the community of mathematicians does not accept conclusions that its members demonstrate are flawed. If different mathematicians advance conflicting conclusions or even if some mathematicians point out that a particular claim is flawed, the community concludes that the problem has not been solved. A recent case demonstrates that point. Andrew Wiles claimed to have proved Fermat's Last Theorem. He published his proof. It underwent the scrutiny of the mathematics community, and a subtle flaw was discovered. Wiles returned to his attic, or wherever he works, and in a year came back with a different proof that has been able to withstand the mathematics community's scrutiny. Wiles and his colleagues did not merely follow the rules of rationality as such; they followed the rules of rationality in mathematics as developed, taught, and practiced in their community, rules that are necessarily different from those in science.

The problem with the encyclopaedists' *unifying synthetic concepts* is that they are based upon rules of rationality that do not provide anyone with the capacity to evaluate and therefore accept or reject them. They have not solved the problem of developing the rationality that is appropriate to their disciplines.

Establishing the validity of *unifying synthetic concepts* presents the same problems in secular moral philosophy and the social sciences as scholastic philosophers faced in attempting to establish the validity of their *a priori* assumptions. Both scholastic philosophers and encyclopaedists failed to establish their source of knowledge and therefore failed to establish the validity of their major assumptions. It is interesting to note that encyclopaedists did not struggle with questions regarding their source of knowledge because they thought they had solved the problem via their understanding of the inevitable, continuous progress of history. Because that assumption was wrong, their confidence in unifying synthetic concepts (their *a priori* assumptions) was misplaced. Our analysis is bound to appear circuitous, but it was they who created the circle. Due to their confidence in the continuous progress of history and to their viewing themselves as being the most advanced group of intellectuals in history, their ultimate test of their own knowledge was whether or not they accepted it.

Again we must note that 19th century *natural scientists* developed knowledge using the epistemology of science. Their conclusions were not valid because they agreed with each other. They agreed that conclusions were derived through adequate methodology and validated in nature. They agreed within the rigorous application of the epistemology of science which had nothing to do with the continuous progress of history or other encyclopaedic claims. However, the encyclopaedists' claim that their success included scientific advances added to their prestige.

In doing secular moral philosophy and social science, the encyclopaedists could not rely on any method but their own, and it failed. What they said, when we remove the rhetorical embellishments is simply, "This statement is right because we said it, and we are right because we are the grandest intellectuals in history. We stand on the shoulders of all who went before us, advancing their knowledge which by definition makes us the most right in history." The problem, of course, is that they had no way of telling whether they were right or wrong.

No success permitted the encyclopaedists to achieve prominence or to endure. No one studies encyclopaedic ethics or social science. But at least 19th century encyclopaedia operated within a well articulated tradition whose values, judgements, and purpose were known and accepted by its members.[11]   They believed that the continuous progress of history made them the reservoirs of truth and they supported their claim with the Hegelian dialectic, Darwin's theory of evolution and the survival of the fittest, and the overall cultural improvement enjoyed in Europe during that time.

However, the support encyclopaedia found in its original historical context has been refuted in the 20th century. World War I produced the lost generation. It was followed by a world wide depression and then World War II. By 1950, confidence in the continuous progress of history had been replaced by the cold war and the very real threat of the complete annihilation of civilization.   Hegel's faith had been destroyed, social Darwinism had been exposed as inept, even monstrous in its application, and scientific achievements had become more notable for producing weapons of mass destruction than for promoting the welfare of humanity or the earth.

It is not hard to understand how 19th century intellectuals could accept encyclopaedia's claims, for the historical and intellectual context in which they lived provided convincing support. What is perplexing is that encyclopaedia has endured after its support has vanished. We must be curious about a view that cannot withstand rational scrutiny but endures as fragments of the tradition in which it was formed.

The tragic events that befell Western civilization in the first half of the 20th century completely discredited the presumption that history inevitably progresses. But these were events. They were not rationally developed arguments, waged among a community of scholars. These events have destroyed the premises of encyclopaedia, but they did not replace it with a better way of thinking.   That nothing replaced encyclopaedia is an especially important point because encyclopaedia was a way of thinking that anointed the elite classes with enormous intellectual authority and ethical righteousness. Predictably, the beneficiaries of that view were reluctant to give it up.

[11] Actually, it is more accurate to say that compared to 20th century encyclopaedists they knew their tradition. MacIntyre points out that 19th century encyclopaedists asserted ethical values disembodied from the religious traditions in which they had been developed and consequently could not explain them to themselves or others.

By 1950, 19th century encyclopaedia's premises had been destroyed. However, its principles and implications had been so institutionalized and had become so much a part of how the elite think, that encyclopaedia persisted as a habit, an unquestioned, unchallenged, routine way of thinking. Any view that persists, especially among the powerful, after its fundamental assumptions have been discredited and obscured, becomes terribly problematic. Encyclopaedia requires some serious consciousness raising, a little de-mooning.

Manifestations of Encyclopaedia in Western Intellectual Life

When I first read *Three Rival Versions of Moral Enquiry* it seemed that MacIntyre viewed encyclopaedia as a transitional phenomenon, important only as an historical influence, not a lasting one. After all, there was very little time between its emergence and Nietzsche's annihilation of it. But I became increasingly uncomfortable with that interpretation because it did not account for why MacIntyre provided such detailed analysis. If he had thought encyclopaedia was merely transitional, he could have treated it in a far more summary fashion. So I started looking for signs of encyclopaedic thinking in what I read and witnessed during political debates and various media commentary. Much to my surprise, I began to see it everywhere.

Economic theory and the principles that define the autonomy of business, the legal status of corporations that give them the same rights as individual citizens, and core economic principles as described in such newspapers as *The Economist*, the *Wall Street Journal*, and the *New York Times* take on very different hues when seen as the products of encyclopaedic thinking. This is not to say that they agree with each other in all cases, but that they are far more similar than different. More importantly, their rationality is the same (if not their journalistic standards). And when their influence enters political debate, which their wealth and power assure that it must, political debate also becomes the product of encyclopaedic thinking.

The point to be made is that when we talk about encyclopaedia, we are not talking about some transitory or defeated view of the past. We are talking about a view that is alive today, and almost uniquely disruptive of rational, courteous, and purposeful discourse in civil society. It is arrogant, dismissive, powerful, and irrational. And it is ubiquitous. But it is largely unconscious, unexamined by its practitioners and unknown by its victims. First we look at its manifestations in the 19th century and then in the 20th century.

19th Century Encyclopaedia

The most obvious expression of encyclopaedia's influence on the 19th century is probably the attitude of the colonial powers toward the people and status of underdeveloped countries. England and Germany justified their economic exploitation, cultural carnage, and personal injustice with the slogan, We must save the savages from themselves. It is important to notice that the elite intellectual, economic, and political class saw themselves as not only right but inevitably right. They were incapable of taking intellectual or personal interest in the ordinary people they encountered at home or around the world. They considered both groups backward and, at best, thought of them as children. Having no interest in other people sets any of us up to see them as objects rather that as authentic persons in their own right. Such a perspective makes it impossible for us even to consider adopting their point of view on anything. One of MacIntyre's most compelling discussions of encyclopaedia analyzes the 19th century European attitude toward Polynesians, especially in Hawaii. He points out that because European colonists had no interest in the Hawaiian point of view, they were unable to notice that what was so devastating to 19th century Hawaiian culture was virtually identical to what was devastating European culture. But Europeans could not recognize the similarities. By refusing to see others as they were, they inhibited their ability to see themselves as they were. As MacIntyre wrote:

> The taboos stigmatized by the contributors of the Ninth Edition as belonging to the primitive and the savage were only seen as alien because of the incapacity for cultural self-recognition and self knowledge which was such a marked characteristic of the society in which they lived. The authors of the great canonical encyclopaedias just because they insisted upon seeing and judging everything from their own point of view turned out to have had no way of making themselves visible to themselves.[12]

---

[12]*Three Rival Versions,* (p. 185). Western Catholic, Evangelical, and Protestant activists are shocked by Islamic fundamentalists. They too seem to have "no way of making themselves visible to themselves."

MacIntyre was interested in far more than the problems of anthropological point of view. He was interested in the detachment of moral rules from the ethical system that gives them meaning.

> The detachment of European moral rules from their place within an overall theological moral scheme, embodying and representing a highly specific conception of human nature, corresponds to the similar detachment of taboo rules, (ibid).

When we are unable to look at others with genuine interest in them as persons, we take an ethical stand that is profoundly flawed. We create such a detached ethical starting point that it is impossible to establish an ethical relationship with the other in theory or practice. Two 20th century philosophers have paid considerable attention to this problem, Martin Buber, who is universally known, and Robert Johann who is less known but whom I find quite interesting.

Both Buber and Johann insist that persons must adopt what we have described as classical realism rather than post-Kantian realism in viewing others. We must see them as they are, from their own perspective. We must not allow ourselves to view others exclusively from our own point of view. Both authors distinguish treating others as objects from treating others as subjects; as existing to meet our needs rather than existing as persons in their own right, manifesting their own dignity and worth. That distinction defines the difference between what Buber called an I-Thou relationship and an I-You relationship.[13] Johann spoke in terms of *intersubjectivity* which means the same as an I-Thou relationship. In an I-Thou relationship, both persons see each other as subjects, initiators of action, existing in themselves, and not merely in terms of the other. The encyclopaedists pronounced themselves the elite class of their elite nation, the holders of truth. They declared everyone else both within their own countries and throughout the rest of the world as underdeveloped and inferior. They established a point of view that treated everyone outside

[13]Buber wrote in French. Translators had to find an English form of the second person pronoun that distinguishes the subjective from the objective case. Thus *Thou* which no one uses. When we note that usage, it is much easier to understand what is meant by treating a person as a subject versus an object and therefore the difference between an I-Thou and an I-You relationship.

their group not only as inferior but as objects whose purpose was to meet their needs. Inevitably, they established one set of ethical standards for themselves and another for everyone else.

In chapter seven we notice that this kind of dual ethical system is characteristic of the ethical development of children in their early teens and is by definition immature. We also establish the importance of understanding that individuals must *learn* mature ethical reasoning and *develop* mature ethical conduct from some source within their culture. By rejecting the principles of mature ethical reasoning and the content of mature ethical systems, encyclopaedists destroyed the capacity of secular ethical institutions and organization to develop and teach mature ethical reasoning. The encyclopaedists destroyed the underpinnings of mature ethical reasoning in Western culture and the genealogists followed by declaring that mature (universally applicable) ethical reasoning does not exist.

When we understand how the encyclopaedists viewed the rest of the world, it is easy to understand the way 19th century industrialists treated factory workers and miners. We understand how colonial powers justified their exploitation of natural resources and people in developing countries as well as their complete indifference to the environment. We also understand the ethical indifference of men to women, and the struggles for civil rights and economic justice that have continued throughout the 20th century.

20th Century Encyclopaedia

It is not my purpose to conduct a full analysis of 20th century culture or elitism, but merely to provide enough analysis for us to be able to proceed with our purpose and for the reader to enjoy the capacity to see encyclopaedia operating in their lives. I could focus the discussion on elitism in education, but it seems more effective to stick with the political topics that have framed our discussion of modern philosophy to this point. To be quite frank, I am reluctant to focus criticism on educators for intellectual problems whose origins lie in moral philosophy and the social sciences in general. I draw my examples of encyclopaedia in the 20th century from political philosophy and economics, in particular, fascism, communism, and capitalism.

Fascism and communism (Marxism) are political expressions of encyclopaedia combined with a dictator. Both rely on the Hegelian dialectic and the continuous progress of history to support their conclusions—recall Marx's dialectical materialism. Even more to the point, both fascism and communism set up one group as morally and intellectually superior to the rest of society, an impossible starting point for any political theory. And by definition, both reject democracy because it frustrates the vital goal of securing the rule of the state by the elite.

When encyclopaedia was applied to political theory in Germany early in the 20th century, it defined the interests of the German people as identical to the interests of the state and the interests of the state as identical to the interests of corporate Germany. It defined the interests of working people with the interests of the rich and powerful. Because this view was taught in universities and supported by the media, it dominated the German people's view of themselves and their country during the first half of the 20th Century.

Communism as defined by Marx and Lenin replaced the domination of society by elite capitalists with the domination of society by the proletariate, which is the flip side of the same error. Fundamental inadequacies in Marxist economic theory have caused totalitarian Marxist societies to play out as societies with failed economies that brutalize virtually everyone. The failure of Marxist societies has eased the task of capitalists who would argue against Marxist theories.

Free market capitalism, especially as practiced in England and the United States, enjoys the enormous advantage of not *defining* any one group as inherently superior to any other group. Thus, it is highly compatible with democracy. And yet the point of view and values of the capitalist elite in those countries dominate economic theory. And both the academy and the media have adopted their point of view.

Every economic system must account for two fundamental processes, the generation of wealth and the distribution of wealth. Marxism has failed to generate wealth and therefore made its claimed capacity to distribute wealth a mute point. But free market capitalism, with its rather astonishing capacity to generate wealth, has increasingly defined the distribution of wealth in terms so beneficial to the elite and so detrimental to working people that its effects cannot be obscured especially during one of the longest periods of economic growth in Western history. The encyclopaedic habits of capitalists combined with the devastating failures of Marxism have allowed capitalists to reject criticism that their theory assures the unjust distribution of wealth. Their replies point at failed Marxist societies and ask, Is that what you would prefer? These arguments jump from the obvious conclusion to that rhetorical question to the assumption that the needs of the working and professional classes are assured when the elite prosper. To be fair, capitalists do not so much argue that point as they assume it and act it out. Rather than legitimately addressing the question, How can an economy best distribute wealth? encyclopaedic capitalists ignore the question and assume that the same market forces that generate wealth so effectively will, in time, justly distribute wealth. They accept that view in spite of contradictory evidence and in spite of their having no way to advance a rational argument that supports it.

However, there is a huge point to be made here. For the same reason I did not want to use elitism in education to frame this discussion, I must let economists and the elite off the hook. Economists and the elite have not failed to develop the secular moral reasoning needed to guide inquiry in economics. Moral philosophers have. Similarly, editorial journalists, who might best be thought of as the applied moral philosophers of democratic societies, have not failed to develop the secular moral reasoning they need to do their work well. Moral philosophers must be held responsible for that failure. Still, it is fair to point out the problems that editorial journalists create when they participate in encyclopaedic elitism.

When the media adopts encyclopaedic habits, it portrays the interests of the people (professional and blue collar workers, racial and ethnic groups, women, environmentalists, teachers, and so on) from the point of view of the elite. The media does not merely help the people understand what is going on in government, it helps us understand ourselves, our culture, and our interests. We the people know ourselves, to a vast extent, by the way the media portrays us. To the extent that the media portrays the people from the point of view of the elite, it is extraordinarily difficult for the people to know *our* legitimate interests. The peoples' knowledge of ourselves is profoundly influenced by an institution that demonstrates virtually no interest, sympathy, or insight into us.

The elite and the media argue that they have not entered into a conspiracy by pointing out that their is no evidence of their doing the things that conspirators do. But when the media, universities, corporate executives, and financiers join, unconsciously, in a way of thinking that assumes that the best way to meet the needs of the people is to pursue the interests of the elite, they do not need to plan or carry out an overt conspiracy. They live the conspiracy without even knowing it.

Because their is no legitimate, acknowledged way of thinking about public policy or conducting discourse in the public square except by using encyclopaedic habits, the people find themselves forming groups that employ this habit of thinking to their benefit. Looking for examples among educational institutions, we notice that the National School Boards Association assumes that the interests of school boards contain the most essential expression of the interests of education, professional educators, and children. The American Association of School Administrators assumes that the interests of school administrators contain the most essential expression of the interests of education, school boards, professional educators, and children. The National Education Association and the American Federation of Teachers assume that the interests of teachers contain the most essential expression of the interests of education, school boards, professional educators, and children. Like the elite classes of society, these organizations and their members have not arrived at their conclusions through a rigorous examination of competing views but as an unexamined habit of thinking.

By way of modeling a willingness to admit to encyclopaedic tendencies, I will now stand up and say,

> Hello, my name is Pat Conroy, and I am a recovering encyclopaedist. Some of the encyclopaedic groups to which I have belonged are: teachers unions, the Amateur Athletic Union (AAU), and several organizations of school administrators and superintendents of schools.

Now you try it. The key is to identify the groups to which we have belonged that think like encyclopaedists.

As we think about the groups to which we have belonged, we realize that the elite have not gone unchallenged. Indeed we gain a useful insight into popular struggles that have been waged throughout the 20th century. The labor movement, the civil rights movement, feminism, environmentalism, and the opposition to the war in Vietnam all rebelled against a kind of elitist-group-think that had virtually no capacity to articulate ethical or practical arguments for their conduct. But the groups that attempted to oppose these views did not discover a better way of thinking just because they rejected these views. Although early on these movements articulated mature moral arguments for their positions, they have had great difficulty maintaining those arguments. We must wonder why these popular and ethically superior movements have suffered a kind of entropy while the elite have gained energy in spite of being grounded in an unethical, unarticulated, and failed view.

The general confusion that plagues secular moral philosophy is a huge part of the problem. In chapter seven, I describe the inevitable, necessary role that mature moral reasoning must play in guiding inquiry in the social sciences and shaping rational, courteous discourse in the public square. But for now we must notice that there is a relationship between the ethics inherent in encyclopaedia and the impact it continues to have on society. But the problems that afflict moral philosophy cannot be explained by encyclopaedia alone. After all, encyclopaedia is a defeated view, and it was defeated both by historical events and an opposing ethical view (genealogy) that has attained a prominent place in secular moral philosophy. We turn now to a discussion of genealogy in order to find out just what it is, but also curious to see how it could defeat encyclopaedia but not replace it in the public square.

Genealogy, The Anti-Epistemology

Genealogy is most easily recognized as individualism. Its is rooted in the work of Nietzsche and is another example of post-Kantian realism. Like other views we have studied, it is more easily understood in the intellectual and historical context in which it developed than by itself. The historical discussion reveals genealogy's place in history and its hold on current thinking in moral philosophy and the social sciences. First we discuss genealogy's source and method of knowledge, which by now are almost self evident, then its place in history, and finally its major manifestations in the 20th century.

Genealogy's Source of Knowledge

Nietzsche rejected the culturally loaded wisdom and smugness of the encyclopaedists and exposed the narrow elitism of their views. Furthermore, he replaced the group, encyclopaedia's source of knowledge, with the individual as genealogy's the source of knowledge. According to Nietzsche, truth does not reside in God or nature or the conclusions of the most advanced scholars of a given time, and not in the autonomy of pure reason. It resides in the *autonomy of the individual.*

Truth results from the unique experiences of each individual in their unique time and place. As MacIntyre explained, according to Nietzsche, truth is not truth as such; truth is true from each individual's view that results from each individual's unique makeup and experiences.[14] Rather than looking for truth in one's own mind, genealogists look for truth in *their person*. Because they claim that the ultimate source of knowledge resides in the individual, they necessarily admit to a vast multiplicity of truths. Some individuals may agree regarding some point, but, at least theoretically, the number of truths can equal the number of individuals.

Like Kant and the encyclopaedists, genealogists believe that rationality exists independent of the physical world, the past, tradition, and community. But they take this independence to the ultimate disengagement. They deny all universal or generalizable conclusions. Rather, they insist that individuals must arrive at individual conclusions.

Many educators may never have heard the term genealogy, but we are familiar with its claims. When we decide that we can never agree on anything and treat that conclusion as the truth about knowledge in education, we find ourselves participating in Nietzsche's genealogy and the conclusion that any view is as valid as any other view. Anyone who has worked for any length of time in a school or taken course work in education has heard the most thoroughly researched and carefully structured arguments dismissed by such statements as, Well, be that as it may, I simply disagree.

The ability of an individual to reject thoroughly researched views with the most casually derived personal opinions results from the assumption that there is no source of knowledge outside the individual. Genealogy elevates the authority of the individual to the absolute, which of course renders all research that is designed to produce *generalizable conclusions* subject to the authority of individual opinion. Research, then, becomes susceptible to the most casual disproof or, more accurately, dismissal. Without generalizable conclusions, there can be no community inquiry, community authority, or deep, powerful, predictive knowledge.

Genealogy's Method of Inquiry

If truth can be known only from the point of view of each individual, then the number of truths, at least potentially, equals the number of individuals. There must then also be, at least theoretically, a multiplicity

[14]Three Rival Versions, (p. 42-43).

of *methods of inquiry* that equals the population. In order to standardize methods of inquiry, we would have to locate the source of knowledge as well as the method of inquiry outside the individual. But that is exactly what genealogy rejects, which means that there is no method of inquiry that can have any more authority than what any individual assigns to his or her personal (not intellectual) conduct. Some of us may choose to employ a method that resembles the scientific method; others may choose something that resembles historiography. But our choices of methodology constitute nothing more than *our* private, personal choices of methodology. Methodology, as such, has no meaning in disciplines that are guided by genealogy.

Much of our discussion of encyclopaedia and genealogy highlights their similarities. As post-Kantian views, both severed inquiry from tradition and community and both ultimately elevated the authority of the individual (or group) to the absolute. It is also important to note their differences which are summarized in the table below.

Clearly, genealogy is an anti-epistemology. It denies the possibility of a source of knowledge and method of inquiry to which a community of scholars could commit. It creates a vast multiplicity of truths and methods defined within the person of anyone who would speak regarding given topics. In education, it precludes community based inquiry, knowledge, and authority. It elevates the most casual views not just of the most indifferent educators, but also of parents and politicians, to the same level of credibility and authority as the most carefully drawn views of our most competent and rigorous researchers and practitioners.

From the point of view of this work, this negative analysis of genealogy is helpful and fair. Our purpose is to overcome the intellectual barriers that prevent educators from integrating research, integrating research and practice, and conducting discourse that leads to agreement, commitment, and action. Genealogy is certainly one of those barriers. However to leave the discussion at that does disservice to genealogy's place in history and gives no insight into its enormous influence during the last quarter of the 20th century. Such a one sided discussion does not answer questions that inevitably arise and must be settled if genealogy is to be rejected where it must be and protected where it must be.

Genealogy's Place in History

One of the great, ongoing intellectual and ethical conflicts in Western culture pits the individual against powerful institutions. The conflict

132

between encyclopaedia and genealogy is probably best understood as a contemporary manifestation of that conflict. Like any great and enduring conflict, this one is sustained by the fact that both sides have legitimate

DIFFERENCES BETWEEN ENCYCLOPAEDIA & GENEALOGY[15]

ENCYCLOPAEDIA	GENEALOGY
Unity of truth and reason and comprehensiveness of the encyclopedic framework.	Multiplicity of perspectives and relativism of truth to those perspectives.
Synthesis, development toward a group truth.	Conflict between perspectives and struggle between rival interpretations.
Truth is known as such. X is X as such.	Truth is known only from a point of view. X is X from this individual point of view at this particular time.
Rules are the rules of rationality as such.	No rules of rationality, rather strategies of insight and strategies of subversion.
Must reject any other view.	Must reject any dogmatic view.

claims. The migration of the Germanic people during the Dark Ages left Europe in chaos. The chaos could never have been resolved by individuals acting separately. It ended when religious and political leaders arranged general peace and instituted a social and economic system called feudalism.

Western political history since the High Middle Ages is largely the story of shifting influence and broadening human rights. It is a story whose dramatic content is structured in the tension between monarchs and the

[15]I have used MacIntyre's analysis and language to create this table.

small group of lords spiritual and temporal who had power over their own lives and the vast majority of people who sought power over theirs.

The Age of Revolution (17th and 18th centuries) introduced ideas that supported the emergence of the individual, but those revolutions were not able to accomplish much more than modestly limit and slightly annoy the elite. However, the growth of democracy during the 18th and 19th centuries presented a massive threat to the elite. At least theoretically, democracy gives the people control of the state, control of making laws and creating institutions that implement those laws. By the 19th century, democracy began to take shape in both North America and Europe. This development put the elite classes at great risk, which explains why the they were highly motivated to accept encyclopaedia as a compelling world view. Encyclopaedia provided an intellectual and ethical view that united and protected intellectuals, financiers, national politicians, and the media. This was the historical context in which genealogy emerged.

Genealogy challenged and rejected encyclopaedia in the university and offered a world view that provided the intellectual and ethical underpinnings needed to advance what came to be known as liberal political and economic theory. The liberal view demanded the acknowledgment of the interests of the individual in all classes. It is important to understand that genealogy has been important because it was successful in promoting the rights of the individual, *but it is ultimately inadequate to that task.* This fundamental inadequacy in genealogy becomes evident in our discussion of genealogy's 20th century progeny, post-modernism.[16]

Post-modernism: Genealogy's Progeny

Post-modernists claim to replace the philosophical views that have prevailed during the modern period. They claim to have ushered in a new era. Of course, accepting that claim requires that we agree about the starting and ending dates and definition of the modern period. I have suggested that 1650 might be a useful date to mark the end of the Middle

---

[16]This term is widely used in academe and the media and includes contradictory views. As such, it is impossible to describe post-modernism without contradicting someone unless one describes every individual view. I only attempt here to provide a general discussion of its place in moral philosophy and the social sciences and its epistemological origins. I do not attempt to resolve or even analyze its current contradictions and certainly do not attempt to explicate its manifestations in historiography, art, architecture, literature, or criticism.

Ages. I have also stressed that one of the most intractable problems in *modern* secular moral philosophy and the social sciences is identifying their source of knowledge. But that is not a modern or post-modern problem. It has confounded philosophers since the 14th century. In addition, much of what the post-modernists assert is grounded in post-Kantian realism and genealogy. Since Kant was an 18th century intellectual and genealogy dates from the 19th century, post-modernism could be said to have begun in the 18th or 19th century. But could anyone claim that the modern era ended in the 18th or even 19th century? It seems more useful to think of post-modernism as post-Kantian efforts to solve modern and lingering medieval problems.

If we accept that post-modernists are better understood as post-Kantian, our earlier discussions of encyclopaedia and genealogy shed enormous light on this late 20th century movement. It seems helpful, for instance, to apply what we have learned about genealogy to post-modern views. We notice that although feminists and environmentalists who call themselves post-modernists offer important new *topics* of inquiry, neither offers a genuinely new mode of inquiry. In addition we notice that like genealogists, post-modernists often set as their purpose to challenge, destabilize, and, as Nietzsche demanded, subvert the status quo, to expose and deconstruct elitist oppression. However, post-modernists are ultimately incapable of offering an alternative set of principles *that can be expressed in laws that can be implemented in institutions.*[17] By challenging encyclopedic elitism, genealogists and post-modernists play a valuable role in the academy and civil society, but by being incapable of institutionalizing change, they permit encyclopaedia to prevail with all of its inadequacy.

Consistent with Nietzsche, post-modern moral philosophers vigorously reject the concept of any moral authority being assigned to society or social groups. They define all such moral authority as oppressive. The most vigorous assertions of this assumption are expressed under such labels as existentialism, phenomenology, deconstructionism, constructivism, feminism, hermeneutics, and critical theory. Like Nietzsche, they claim that there is no moral truth as such, there are only moral truths as identified by individuals informed by their unique experiences and personalities.

---

[17] Admittedly, some social scientists and especially some feminists and environmentalists are attempting to articulate principles and create institutions that can benefit society. Some have begun to revisit ethics and moral philosophy.

An example might be helpful so that we do not assume that these views are merely ridiculous. Say you are riding cross country on a train and find yourself seated across from two women. It is a long trip, and eventually, in a desperate attempt to avoid boredom and comforted by the anonymity of strangers traveling together, conversation touches the deeper topics of human interest. You begin to discuss the nature and meaning of love. Now assume that you had read C. S. Lewis's *Four Loves*, Martin Buber's *I and Thou* and maybe even *The Meaning of Love: an Essay Towards a Metaphysics of Intersubjectivity* by the American Jesuit, Robert O. Johann. You would certainly be steeped in universal principles and promises of love.

But let us consider the two women with whom you are speaking. One grew up in a loving home. Her mother and father loved each other and their children. The children loved their parents and learned to respect and look out for each other and, as they grew older, came to love each other. As a child, this woman had many friends, both boys and girls. As she got older, many young men expressed fondness for her. Eventually she married a man who has loved her and their children. She is returning to their home, anxious to rejoin him after visiting one of her sisters.

The other woman has lived a very different life. She was raised in a brutal home where her father beat her, her mother, and her siblings. When she was 14, an uncle raped her. When she was 15, her father drove her out of her house. A pimp saved her from starvation and she worked for him for ten years. She bought a ticket on this train in a desperate attempt to get away, to start a new life.

Phenomenologists would ask, What use do the universal definitions of love bring to the conversation you are about to have with these women? Love means such entirely different things to them that your only purpose can be to come to know what they know from their particular points of view. Furthermore, you inevitably interpret what they say according to your own experiences. Even the reality of their lives, however compelling, cannot be known as such by you. You can only know your interpretation and reaction to their stories.

The conclusion made by Nietzsche, genealogists, and post-modernists is that there is no such thing as universally valid moral statements or universal moral truths. There are only individually known moral statements. There is only my moral truth and your moral truth. Even texts do not exist as such but only in relationship to readers, and therefore the content and meaning of texts varies from reader to reader. Textbooks that attempt to carry on the culture and tradition of nations are particularly oppressive for they use the power and influence of the elite intellectual class to impose their particular views of history and truth on their country folk. As women, the poor, and people of color point out to the predominately white male authors of cultural history and ethics, Your history is not our history, and your ethics are not our ethics. Advocates of critical theory seem to have most completely dedicated themselves to Nietzsche's call for the subversion of history and any form of moral tradition, but all post-modernists contribute to that end.

Before we turn to a discussion of hermeneutics and critical theory, it would probably be helpful to return to our train trip and explain why an encounter with such disturbingly different personal experiences with love does not destroy the meaning of universal statements about the nature of love but actually adds to them.

One only concludes that there is no valid universal truth about love if one allows any interpersonal experience to qualify as a valid definition of love. It is more helpful to our understanding of language, concept formation, and the meaning of love, however, if we acknowledge that only some interpersonal relationships can be defined as loving. Others are far better understood as expressing the absence of love, and some express the opposite of love, hatred and violence. To treat the experiences of these two women as expressions of love is to treat love and hatred, kindness and abuse as identical terms. When our definitions of words do not describe both what the concept they signify means and what they do not mean (in this case, what is love and what is not love) it is impossible to think with any clarity for we cannot construct genuine concepts. Classifications and genuine concepts, as Aristotle and Vygotsky teach us, must include what the concept includes and exclude what the concept excludes.[18] This requirement applies to concept formation in the natural sciences, mathematics, history, moral philosophy, and the social sciences.

Furthermore, Aristotle's structure of ethical reasoning helps us interpret the experiences of the two women. If we identify the purpose of family, or what it means to be a good family, there is room for creativity and individual difference, but it is impossible to agree that the purpose of families is advanced by conduct that destroys the humanity of the people who occupy them. Whatever ethical purpose one might identify for families, love must

---

[18]I discuss Aristotle and Vygotsky on this point in chapter seven.

universally be understood as a virtue, or something that leads toward that purpose. And hatred and violence and other destructive behaviors must universally be acknowledged as vices, or conduct that destroys the meaning and purpose of families. In our example, one woman experienced love. The other experienced hatred and violence. To confuse the two as expanded or individual meanings of love is to destroy the meaning of language, the capacity to reason, and the foundations of moral philosophy. It constitutes a mammoth intellectual error that threatens individuals and society. Tolstoy demonstrated an understanding of the universal quality of the good as opposed to the chaotic, unpredictable variety of vice in the first sentence of *Anna Karenina*: "Happy families are all alike; every unhappy family is unhappy in its own way."

Two forms of post-modernism seem currently to exercise particular influence on education: hermeneutics and critical theory. Existentialism has been important, but it is generally understood as an elaboration of Nietzsche's view. Feminism has been enormously influential in many schools, but it is so dynamic a movement as to defy definition. Probably the most important topic in feminism *for our discussion* is feminism's hermeneutics which is adequately discussed under the unrestricted term.

Hermeneutics

The classic definition of hermeneutics is the science or art of interpreting scripture. Schillebeeckx's definition is helpful:

> Hermeneusis is 'explanation'; hermeneutics is 'the science of explanation', which examines the prior factors necessary to achieving a hermeneusis or explanation (for instance, understanding of the Bible). This study is necessary because of the ever-growing experiential and intellective horizon of our experiences, our thinking and our ways of verbally expressing these.[19]

Any method of inquiry that helps us work through the myriad ways of thinking and expressing ourselves in texts, that gets to the root of various experiential and intellective differences to form meaningful explanations of texts, rightfully attracts the attention of scholars.

Social scientists and educators tend to identify this method with history and psychology while almost ignoring its relationship to theology.

[19] *Jesus: An Experiment in Christology*, (p. 745).

However, if we check the background of the early proponents of hermeneutics in the modern era, we notice that they were not historians or psychologists: Friedrich Schleiermacher (1768-1834) was a German philosopher and theologian. He taught theology at the University of Berlin from 1810 until his death. Edmund Husserl (1859-1938) was a German philosopher most noted as the founder of phenomenology. Martin Heidegger was born in the late 19th century but is known as a 20th century existentialist. It is important to note the traditions out of which these three scholars came. Their backgrounds highlight the problem with the source of knowledge from which hermeneutics suffers *when used in education or the social sciences in general* or in moral philosophy.

Hermeneutics, when used in its classical setting of scriptural study, does not suffer from problems with the source of knowledge, because theology does not suffer from problems with the source of knowledge. Scripture scholars using hermeneutics or any other method of inquiry do not claim that their conclusions stand on their own. They claim that their conclusions can withstand the scrutiny of other scripture scholars when examined against scriptural texts. Regardless of the character of the engagement with the text (exegesis, criticism, or appropriation) scriptural texts contain an authority that permits scholars to go behind each other's arguments and seek support or refutation. Consequently, hermeneutics, when used in theology, has always and continues to frame lively and useful discourse.

When historians use hermeneutics in the study of history they encounter compatible epistemological circumstances. A historical text, once validated as a reliable primary or secondary source, needs only to be studied and its meaning revealed. Of course different historians may attach different interpretations to the same text, but those differences are resolved (if any resolution is possible) in debates regarding the context and content of the text. Hermeneutic methods can be helpful in that kind of inquiry.

But if we apply the hermeneutic method to secular moral philosophy or education or the social sciences, we must notice that we do not study texts that hold any of the authority contained in scriptural, literary, or historical documents. One can study educational texts as part of the historical record, and in that case the hermeneutic method can be useful. But then one is conducting historical inquiry, albeit the history of education. One is not doing the fundamental, defining work of education which is to understand learning and develop and use instructional methods that work.

To succeed in the social sciences, an epistemology must not merely guide research, it must integrate research and research and practice. Because of the predisposition of social scientists for individualism, when hermeneutics is used in the social sciences it is often conducted in a manner that isolates inquiry from anything outside the reader and the text, from other research, and from practice.

Hermeneutics is an appropriate *method* when used in historical kinds of research in education, but *it is clearly not an epistemology and it is clearly not a method that delivers primary answers in education.* Any attempt to elevate a method of biblical study to an epistemology of the social sciences where it has no source of knowledge inevitably destroys itself in practice. It has no capacity to guide inquiry or promote agreement, commitment, and action. Hermeneutics is different from critical theory mainly in limiting itself to texts instead of the underlying motives of a discipline.

Critical Theory

Critical theory can best be understood as reflecting Nietzsche's belief that inquiry must subvert the past. Nietzsche railed against an intellectual tradition that was grounded in encyclopaedia. He rejected all intellectual authority as oppressive and asserted the complete independence and autonomy of the individual. When we consider the racism, economic exploitation, and other forms of injustice that the rich and powerful continue to impose on the most vulnerable members of society, when we consider the eroding status of an increasing majority of citizens in the United States,[20] we must acknowledge that Nietzsche's work continues to be important. Furthermore, we understand why many social scientists have adopted his views. They break down the elitist façade that claims the high ground but is in effect oppressive. Typically, critical theory aims to destabilize and deconstruct the elite forces that mis-serve society. However, it fails even to claim a source of knowledge, and suffers from virtually all of the same epistemological problems as hermeneutics, which I do not repeat.

The attraction of critical theory is that it seems to get at the truth by unveiling duplicity, hypocrisy, and oppression. Although it is impossible to reveal a lie without revealing some aspect of the truth, it is quite possible to reveal hypocrisy or oppression in the social sciences without revealing what would actually work. Critical theory suffers from what one might call the

---

[20]See: Mishel, Bernstein, and Schmitt, *The State of Working America;* or "Pay: The best . . . and the rest," *The Economist,* May 8-14, 1999.

skeptic's fallacy. Skepticism alone is entirely inadequate as a motive or outcome of inquiry in the social sciences and moral philosophy. Pascal and Hume were right in complaining that natural science could not solve the problems faced by moral philosophy and the social sciences, but their skepticism was incapable of suggesting an alternative. I do not reject the value of skepticism, for it is a prerequisite to rigor. Curiosity and skepticism drive learning. Curiosity gets us started and keeps us going. Skepticism imposes rigor. Both depend upon some other form of inquiry, one that can generate solutions.

Ironically, by separating the social sciences from moral philosophy and denying the capacity of intellectuals to develop mature moral reasoning and universal ethical principles, secular moral philosophers and social scientists directly contribute to the conditions that permit injustice and oppression. Because moral philosophers and social scientists are by definition the ones able and responsible for providing ethical as well as intellectual leadership in the academy, government, and the public square, a major share of responsibility for the absence of mature moral reasoning and ethical conduct in Western societies must fall on them. It is painful and infuriating to witness ethical nihilists in moral philosophy and the social sciences decry the unethical conduct that they see in economics, politics, civil society, or in the conduct of children.

Both hermeneutics and critical theory raise interesting concerns about bias and offer skills that enhance one's engagement of texts. However, they use these skills in the context of epistemological assumptions that place the source of knowledge in the individual or in the individual's encounter with the text. No authoritative conclusions can come from such study.

One might legitimately wonder how it is possible that post-modernism seems to be taking hold in schools of education. One answer is that there is no competing view. There is no epistemology in education that identifies a source of knowledge other than the individual or the beliefs of the most powerful group. Post-modernism seems to convey legitimacy on the chaos that plagues inquiry in education. Furthermore, it is compatible with one of the great values in the university, academic freedom. Why do schools of education encounter virtually no intellectual conflicts around topics as dicey and compelling as cognitive psychology and pedagogy? Not because we have overcome our disagreements or defined the terms of our disagreement as the framework for research (which is the general condition of discourse in the natural sciences), but because we have *agreed to disagree*. And the slogan we use that permits and ennobles such a meager intellectual stand is academic freedom.

What many social scientists and moral philosophers seem not to notice is that principles such as academic freedom or the inalienable rights of individuals or the inherent dignity and worth of every person cannot be sustained in a world view that reduces all truth to individual opinions. Many individual opinions hold most persons in low regard and make no concessions to academic freedom or individual rights and dignity. The great irony of individualism as an epistemology has been the damage it has done to our national commitment to *principles* of individual dignity, rights, and justice. I have listed three tasks that have confronted intellectual leaders in the social sciences since the 17th century: 1) Articulate secular moral principles upon which society can be based, 2) Translate those principles into laws, and 3) Invent the institutions that implement those laws. Individualism, while asserting the central place of the individual in society, cannot articulate principles that can be translated into laws and certainly has no capacity to guide the invention or conduct of institutions.

Understanding this incapacity provides an interesting lens through which to view 19th and 20th century liberalism. Clearly, early liberals possessed the moral high ground when they fought for child labor laws, the rights of workers to collective bargaining, social security, Medicare, environmental protection, women's rights, civil rights, and medical justice. But they seem to have lost their hold on the public's imagination and influence in political discourse. Greed and dispassionate capitalism have replaced the social ethics that inspired liberalism. But how can greed trump justice in a democratic society? Liberal intellectuals and activists abandoned the universal ethical principles that provided the foundations of the liberal tradition, not deliberately or consciously, but as the unintended consequence of asserting genealogic ethics. As individualism eroded social ethics, liberalism lost its foundations, clarity, and energy. Liberals created their own intellectual and ethical vacuum. Encyclopaedists filled the vacuum. Lacking universal ethical principles, the liberal tradition became incapable of providing a compelling counterbalance to the self-interest of the elite in spite of the fact that historical events destroyed encyclopaedia's premises. The elite employed a habit of thinking that generates unsupported and unsupportable principles that inform laws and design institutions to the benefit of the elite. That is how greed won.

Factions of evangelical Christians and the Catholic hierarchy have stepped into this ethical void and attempted to reassert the central role that moral theology and religious moral philosophy played in the Middle Ages. But the conditions created by the Protestant Reformation that reached their brutal conclusion in the Thirty Years War have not gone away. Indeed, if anything, civil society is religiously more diverse today than during the 17th century. Attempts by various religious institutions to impose their views on civil society are bound to fail. That is predictable. What cannot be predicted is the extent of the hostility and damage that will ensue before this trend is stopped.

Genealogy is probably the most obviously inept rational system operating in education today, but the encyclopedic view is equally problematic. Because it is so little understood, it may constitute the greater challenge to intellectual leaders. Both have devolved into the anti-rational methods of individualism, which raises an obvious question: What has academic philosophy been doing in the 20th century? We have already noted that encyclopaedia has endured as an unexamined way of thinking. It does not exist as an operating *philosophical* system in the university. On the other hand, the influence of Nietzsche has thrived in various forms of what we have discussed as post-modernism. But post-modernism is a fairly recent phenomenon. The major academic view that attempted to prevent philosophy's devolution into individualism was lead by Bertrand Russell and is called analytical philosophy. Analytical philosophy has dominated moral philosophy and epistemology in England and the United States during the 20th century. We must understand the terms of its failure in order finally to establish the complete inadequacy of secular moral philosophy at the end of the 20th century.

Analytical Philosophy

The scholars who have dedicated themselves to making philosophy truly scientific are called analytical philosophers, their work, analytical philosophy.[21] Our discussion of this view again focuses on questions regarding the source of knowledge and method of inquiry. Analytical philosophy rejected the whole line of thinking that we have followed from Kant through genealogy. Rather it joined the tradition of empiricism founded by Bacon and Newton. These philosophers attempted to make philosophy scientific and especially mathematical.

---

[21]I include in this term logical positivism and positivism.

Mathematics and philosophy provide an interesting comparison. Both find their greatest expression in providing essential intellectual tools and solutions to other disciplines. Both are highly susceptible to arcane lines of inquiry that become so recondite as to interest no one but professional mathematicians or philosophers. Both, when operating alone rather than in the context of an applied discipline, are highly susceptible to statements that have no reference in reality. Indeed, if mathematics did not contribute to some other discipline, if it did not provide useful tools for inquiry and daily life, it would have to be considered useless, or at best a mere game, like checkers or chess. Similarly, *to the extent that we find secular moral philosophy useless in other disciplines, we must conclude that it is useless.*

Importantly, mathematics had a continuous content from Euclid until the 17th century when it began to expand its content and to provide a defining component of scientific inquiry. Although mathematics appears to be exhausting its possibilities for generating new mathematical knowledge by itself, in its relationship to science, it continues to be indispensable and inventive.

Philosophy's content, on the other hand, has been dramatically reduced since the 17th century. Natural philosophy invented its own epistemology and became natural science. The social sciences emerged and distanced themselves from moral philosophy in order to be more like natural science, thus the name. Psychology took a huge area of inquiry away from moral philosophy, as did economics, education, sociology, anthropology, and law. These disciplines did not merely diminish philosophy's content, they insisted that philosophy could not contribute to their work. Even the humanities, which philosophy has become, and the fine arts, long interested in aesthetics, ignore philosophy. Two areas of inquiry seem to provide the content of moral philosophy, epistemology and ethics.

In chapter seven, I argue that from an epistemological view, secular moral philosophy is as indispensable to the social sciences as mathematics is to the natural sciences. But secular moral philosophy has *failed to become* indispensable to the social sciences. Secular moral philosophy's failure to be adequate to this challenge accounts, in large measure, for the inadequacy of the social sciences. Moral philosophers often complain about the immorality of economics without seeming to notice that it is not the job of economists to develop the system of mature secular moral reasoning that they need in order to assure moral conduct and moral teaching in economics.

Because mathematics is indispensable to natural science, natural science could not function without the development of competent mathematics. To their good fortune, mathematicians have developed useful tools for scientists. Mature secular moral reasoning is indispensable to the social sciences. Because moral philosophers have failed to develop a system of mature secular moral reasoning, the social sciences have failed to develop. Of course, it was impossible for analytical philosophers to see this problem because they excluded *ethics* and *moral* from *philosophy*.

Analytical philosophy failed to guide the social sciences because it failed to distinguish the source of knowledge in natural science from the source of knowledge in the social sciences. Rather, analytical philosophers adopted the epistemology of natural science and thereby became merely philosophers of science. Philosophy departments in the great universities of England and the United States have dedicated themselves to answering the questions that Bacon and Newton pretty well exhausted in the 17th century. The source of knowledge in science is nature and the method of inquiry is empiricism grown into the scientific method. Analytical philosophers have not improved upon the epistemology of science. And by being merely philosophers of science, they have not improved upon inquiry in the social sciences. They have proven to be quite dispensable indeed and therefore must be considered a failed experiment in modern philosophy.

Because many of the most prestigious philosophers in the United States and England claim to be analytical philosophers, the reader may expect a slightly more convincing argument regarding their failure than I have just provided. Fortunately two major American analytical philosophers recently described the last 50 years of their field in a manner that makes the argument for me.[22]

Hilary Putnam is Cogan University Professor at Harvard University. His article in *Daedalus*[23] is admittedly autobiographical and far more descriptive than critical. The major point I would draw from his article responds to the following statement he made regarding the importance of W.V. Quine:

---

[22] *Daedalus: Journal of the American Academy of Arts and Sciences* (Winter, 1997).

[23] "A Half Century of Philosophy, Viewed from Within."

I defended Quine's 'indispensability argument' in the epistemology of mathematics—the argument that the justification for accepting mathematics is simply that it is indispensable in sciences that are unquestionably empirical, in particular in physics, (p.186).

It is rationally impossible to defend Quine's *indispensability argument*[24] regarding mathematics and ignore analytical philosophy's persistent dispensability. Not only is analytical philosophy irrelevant in all other disciplines, many analytical philosophers treat the *inaccessibility* of philosophical statements as evidence of their *indispensability*. For that more reflective analysis we must turn to Alexander Nehamas, a chaired professor in the humanities at Princeton University.

If Professor Putnam appears the unreflective chronicler, Professor Nehamas exhibits analysis, self-consciousness, and wit. A single quotation from his *Daedalus* article[25] reveals all three:

> That has lead to what I believe is a dangerous fragmentation in the field, with people who teach together in the same department having neither any idea of what their colleagues are doing nor any interest in ever finding out. To see this point, it will help to discuss for a moment the canon of analytical philosophy.
>
> The problem is that no such canon exists today, (p. 221).

Describing the fragmentation of analytical philosophy and the lack of a canon, a core set of beliefs, is another way of saying that analytical philosophy has devolved into a form of individualism. Unlike genealogy, analytical philosophy does not start with assertions such as X is X from a multiplicity of views. However, the inability of analytical philosophers to establish a canon combined with their ability to continue as the major philosophical force in major universities means that there has been an unstated, undocumented accommodation of a multiplicity of X's in analytical philosophy.

There is no end to the irony in this story. G. E. Moore, Bertrand Russell, Ludwig Wittgenstein, A. J. Ayer, and others sought to bring

---

[24]W. V. Quine, "On What There Is."

[25]"Trends in Recent American Philosophy," in *Daedalus*.

mathematical and scientific rigor to philosophy. But they focused exclusively on method, asking how to design more precise statements and liberate inquiry from all the impossibly undefinable language that provides the content of philosophical debate. By not establishing an authoritative source of knowledge, they could not achieve an authoritative method.

As MacIntyre would say, analytical philosophy consists of contradictory, incompatible, incommensurable, and untranslatable views. According to Nehamas, the contentiousness that might exist among advocates of such disparate views, at least as they might exist under normal conditions of intellectual engagement, have been precluded by isolation. Like educators, analytical philosophers do not argue. They do not suffer conflict, because they have accepted the conclusion that there is no way to resolve their differences. Without conceding to having become genealogists, they have arrived at the same conclusion. There is no single correct view and there is no possibility of reaching a single correct view. Multiple truths exists in analytical philosophy's multiple views.

Analytical philosophers so completely lack agreement that it would be impossible for analytical philosophy to guide other disciplines. As MacIntyre has pointed out, contemporary philosophy reminds us of the marginalization of theology that began in the 14th century. Now, just as then, the presence of intractable conflicts causes contradictory views to exist side by side and makes it impossible for other departments in the university to turn to philosophers for the products of their work. Again we note Quine's indispensability argument and the contradictory claims regarding the inaccessibility of philosophical statements.

Nehamas points out that analytical philosophy even when addressing "issues of great interest to a broad audience" does so in "extremely technical terms and [is] unable to explain [its] inner workings to outsiders," (p. 215). Its statements are inaccessible. Astonishingly, both Putnam and Nehamas seem to accept the improbable analogy that analytical philosophers have drawn between the inaccessibility of deep science and the inaccessibility of philosophy. Quine's indispensability argument seems to have lost all meaning to them. Because airplanes successfully take off and land, bridges hold, rockets go into orbit and space shuttles return, one is inclined to trust mathematics and science. Add to those achievements the ability to turn new knowledge into astounding personal conveniences–not only the personal computer, but spell check too! Our daily lives are continuously made more convenient and interesting because of science.

Furthermore, many of us who lack even introductory knowledge in science can be swept away by such scientific works as Stephen Hawking's *A Brief History of Time*. We know that scientific inquiry as it is actually practiced by scientists is beyond our ken, but scientists are able to find language and images that engage our imaginations without diminishing their work.

Contemporary philosophers, on the other hand, leave no record of their achievements either in academe or civil society. Even the work of Quine and others who have claimed that "philosophy of science is philosophy enough," and have rejected the role of philosophy in such mundane and inherently inadequate disciplines as economics and education, must ultimately face the fact that Nehamas noticed, "Working natural scientists were never very interested in what their philosophical colleagues were telling them about their own disciplines . . ." (p. 214). Analytical philosophy which is only the philosophy of science has not even contributed to scientific inquiry.

Again we must notice that to the extent that we find philosophy useless in other disciplines, we must conclude that it is useless in itself. Rather than contributing to philosophy's usefulness, analytical philosophy and positivism have contributed to it marginalization. Each has dissolved into atomized groups of thought and individual opinion.

Conclusion

The lasting achievements of the period known as the Enlightenment were made in natural science which successfully replaced rationalism with empiricism grown into the epistemology of science. This epistemology has permitted the natural sciences to enjoy continuous progress into the present. Assuming that the modern period began with the Enlightenment, it has not ended for the natural sciences. Natural science continues to be enlightened by its intellectual community and its epistemology which remains unchallenged. The only persistent intellectual error made by natural scientists occurs when, frustrated by the inability of moral philosophy or social science to provide adequate leadership in applying scientific knowledge in society, they respond by attempting to conduct moral philosophy or social science in a manner that pays no attention to the epistemological problems in these disciplines. However, as we see in chapter seven, that error must be understood as a product of the failure of secular moral philosophy to guide ethical inquiry and the failure of the social sciences to ground themselves in ethical purpose. It is not the product of the failure of natural scientists to conduct moral philosophy or to answer ethical questions raised by scientific discoveries.

On the other hand, the modern era has not been as modern as social scientists and moral philosophers would wish to claim and post-modernism is very much a part of the modern tradition. Moral philosophy (since well before the Enlightenment) and social science (since the Enlightenment) have failed to achieve full development. Rather, they have bequeathed Western culture at the end of the second millennia with two poorly understood, deeply contradictory, and enormously flawed ways of knowing. Encyclopaedia has provided the vehicle for transporting medieval and Renaissance aristocratic elitism into the foundations of democratic governance. Although early on genealogy joined Western religious traditions to assert the rights and stature of individuals, it has subverted those principles and proven itself incapable of advancing principles, laws, and institutions that can sustain the liberal tradition. Rather than challenging the West's increasingly elitist institutions, genealogy has created the philosophical, legal, and institutional vacuum that the elite have filled with unexamined, unarticulated, indefensible, self-serving laws and institutions. While giving voice to the dignity and rights of working people, the poor, women, ethnic and racial minorities, and the environment; genealogy has been helpless to do anything to advance their rights and dignity. Unable to articulate universal principles, it has been unable to create laws, and without laws, it has been incapable of developing or changing institutions.

Admittedly, legal and institutional conflicts do occur and attract our attention, but they are best understood as conflicts that are waged among the elite. Elite corporate views confront elite government views, but neither represents working people, the poor, women, racial and ethnic minorities, or the environment. They represent the interests and policies of elite corporations and elite politicians and elite bureaucrats and elite religious leaders, as reported by the elite media.

Of course, exceptions can be made to such broad generalities. Some elite religious and political leaders have institutionalized assistance to the poor. However, the poor and especially working people who do the work of those institutions or pay a disproportionate share of their costs, have no trouble recognizing the reality. These charitable institutions provide a balm to the consciences of the elite who continue to ignore the economic principles and institutions that create poverty and cheat working people.

Charity and justice are different virtues, each with its own definitions and content. Charity is not some humiliating substitute for justice. But it is easier to see hypocrisy and injustice than to analyze it in a way that begins to suggest an alternative. That is why understanding encyclopaedia is revealing, explanatory, and important. Encyclopaedia operates as a world view that guides the thinking of elite Western individuals and institutions and produces highly authoritative, prestigious conclusions the basis for which are astoundingly self-serving while remaining largely indefensible and inexplicable.

The issue is not that the interests of the elite should be ignored. As mentioned earlier, Marxists have made that mistake with devastating consequences. Indeed, the 20th century political revolutions in South America provide a lengthy, tragic example of the inability of competing encyclopaedic groups to communicate or reach common ground. Anyone who has found it impossible to keep track of which were the good revolutionaries and which were the bad revolutionaries in South and Central America can be comforted in realizing that none were good. They were either fascists, who tended to enjoy the support of the American elite, or communists, who tended to enjoy the support of some terribly naive American leftists. Rather than succumbing to economic theory that chooses winners and losers, we must have a way of thinking about and conducting moral philosophy and social science that reveals and balances the needs of everyone. A solution that disregards the interests of the elite must be seen as failed *for the same reason* as views that disregard the interests of working people and other disenfranchised groups. All the permutations of encyclopaedic dice must be rejected.

In chapter seven, we discover that encyclopaedic thinking has succeeded because moral philosophers have not developed mature levels of moral reasoning. In chapter eight, we discover that economists, educators, and other social scientists have not developed mature levels of cognition, what Piaget called *formal operations*. Because our topic is education, we do not attempt to meet the intellectual challenges presented by attempts to reach full cognitive development in economics or the other social sciences. But our general discussion of the role of mature ethical reasoning inevitably applies to economics and the other social sciences in a way that makes it possible for readers to move independently toward ethical solutions in those disciplines. But again, we do not attempt specific ethical solutions in those disciplines. On the other hand, genealogy has presented an entirely different set of problems to Western moral philosophers and social scientists.

By locating the source of truth in the individual, genealogy and its many variations deny the possibility of articulating any form of social ethics or institutionalized social policy. What cannot be articulated cannot be expressed in law. What cannot be expressed in law cannot be institutionalized.[26] The two great revolutions in the history of Western culture, the Protestant Reformation and the English-American political revolution, succeeded not merely because they rejected institutionalized oppression. They succeeded because they rejected institutionalized oppression and replaced it with new and more effective institutions. Encyclopaedia has endured in spite of all of its fundamental assumptions having been discredited because no philosophical alternative has been advanced.

In order to survive in such an environment, public educators have attempted to accommodate both views. We have created encyclopedic institutions such as the National School Boards Association, the American Association of School Administrators, the National Education Association, and the American Federation of Teachers. Only the most unaware observer can view these institutions as different from the institutions that support elite corporate or political or social interests. They are indistinguishable from the elite corporations and institutions in their group directed interests. They have an encyclopedic purpose: to advance the interests of their group and define the interests of their group as applicable to as broad a spectrum of society as possible. However, in the current social and political environment, education and society would be diminished if any of these educational institutions were weakened.

In addition, educators have assented to genealogical and post-modernist views by defending the rights of researchers, teaching faculty, school administrators, and school teachers to look upon all research and methodology from a post-Kantian perspective. What the research says, as such, is not as important as how the individual encounters it or what the

---

[26] For all that the media and others denounce institutions, the elite have no trouble writing laws and creating institutions that serve their needs. The media's attacks on the value of laws and institutions has proven to be a very effective means of furthering the authority of the elite and undermining the interests of working people, disenfranchised groups, and the environment.

individual chooses to use. From this end of the intellectual spectrum, there is no need or capacity for intellectual authority or institutional coherence.

Education is a discipline deeply entrenched in the Western intellectual tradition and as such is struggling to overcome intractable problems that have frustrated Western intellectuals for 700 years. When principals and teachers meet and encounter intellectual problems that confound discourse and make agreement seem impossible, they encounter the same intellectual problems that undermine inquiry in secular moral philosophy and the other social sciences. Educators might wish to turn to moral philosophy and social science for assistance, but there is nothing to encourage us to do so. Rather, we must find our own solutions. We turn now to that challenge and its vast promises.

Part II

An Epistemology for Education

7

The Source of Knowledge

By now our challenge is clear. Educators must develop, commit to, and use an epistemology that is appropriate to our research and practice. It must allow us to integrate research, integrate research and practice, and conduct discourse that leads to agreement, commitment, and action. Before we begin to discuss the specific components of *this epistemology*, it is important to establish, at the *formal* level, the components of *an epistemology*. I use the term formal in the same way Kant and Piaget did when they talked about thinking about thinking. In distinguishing concrete operations from formal operations, Piaget contrasted using an hypothesis from thinking about hypotheses as such. We make the same distinction when we begin this discussion by establishing what we mean by epistemology in general and then arguing for a particular epistemology.

Its seems clear that the epistemology of any *inquiry based* discipline[1] must provide answers to three questions: 1) What is the source of knowledge in this discipline? 2) What is the formal architecture or structure of knowledge in this discipline? 3) What is the method of inquiry in this discipline? Different disciplines are identified and defined by the different answers they provide to those three questions. Furthermore, the strength and clarity of the answers that each discipline advances predicts the depth of commitment to its epistemology and the level of intellectual authority each discipline can achieve.

Below, I provide the answers that natural science has advanced to these questions along with the answers I suggest for the social sciences. Again, these questions provide the formal structure of epistemology that guides epistemological discourse in all inquiry based disciplines.

In this chapter, I argue that an ethically grounded purpose provides the source of knowledge in the social sciences and I demonstrate that it is

---

[1]As I noted earlier, art, dance, music, and even literature seem to be grounded in expression rather than inquiry and therefore would require a different formal definition of epistemology if they were to benefit from epistemology at all. Aesthetics may guide their efforts more usefully and clearly than epistemology.

THE EPISTEMOLOGIES OF
NATURAL SCIENCE AND SOCIAL SCIENCE

SOURCE OF KNOWLEDGE:

Natural Science:
Nature

Social Science:
Ethically Grounded Purpose

FORMAL ARCHITECTURE AND STRUCTURE OF KNOWLEDGE:

Natural Science:
Scientific Paradigms

Social Science:
Theoretical Models

METHOD OF INQUIRY

Natural Science:
Scientific Method
(Quantitative Analysis)

Social Science:
Social Science Method
(Qualitative and Quantitative
Analysis)

possible to develop a system of mature secular ethical reasoning. In chapter eight, I describe a formal architecture that allows *educators* to integrate research and to integrate research and practice. In addition, I demonstrate that the organization and structure of knowledge are inseparable from the intellectual and social integration of a professional community. The integration of research, the integration of research and practice, and the integration of a professional community must be treated as inseparable tasks. Both knowledge and communities must be formally integrated by the formal architecture of knowledge in a discipline.

In chapter nine, I discuss the method of inquiry in the social sciences. Resolving issues in research methodology involves clarifying what is already known rather than inventing what is not known. I also discuss *research and development* which are highly advanced and integrated in natural science and commerce but terribly underdeveloped and disjointed in education. Admittedly, I recommend enormous change, and as we all know, it is currently impossible to institutionalize discipline wide change in education. However, I demonstrate that most of the problems that we encounter when attempting to lead change result from the intellectual problems that prohibit the integration of research and practice. Those intellectual inadequacies produce such an irrational environment that change often requires educators to stop doing what they believe in and start doing what they do not believe in. Paint it any way we want, change that cannot be defended rationally and persuasively must be imposed or left to chance. It is either resisted or ignored. I end chapter nine with a discussion of how the epistemology of education permits educators to re-think change.

Now we turn to the most dramatic task we face, resolving the 700 year old problem regarding the source of knowledge in education.

Resolving the 700 Year Old Problem

Throughout this text, we have acknowledged that education cannot use the epistemology of science. Now I can provide an argument that supports that conclusion. During the years that have been occupied by this project, I spent quite a lot of time struggling with the epistemological differences that distinguish natural science and the social sciences. I do not recall when I made the formal distinction between source of knowledge and method of inquiry in epistemology, but I remember vividly the day I found a resolution to the difference between the source of knowledge in natural science and the source of knowledge in the social sciences.

I was reading Kant's "Preface" to *Fundamental Principles of the Metaphysic of Morals* and unexpectedly found the distinctions that had eluded me. I invite the reader to develop some sense of excitement over participating in the discussion of a solution to an intellectual problem that has troubled Western intellectuals for 700 years.

Above, I referred to Piaget and Kant's use of the term formal.[2] It is important at the outset of this discussion to note what Kant meant by formal knowledge and to do some work with his definition. Kant distinguished formal knowledge from knowledge about things when he wrote:

---

[2] When Piaget discussed *concrete* operations and *formal operations*, he claimed to be doing *genetic epistemology*.

> Ancient Greek philosophy was divided into three sciences: physics, ethics, and logic. This division is *perfectly suitable to the nature of the thing*; and the only improvement that can be made in it is to *add the principle on which it is based*, so that we may both satisfy ourselves of its completeness, and also be able to determine correctly the necessary subdivisions.[3]

Kant's *division* of knowledge into physics, ethics, and logic is not perfectly suitable to the nature of knowledge as modern intellectuals have organized it. However, Kant provided the key to unlocking the epistemological riddle regarding why different disciplines require different sources of knowledge. If logic, physics, and ethics are inherently different disciplines, they must require different epistemologies. By understanding the different ways they answer epistemological questions, we are able to discern *the principles* that determine those differences.

Kant's first distinction focused on the difference between logic as opposed to either physics or ethics.[4] Kant began his discussion of these differences by writing:

> All rational knowledge is either *material* or *formal*: the former considers some object, the latter is concerned only with the form of the understanding and of the reason itself, and the universal laws of thought in general without distinction of its objects. Formal philosophy is called logic, (ibid.).

According to Kant, knowledge can be divided into: 1) Knowledge about how we know, the nature of reason and how we reason, the form of understanding or the form of cognition, and 2) Knowledge about things (material knowledge). Formal knowledge is concerned with the form or architecture of cognition itself, what I call epistemology. The only formal

---

[3] P. 253, emphasis added. Kant used italics for emphasis and sometimes I do. Whenever I use them, I note that they were added. Otherwise, they were used by Kant.

[4] What Kant called physics, we call natural science, and what Kant called ethics here he later refers to as moral philosophy which we call social science.

knowledge Kant acknowledged was logic. I think we can improve upon Kant's description of formal knowledge.

Ultimately, all intellectual activity must be logical. I make no attempt to improve upon that point. However, the object of inquiry impacts how we define and characterize our logical processes. The object of inquiry in natural science and the social sciences are very different (a point that becomes clear in our discussion of *their* sources of knowledge). Obviously, those differences demand that we develop different epistemological components for the two disciplines. All epistemologies must account for their discipline's source of knowledge, formal architecture or structure of knowledge, and method of inquiry.

That different disciplines require different *epistemologies* becomes evident in the fact that they must have different *sources of knowledge* or different *structures of knowledge*, or different *methods of inquiry*. Our definition of epistemology consists of these three components. We admit that these components are *real* because they provide the basis for distinguishing whole frameworks of inquiry (natural science from social science) and disciplines within those larger frameworks (i.e. sociology vs. economics vs. education). The recognition that there are no differences among these components of inquiry in biology, chemistry, and physics helps explain why those disciplines have increasingly been recognized as inseparable. On the other hand, there are real differences between inquiry in natural science and inquiry in the social sciences. Those differences must be accounted for in their epistemologies. Kant called natural science physics, which seems prescient, and the social sciences ethics, which also seems prescient the more we understand his view.

Two Kinds of Material Knowledge: Physics and Ethics

Having expanded Kant's description of formal knowledge, we turn to his discussion of the two kinds of material knowledge. Material knowledge is concerned with objects in the physical world. In distinguishing two kinds of material knowledge, Kant answered our question regarding why science and the social sciences cannot use the same epistemology.

> Material philosophy, however, [which] has to do with determinate objects and the laws to which they are subject, is again twofold; for these laws are either laws of *nature* or of *freedom*. The

science of the former is physics, that of the latter is ethics; they are
also called natural philosophy and moral philosophy, (ibid.).

I explain that statement, but I do not attempt to improve upon it.
When we conduct inquiry into the material world (the task of natural
science and the social sciences), we study objects in the physical world
that are governed either by the laws of nature (natural science) or the laws
of freedom (the social sciences). But what does freedom have to do with
the social sciences?

The social sciences study those principles, laws, and institutions that
occur in the *physical world* and have been *created by humans* to help us
assure such social achievements as peace, prosperity, and justice. *None*
of these phenomena exists independent of human action. *Nature's* laws,
even though they require humans to notice and articulate them, are
inherent in the physical world. Gravity did not depend upon Newton's
describing it in order to function. But no social principles, laws, or
institutions exist until humans describe and actualize them. What the
social sciences study in the material world are things that humans have
invented.

But what does the fact that the social sciences study what humans
have invented have to do with ethics? Why does Kant call this inquiry
moral philosophy? Again, he is clear:

> Natural[5] and moral philosophy . . . the former, however, being
> laws according to which everything *does* happen; the latter, laws
> according to which everything *ought* to happen, (ibid., emphasis
> added).

How does one study the laws according to which everything *ought* to
happen? Kant stresses that *the starting point* of any rational method that
asks the question, What ought to be? is ethics. What ought to be? is an
ethical question and answering it requires ethical reasoning. Clearly, what
Kant has suggested and what we act upon is shocking to many social
scientists who have defined their disciplines as science in order to
distinguish them from moral philosophy. But we begin to see that social

---

[5] Again, natural philosophy is the term scholastic philosophers used for
what we call natural science.

scientists make a grave error when they distance their disciplines from moral philosophy. It is important to recall why social scientists got caught up in such an error. We must recall that they faced real problems that face us today, for we must solve those problems when we reconnect the social sciences with moral philosophy.

As we have seen, scholastic philosophers failed to develop a source of knowledge that was independent of theology. As a practical matter, medieval moral philosophy was more a variation of medieval moral theology than a legitimate, independent intellectual enterprise. As a result, the Protestant Reformation *divided* both theology and *moral philosophy* along religious, sectarian lines. Medieval moral philosophy was as dogma bound as theology, so when the Protestant Reformation produced institutionalized divisions in Christian dogma, it produced institutionalized divisions in moral philosophy.

Since the content of moral philosophy is what today we call the social sciences, dividing it along religious, sectarian lines created intractable political conflicts. Citizens, politicians, and intellectuals were forced to remove theology from the social sciences which also forced them to distance the social sciences from moral philosophy. Society had to develop principles of tolerance for different religious views, but they also had to develop *shared secular* principles that united civil society. In order to describe accurately their disciplines, scholars interested in the human condition stopped calling themselves moral philosophers and began calling themselves social scientists. During the entire history of social science, social scientists have attempted to conduct inquiry independent of moral theology *and moral philosophy*.

In the meantime, secular moral philosophers have completely failed to develop a system of moral reasoning or moral content that can build consensus in the public square or assist inquiry in the university. The ineptitude of secular moral philosophy explains why social scientists have distanced themselves from it. More recently, some social scientists have shown interest in ethics, but they have found that secular moral philosophy is inadequate to their tasks. As we begin to understand that mature moral reasoning is as indispensable to the social sciences as mathematics is to natural science, we realize that we are faced with the dilemma of developing forms of moral reasoning that do not exist in religious or secular moral philosophy.

The Indispensability of Ethics to the Social Sciences

Existentialists' claim that humans are *doomed to freedom*. That is certainly true about social scientists and educators. We may notice injustice in the financing of health care, attempt to fix it, but encounter political opposition carried out in national advertising campaigns. We sense that we have lost the ability to conduct the kind of public discourse necessary to understand and solve the problem. The opposition's irrationality and financial resources may seem overwhelming and in our discouragement we might quit the fight. But that does not change the injustice. It merely means that we have chosen to live with the injustice rather than fight the political fight, do the intellectual and political work, needed to resolve it.

Social scientists and educators can choose to act or they can choose to do nothing, but they cannot avoid the fact that they are responsible for the consequences that result from their choices. It is surprising to notice how casually many secular moral philosophers and social scientists treat their freedom, how much they demand it, and how little they account for it.

There is a vast history of social scientists and politicians who have worked hard to serve people and society, but others have made decisions motivated by self interest, greed, power, ignorance, and indifference. When social scientists study what exists in society, it is absurd to treat it as if it were necessary, as if it were real in the same unalterable fashion in which nature is real. To treat natural phenomena as if they contain the source of knowledge for social science is sometimes called the *naturalistic fallacy*.

Because social scientists spend the vast percentage of their time studying the material things that define the *activities* of the social sciences, it is easy to commit the naturalistic fallacy. For example, educators commit the naturalistic fallacy when they assume that all the material things that impact education (school finance, governance, research, curriculum, and pedagogy) are as natural, inevitable, and unalterable as gravity. They assume that they can study their history or current practice and discover their underlying reality. But those events are not natural and they have no underlying reality in the way that gravity does. They are all the result of human choices, human action—whether deliberate or unintended, conscious or unconscious, conscientious or indifferent. Some choices were made with the kind of determination that insists, "We must do something, even if it is wrong, we have got to make a decision!" To treat the material manifestations of these or any human choices as if they contain our source of knowledge, as if they are as necessary and unalterable as the truth of nature, is indeed folly.

Social scientists must create their own source of knowledge. They must identify what it is that *ought to be*, and, even more difficult, they must treat their description of what ought to be as their standard of knowledge. Educators, for example, must continue to study school finance, governance, research, curriculum, and pedagogy, but they must study these topics in terms of how they contribute to what they have decided ought to be in education. Each discipline must identify its own source of knowledge and use it in the same way that scientists use theirs. Social scientists must not confuse what exists in the social sciences with their source of knowledge. Like natural scientists, they must use their source of knowledge as their standard of knowledge. But unlike natural scientists, they must *develop* or *select* their source of knowledge. They must develop the answer to the question, What ought to be? But why must the answer to this question be an ethical statement?

Attempts to answer questions regarding what ought to be in any of the social sciences evoke two very different questions: 1) What *can* we do? and 2) What is our ultimate goal or purpose? The first question frames the issue in a manner that feels safe and is so practical that it must be the essential question. The second question demands attention not just to what we do not know but to what might very well be unknowable. It sounds so impractical that it cannot be the essential question. At first glance, it would seem that social scientists would do well to limit their description of what ought to be to what they know how to do, but that conclusion is not as useful as it might seem.

As a source of knowledge, the statement that describes what ought to be must guide both *research and practice*. If it were defined in terms of doing what practitioners already know how to do, there would be no need for research or program development or staff development. The statement of purpose would preclude the need for development which would destroy inquiry and practice.

When social scientists accept that we conduct inquiry into the laws of freedom and that our disciplines must accept responsibility to choose not only what we can do, but also what we *ought* to do, we make an enormous change, a change that challenges us both ethically and intellectually. We define our source of knowledge as *what ought to be* rather than *what is.* In making that choice, we invigorate our freedom and overcome the naturalistic fallacy. We accept that our source of knowledge is our ethically grounded purpose. In referring to the source of knowledge in the social sciences, I use the terms *telos* and *ethically grounded purpose* interchangeably. *Telos* is helpful because it is the term Aristotle used and reminds us that we are grounded in a secular ethical tradition of long standing. In addition, it requires just one word. *Ethically grounded purpose* is useful because its meaning is so clear.

Since our source of knowledge is our *telos* or ethically grounded purpose, in order to identify it, we must employ a system of ethical reasoning. We must develop a system of ethical reasoning that can win consensus and commitment in the social sciences. Otherwise, we cannot agree on what ought to be; we cannot agree on our source of knowledge; and we cannot agree on standards of research or practice. Ethical reasoning is as indispensable to the social sciences and education as mathematics is to the natural sciences. But can we develop a system of ethical reasoning that can win consensus? First we develop the framework for a system of mature secular ethical reasoning that can be used in all of the social sciences, then we discuss how we can use mature secular ethical reasoning in education.

Developing Mature Secular Moral Reasoning

Our task is to describe a *system* of *mature secular* ethical reasoning that can be used by social scientists to *produce a canon* or ethical content to which all social scientists can commit. Aristotle provides the *system* or *ethical structure* we use. Educators know a lot about *mature* ethical reasoning through their study of Piaget and Kohlberg. Their work plays a significant part in this project. *Secular* has to do with source of knowledge. Kohlberg helps us solve that problem by replacing the expectation that our source of knowledge has an ontological origin with the understanding that it is developmental. *Agreement and commitment* actually have as much to do with how we learn moral reasoning and what we expect of moral reasoning as they do with the structure of moral arguments. Vygotsky and MacIntyre help us with how we learn and our willingness to learn ethics. Kant provides the *method* of ethical reasoning that *produces an ethically grounded purpose and a canon* to which social scientists can commit. Two separate commitments must be won, first to *the system* and method of ethical inquiry and then to *the canon* or content produced by the ethical system. My purpose is to describe a general framework for the system and method and to explain the role of research and teaching in ethical development so that social scientists can develop a competent system of secular ethical reasoning and a just canon. I do not attempt to develop the complete system or canon for those tasks require a major research and development project with broad participation among social scientists and moral philosophers.

Aristotle's Ethical System

As we have seen, Aristotle's ethical system was composed of: 1) The *good*, an ethically grounded purpose, or what he called the *telos*; 2) *Virtues*, conduct that leads to the good; and 3) *Vices*, conduct that leads away from the good.

The immediate attraction of Aristotle's system is its simplicity and clarity. It tells us what to study and promises that if we are successful we can develop ethics that establish what we ought to achieve ultimately, what helps us achieve it, and what gets in our way. The simplicity of this system precludes our having to discuss it in any detail. The argument for its efficacy is contained in its application to the development of mature ethical reasoning and the development of a formal architecture of inquiry and knowledge contained in chapter eight. The structure of ethical reasoning that we have borrowed from Aristotle focuses our attention, but it does not reveal the ethical content social scientists need to guide our professional conduct. It does not tell us what *the good* is, nor does it identify virtues and vices. By the end of chapter eight, however, we see how this simple framework has directed us to develop a mature system of ethical reasoning, the *telos*, or ethically grounded purpose of education (the good), and the formal cognitive operations required to identify what educators must do to achieve our purpose (virtues) and what we must not do (poor practices, or in Aristotle's terms, vices).

Recalling Aristotle's enormous confidence in reason, inquiry, and teaching; we recognize that not everyone can design an ethical system or develop a just canon, but many can learn both. However, as we learned from studying the encyclopaedists, folks who take responsibility to invent or develop what others must be taught must avoid developing a system that serves them at the expense of everyone else. Our challenge, then, is to develop a system of mature secular ethical reasoning that produces a just canon. This challenge is aided by the work of Kohlberg and Kant. First we review the work of Kohlberg, then Kant.

Kohlberg's Theory of Moral Development

That the capacity to reason ethically follows a developmental sequence is well known among educators familiar with Piaget's work in cognitive development and Kohlberg's work in moral development. Piaget observed that as children get older, they become able to perform cognitive functions that earlier had been impossible. His four stages of cognitive development include: sensory-motor (birth to age 2), pre-operational (age 2-7), concrete-operational (7-11), and formal-operational (11-15). These stages have been confirmed in various studies, one of the most interesting of which was conducted by H. T. Epstein, a neuro-physicist who established stages of brain and skull growth that matched Piaget's stages of cognitive development.

Kohlberg identified stages of *moral reasoning* or *moral development* that, not surprisingly, display a high correlation to Piaget's stages of cognitive development. Two things are of great interest in Kohlberg: first, the kind of moral reasoning that children exhibit at different developmental stages provides a compelling set of definitions of moral reasoning arranged in a hierarchy from the immature to the mature. This point does not require much discussion, but we eventually rely on it when asking educators to accept that ethical conclusions based on immature reasoning cannot be treated as equal or superior to ethical conclusions based on mature reasoning. That is not a startling expectation. We do not allow immature logic to prevail over mature thinking in science or mathematics or history. It makes no sense to let immature logic prevail in ethical reasoning.

Second, both Piaget and Kohlberg treated the stages of cognitive and moral development as dependent upon biological prerequisites. In other words, children cannot learn anything that requires cognitive functioning that is beyond their biological maturation. Epstein supported Piaget's view by confirming that neither brain growth nor cognitive development occurs before the threshold years identified for each stage. According to this developmental view, the critical event in cognitive development is *biological maturation.* In other words, if a child is not *biologically* ready to learn something, there is virtually nothing for the child, parent, or teacher to do but wait until the child has developed biologically, *and then they can learn.* This assumption makes patience an important part of bringing children along cognitively and ethically.

But there is a huge theoretical problem in all of this. Anyone who has worked with children and paid attention to their cognitive functioning knows that age is no guarantee of development. Children can be old enough, but still not be able to perform at the level of cognitive development their age would indicate. Dansen[6] found that only 30 percent of adults can operate at the level of formal operations, which according to Piaget becomes possible between the ages of 11 and 15 years. Piaget and Epstein seem to have identified something that is important and real about cognitive development: biological maturation is required to function at various cognitive levels. But they did not explain why, once that level is reached, some children actually develop the higher cognitive functions and others do not. They did not explain why only 30 percent of the adult population achieves formal reasoning in spite of the undeniable fact that 100 percent of the adult population is older than 15.

Initially, Kohlberg seemed to get caught in the Piagetian trap: If no one can function at a higher level of moral reasoning than is made possible by their biological maturation, but if biological maturation does not assure that the person actually is able to perform at those levels, then some variable(s) in addition to biological maturation must impact cognitive and moral development. Without accounting for those variables, one cannot explain cognitive or moral development.

In 1966, Turiel (one of Kohlberg's colleagues) in attempting to confirm that children move sequentially through Kohlberg's stages, conducted a study in which he investigated the impact on children's moral reasoning when they receive instruction at one stage above their current level of moral reasoning, one stage below, and two stages above. He found that children are most influenced by instruction that teaches them to reason morally at one stage above their current *operating* level. Turiel found that instruction at one stage above their current operating level was likely to result in their actually moving up. He proved that children do not leap any of the stages even if given instruction at higher levels, that was the purpose of his study. But he also demonstrated that *instruction impacts development.* He demonstrated that children do not either mature

---

[6]Dansen, Pierre R.; "Cross-cultural Piagetian Research: A Summary;" Journal of Cross-cultural Psychology, N. 3, 1972.

mentally and morally or not. Some children seem to mature quickly and learn many things on their own. That is no secret. But Turiel demonstrated that if children are not able to develop cognitively or ethically on their own, they are not just flat out of luck. He proved that instruction has a direct influence on learning and development.

In other words, Turiel confirmed what Plato, Aristotle, Aquinas, and MacIntyre agreed about:

> The human being who has *acquired the necessary education* in the intellectual and moral virtues *and who thereby apprehends* what his or her true good is acts so as to achieve that good.[7]

Kohlberg's Levels of Moral Development

Kohlberg described three levels of moral reasoning.[8] The first level is called *pre-conventional*. That very young children use immature reasoning is not the really arresting issue. More to the point, they are egocentric. They are only interested in having their own needs met. Because they are undeveloped physically, they have to depend on others to meet their needs. Adults are far more likely to meet their needs than their peers or older children. Logically, their physical, social, and psychological development drive them to please adults, and typically that means they willingly follow adult rules.[9] The ethical decisions and habits

---

[7]MacIntyre, *Three Rival Versions*, (p. 154, emphasis added).

[8]Each of Kohlberg's levels of moral reasoning contains different stages. In the interest of brevity, I have described the levels generally. This decision is not terribly noticeable until I describe the post-conventional level in terms of the social contract. That is actually only a mid-range stage of development in that level, but I think it is fair to say that individuals, professions and society would function magnificently if we all operated at that stage.

[9]This level of moral development operates within adults who are egocentric, feel helpless, and logically (albeit unfortunately) follow the dictates of religious, corporate, and political leaders in hopes of getting their needs met. They are incapable of the moral reasoning that defines a responsible adult. These are the adults who constitute the loyal workers who support just and unjust leaders. They give and take lives for causes others define, unable to evaluate the justice of the

of young children are therefore almost entirely dependent upon the ethical expectations of the adults upon whom they depend for their physical, intellectual, and moral development. Assuming competent adult supervision, that is all well and good; but, in any event, this level ends when children enter their early teens.

In their early teens, children enter the level of moral development that Kohlberg called *conventional*. They begin to think for themselves. This change allows them to develop from compliant, obedient, dependent children to self-actualizing, self-determining, independent, responsible adults. Unfortunately, this transformation begins, whether we like it or not, before children are ready to handle it. The biological maturity required for *formal reasoning* occurs as early as age 11 and no later that 15. In their early teens, most children begin to be able to conduct formal reasoning and therefore they begin to think differently. They begin to create their own ethical systems, and they begin to apply their nascent reasoning skills to ethical questions which they are inclined to answer for themselves.

Our purpose in this discussion is to establish the fact that moral reasoning is better understood in terms of a developmental construct than as materialistic ontology and to gain insight into various levels of development so that we can understand and pursue mature levels of moral reasoning. But since we are educators, we must be interested in the ethical development of children as well as the ethical development of our profession. In addition, the level of ethical reasoning children use in their early teens is the level of ethical reasoning that most adults employ. So we need to give this level special attention.

Piaget observed that when children mature cognitively from pre-operations to concrete operations, they restructure *everything they know* into concrete operations. Similarly, when children move from pre-conventional to conventional levels of moral reasoning, they restructure everything they know—all of the ethical rules they have been taught by adults—into the new ethical principles they are now able to form *for*

causes or the competence of their leaders. Democracy demands that leaders limit their authority by developing competent moral reasoning in as many adults as possible. Unfortunately, many leaders have not established protecting democracy or developing citizens as their ethical purpose. Their unethical purpose is to garner power for themselves or their group.

themselves. But the ethical system they employ is immature and therefore inadequate to the ethical decisions they must make in school, at home, and in society. Two huge developmental issues impact schools: 1) When students enter the conventional level they reject all of the ethics they have been taught and replace them with their own ethics, and 2) Their level of moral reasoning is immature and inadequate to their ethical needs.

More than one parent or teacher has complained that when children enter their early teens, they seem to go brain dead. They forget what they have known since first grade. But they have not forgotten; they have begun to restructure their entire ethical system. Be home by 10:00 p.m. on Friday night. Not only is the conclusion wrong, the parent has lost the right to make such a decision. But the person we are talking about is not an eighteen year old senior who has a good job or has been accepted to college. We are looking at an obdurate twelve year old, or a sixteen year old with a car, or any child with a gun. Being a parent of children in their early and mid teens is terrifying. [10]

Simply put, children and adults who function at the level of *conventional* moral reasoning employ an ethical system that has two different canon, two sets of content: 1) The ethical rules they apply to themselves and their friends, and 2) The ethical rules they apply to everyone else. For children, this level constitutes important development, because it means that they have left the egocentric world of early childhood in which they sought to please adults for personal gain and have *developed a social reference* that includes themselves and their peers. Establishing a social reference rather than an individual reference constitutes development, but as long as their social reference distinguishes the ethical status of individuals in their group from everyone else, their reasoning must be considered immature. It is no longer individual, but it

---

[10]There are enormous implications of this theory for educators who design curriculum and instruction or attend to the culture of middle schools, junior high schools, and high schools. All of us must understand the complex impact of cognitive, ethical, and social/psychological development on children and young adults. That understanding clarifies what we can expect of children, what we must teach, and how we must design schools and programs. Most important, this understanding clarifies the urgency connected to professional educators' agreeing on, teaching, and acting *consistently* regarding these issues. Unfortunately, that discussion is beyond the scope of this text.

is still subjective—based upon my group rather than on me. Mature moral reasoning generates objective, universal principles, a point that we establish with the help of Kohlberg and Kant.

Kohlberg called his third and highest level of moral reasoning *post-conventional* or principled moral reasoning. Simply put, principled moral reasoning acknowledges the social contract. We have seen that the social contract does not, by itself, assure high levels of moral reasoning. Hobbes described a social contract in which all of the empowering terms were on the ruler's side and all of the oppressive terms were on the people's side. Encyclopaedists have vitiated the social contract in Western democracies by making it one sided. We know, then, that debate about the terms of the social contract must be guided by mature moral reasoning. Kohlberg's analogy is helpful, but not adequate to the development of mature moral reasoning. It gives us a picture of what we are trying to achieve, but not the logic that allows us to achieve it. The logic of this level comes from Kant whom we visit shortly.

The significant distinction we must take with us from our discussions of Kohlberg's hierarchy of moral development is the difference between Kohlberg's second level of moral reasoning, *conventional* moral reasoning; and his third level, *post-conventional*. In the second level, the ethical stature of individuals depends upon the group to which they belong. In the third level, all humans enjoy the same ethical stature. Mature ethical reasoning cannot be developed from the subjective point of view of either the group or the individual. Mature ethical reasoning must be developed from an objective, universal point of view.

Most important, we notice that ethics, ethical systems and content, must be *developed*. Once we accept that premise, we overcome the major opposition in secular moral philosophy to the acceptance of mature moral reasoning. By understanding that the existence of mature ethical reasoning and conduct lies in development and teaching, we realize that mature moral reasoning and the canon of a mature ethical system are not material things; they do not exist anywhere; they are developmental constructs. This distinction requires our attention.

Ethical Development vs. Materialistic Ontology

Currently, secular moral philosophers argue for the necessity of ethical nihilism. Nihilism presents three positions: 1) There is no ethical truth extant to be known. 2) Since there is no ethical truth that exists independent of humans, each individual must create his or her own truth.

3) Any ethical statement developed by anyone or any group can only be required of that individual or that group, for broader application of individual and group opinions necessitates coercion and oppression.

The first statement is true. Ethics do not exist. But where secular moral philosophers see this as an ontological problem, we see it as a developmental problem. Predictably, many natural scientists and moral theologians may be quite dissatisfied with our answer, but that is their problem. Neither is capable of developing mature *secular* moral reasoning within their epistemology. They can complain or ridicule all they want, but left to their own devices, they cannot help.

The prestige, success, and, in some cases, arrogance of scientists has pushed and shamed secular moral philosophers and social scientists into trying to ground our inquiry as *firmly* as inquiry in science. Empiricists and analytical philosophers in particular have fawned over science and consistently committed what we have called the *naturalistic fallacy*. Genealogists have also been susceptible to the material bias of scientific epistemology, for they have *located* the source of knowledge in the individual which is also a materialistic solution. We do not reject the statement, There is no ethical truth extant. We agree. But we interpret its consequences differently. We do not accept their next statement, that each individual must create his or her own truth. Rather, we claim that ethics like other social achievements must be *developed*, and, as with other social achievements, we deny that individuals must develop them on their own.

There are no economic theories, laws, or institutions extant for us to discover and use, and it is impossible to think of economics as being conducted according to various designs that emanate from individuals. No one would suggest that only individuals can describe economic theory and practice or that an economic theory can only apply to the individual who asserts it. No one would suggest that each individual must develop his or her own political theories or that those theories could only apply to the individual. And yet we are asked to endure a view of moral reasoning that claims that every individual must create his or her own ethics, and that those ethics can only apply to the individual who asserts them.

It seems important to consider that it actually makes sense that across the world masses of people are increasingly attracted to dogmatic moral theology. Regardless of the religion, dogmatic moral theology offers concrete, universal rules with the promise that those who follow them are set apart from, morally superior to, the rest of humanity. Dogmatic moral theology resonates within pre-conventional and conventional moral reasoning. Ethical nihilism defies pre-conventional, conventional, and post-conventional levels of moral development. It offers nothing for children to follow, undermines the social perspective of conventional moral reasoning, and offends the adult who strives for the objective and universal ethical principles of post-conventional moral reasoning.

Again, we find that we can argue against a philosophical view, but what really matters is that we replace it. If we can develop a system of mature secular ethical reasoning and a just ethical canon, the nihilistic argument can be destroyed and replaced. Obviously, the success of moral reasoning has great implications for the success of moral teaching and on the willingness of colleagues and graduate students freely to accept what is taught. But that is true of all knowledge and all teaching.

I present Kant's method as a foundation upon which secular social scientists can develop mature secular ethical reasoning. I welcome arguments that improve upon Kant's methods or replace them with something better. Whatever it turns out to be, social scientists must find a *secular method of ethical reasoning* that can win consensus for the canon of professional ethics in the social sciences and the *telos* of each discipline.

Kant's Categorical Imperative

Kant constructed *universal secular* ethical statements that overcome individualism and elitism. Only *universal* ethical statements have the capacity to establish consensus and win commitment. Only universal ethical statements can form the canon or content of an ethical system. And only *secular* ethical statements can form the content of an ethical system used in universities and the public square.

Kant emphasized the distinction between an ethical statement that is valid for the individual who asserts it as opposed to an ethical statement that is valid to every rational being. The first he called maxims, the second laws. These laws, with their objective rather than subjective validity, he called *categorical imperatives*. Kant is clear in his attitude toward ethical statements that are grounded in the individual.[11] Yes, he

---

[11]Kant pre-dated the encyclopaedists and did not anticipate their assent to *group ethics*. He acknowledged the prestige of private ethics in private matters, but he demanded *universal* ethics in society.

would admit, each individual is capable of developing ethical statements that are valid privately, but they enjoy only a subjective or personal validity. Higher level, more useful ethical statements have objective reality. They do not depend upon the individual. They are valid in themselves, apply universally, and are grounded in a different kind of rationality than individual beliefs. He used the term *categorical* to emphasize the objectivity and universality of these statements.

According to Kant, *categorical* imperatives, "are objectively and universally valid only when they hold without any contingent subjective conditions, which distinguish one rational being from another,"[12] and therefore are "valid for the will of every rational being," (ibid., p. 297). In other words, by being *categorical* these ethical statements apply, without qualification, to every human being in every culture and at every time regardless of variations in personal experiences. Further, a *categorical* imperative provides an ethical standard that is valid whether one is able to achieve it or not. The occasion of one's being a coward, regardless of how understandable that conduct might be, regardless of how much I might admit that I would behave that way in those circumstances, does not alter the standing of courage as an ethical principle. Nor do cowardice or hatred or duplicity become universal ethical principles by being universal conduct. Courage, charity, and justice constitute universal ethical principles, regardless of the extent to which any of us might be capable of achieving them. Kant emphasized the independence of ethical principles from individual opinions, experience, and capacity. That is what he meant by their being *categorical*.

By being *imperatives*, these laws *command the will*. Kant's meaning of *imperative* is indistinguishable from what Plato, Aristotle, and Aquinas meant when they taught that if a person knows what is right they need no other motive to do what is right. The difference is that they placed enormous importance on humans' ". . . acquiring the necessary education in the intellectual and moral virtues."[13] Kant expected even more of the will and intellect than Aristotle and Aquinas, because he assumed that humans enjoy a natural understanding. We can improve on that point

---

[12]Critique of Practical Reason; Part I, Elements of Pure Practical Reason; Book I, The Analytic of Pure Practical Reason, I Definitions, (p. 298).

[13]*Three Rival Versions,* (p. 154).

without altering the rest of his ethical methodology. We agree that if a moral law applies without condition to all rational beings, then when faced with a moral choice that involves a categorical imperative, the individual's will must be directed by the imperative, so long as the person has acquired an adequate ethical education.

Kant may have expected natural understanding to assure assent to mature ethical statements, but, as we noticed in chapter six, he did not expect *ethical inquiry* to proceed naturally. He stressed the need to employ reason and conduct rigorous inquiry. He specifically rejected descending to the realm of popular opinion[14] or popular argument while attempting to conduct such inquiry, and he provided the essential intellectual tool required for that inquiry.

If we wish to know if a moral statement is merely a subjective maxim (a personal belief that does not apply to anyone else) or a categorical imperative, Kant instructed us to ask, What would happen if the statement was applied universally? For example, the moral statement, "Always act so as to assure your own pleasure." is often cited as a universal moral guide. But as Kant pointed out, when applied universally it destroys itself in practice. The pursuit of pleasure involves the pursuit of physical objects and since physical objects are limited and human desire for pleasure is less limited, it is inevitable that one person's pursuit of pleasure, at some point, must conflict with another's. Such conflict does not contribute to harmony (a *permanent order of things*) which is the *telos* of Kant's ethical system. Any moral assertion that *must* lead to conflict when applied universally cannot serve as a categorical imperative.

But how can we act so as to assure that our decisions will lead to justice and harmony rather than injustice and conflict? Kant tells us: "Act so that the maxim of thy will can always at the same time hold good as a principle of universal legislation," (p. 320). In *The Metaphysic of Morals*, Kant states this principle in a slightly different but highly revealing form: "I am never to act otherwise than so *that I could also will that my maxim should become a universal law*," (p. 260).

Kant's use of the term *will* in this second quotation is especially helpful. It is not at all similar to, Am I *willing* to take my chances that others might behave this way? Many would say yes, emboldened by the general moral conduct of their neighbors. That is an entirely different

---

[14]*cf.*, p. 112.

question from, Is it rational for me to insist that this behavior become a universal, legislated mode of conduct? That question eliminates chance from the issue. It asks, Would I insist that others act in this way toward me and everyone else?

It does not mean that I would will it knowing that my political, economic, or physical power means that in reality others could not treat me that way and so I would actually risk nothing. And it does not mean that I would will it knowing that my natural talent would protect me from its consequences. Understood properly, Kant's imperative does not leave room for chance or power or talent or any other social variable. It insists that the conduct one brings to others must be brought back directly to oneself, that it must define the nature of all relationships. It is rationally impossible to insist that unethical acts be demanded of oneself and others.

Notice, we do not expect all people to act in this highly rational manner. We are describing a methodology that intellectual leaders can use to develop a system of mature ethical reasoning and its canon. Importantly, like Kant, we can use his question (Would I demand that this principle be universally legislated?) as the essential *tool* in evaluating statements to determine whether they qualify as categorical imperatives, laws that apply universally. It helps us identify our *telos* and it helps us articulate our canon.

Winning Consensus to a Secular Ethical Canon

Critical to winning consensus for secular ethics is to win the argument for the preference of universal virtues over vices in general and for a specific list of universal virtues in particular. That task goes to the heart of attempts to build consensus for the canon of an ethical system. Three bad habits have undermined attempts to win this argument: 1) We have paid too much attention to vices and not enough to virtues. 2) We have treated as vices insignificant conduct and sometimes conduct that is at least neutral or, arguably, even ethical. 3) We have brought to the public square intractable ethical questions and have allowed the uncertainty that surrounds them to reduce the clarity and authority of indisputable ethical statements.

Too much attention paid to vices leads us away from our purpose. We are better off identifying our *telos* and the most powerful, influential, important kinds of conduct that lead us to that end, than fussing over the definition of vices. Dedicated distance runners spend virtually no time thinking about the fact that smoking reduces the efficiency of the cardio-vascular system. They do not seek nuanced definitions of when smoking begins to have a negative effect. They are far more interested in the training techniques that maximize cardio-vascular efficiency. Woodworkers do not concentrate on not making bad cuts. What would they concentrate on? They concentrate on making clean, accurate cuts. "Measure twice and cut once," describes a virtue, not a vice.

Moral philosophy and ethics have been done great harm by placing too much emphasis on insignificant ethical distinctions. Careless use of such questions as, What would happen if everyone should do that? earned a bad name for the logic of the categorical imperative, especially when students or teachers rejected the ethical premise of the question and replied, It would be a more interesting class! or This would be a much better place to teach! Ethical demands that cannot be supported rationally must be rejected. Such statements may accurately describe conduct that displeases a principal or teacher, but if we cannot demonstrate rationally that they detract from the school's *telos*, they cannot be made part of the school's ethical canon. That rule may seem permissive, and it would be if that were all there is to it, minimize prohibitive rules. However the more important point is to identify and teach virtues. After all, virtues, positive ethical conduct, provide the rational motivation of any ethical system. If one is committed to an ethical goal, virtues contribute to the achievement of that goal and therefore are interesting. Vices hinder the achievement of that goal and therefore are not interesting.

On the other hand, as a practical matter, we must draw the line on conduct that inhibits a positive learning and social environment. An essential part of the process older children use to invent their own ethical system demands that they test the efficacy of virtues and vices. Adults are pleased, and may not even notice, when children test virtues to see if good things actually result. But adults are quick to note when children test vices to see if they produce negative consequences in their relationships with their peers. To the extent possible, educators must define vices that permit children to conduct tests that engage our attention while assuring the safety of everyone. If the only rule educators set is that children cannot seriously harm other children, children cannot test the limits of adult rules without doing serious harm to other children. Again, the social, psychological, and ethical development of children and its impact on the design of schools requires far more attention than we can give here.

Finally, by including very difficult, unresolved ethical problems in the content and teaching of ethics, we locate inquiry in the public square, or as Kant would say, we descend to popular opinion before we have resolved these questions rationally. These questions are best confined to the research conducted in what we might call speculative moral philosophy or classes in ethics taught by able ethicists to mature students and professionals. Clearly, rigorous moral inquiry cannot be conducted in the public square any more than can any kind of deep inquiry. Careless ethical claims and casual ethical speculation do great damage to ethical teaching and ethical authority. Rather, we must focus on our *telos*, on the virtues that are revealed by the logic of the categorical imperative, and by appropriate attention to vices. Our canon must be rational, meaningful, and just. Then it can win consensus in the university and the public square. Aristotle, Aquinas, and Kant would say that it would rationally demand consensus because one would have to be immature or obdurately irrational to withhold consensus. However, there may be a more subtle point to make. Many educators and social scientists have not developed the capacity to conduct mature moral reasoning. Leaders must develop social and intellectual norms that prohibit members of the social sciences from imposing immature moral reasoning and immature moral conclusions on our disciplines. We must develop and teach mature moral reasoning so as to assure the ethical development of social scientists and the social sciences. But we must also prevent our disciplines from sinking to the lowest common denominator. We must take mature intellectual and ethical stands.

When we combine what we learned from Kant with what we learned from Kohlberg's hierarchy of moral reasoning, we notice that secular moral philosophy has devolved during the 19th and 20th centuries. Kant described the universal, objective conclusions of the categorical imperative. Encyclopaedists have reduced truth to the truth of *my group* which manifests the ethical reasoning of children in their early teens. Their ethics are so unsatisfactory that genealogists have reduced truth to the incontestable uniqueness of the individual, which manifests the egocentric reasoning of young children. If somebody doesn't do something, we are headed toward single cell moral reasoning. We must develop a system of mature secular ethical reasoning, use it to conduct rigorous research and development aimed at articulating our *telos* and canon, and then teach all that we have learned. And we must establish mature moral reasoning as a standard that must be met by anyone who wishes to be a social scientists. Natural scientists do not alter their research standards for would be scientists who cannot get their math right. Social scientists cannot alter our standards for would be social scientists who cannot get their ethics right.

Clearly, we must develop and teach a system of mature secular ethical reasoning and its canon to educators, but what are the limits of that canon? Are we interested in the personal ethical conduct of educators? Of course not. We must develop a canon that guides the professional conduct of educators, both researchers and practitioners. But our discussion of teaching ethics to children makes it clear that we cannot avoid the task of developing and teaching social ethics. Developing the canon of professional or social ethics is a huge task with substantial opposition. We must overcome that opposition and maximize the opportunities that a mature secular ethical system and canon offer.

Opposition to Ethical Inquiry in the Social Sciences

A major purpose of Part I was to provide the information needed to identify and overcome the opposition to social scientists' developing mature secular ethical reasoning. To understand this opposition, we must expand our understanding of why the social sciences distanced themselves from ethics. Three disciplines study ethics: moral theology, religious moral philosophy, and secular moral philosophy. Each has a long standing place in the university, and yet none contributes to inquiry in the social sciences or any other department in the university.

As we have seen, moral theology, regardless of the religion in which it is practiced, uses revelation as its epistemology, which means that its source of knowledge is God, sacred texts, and sometimes tradition. The first and ultimate act of moral theologians is an act of faith, the acceptance of a particular view of God whether Moslem, Jewish, Mormon, or Christian.[15] As long as moral theology is conducted within a single faith community, it enjoys tremendous intellectual authority, but that authority is based on faith in and commitment to the particular view of God and the

---

[15] I should acknowledge that I have deliberately limited this discussion to the major Western religions that have developed ethical systems. Any improvement that can be made to this work by bringing insights from other traditions is welcome, but it is irrational to dismiss this work simply because it did not address the Hindu or Buddhist traditions.

dogmatic tradition in that community. When moral theologians step outside their faith communities, they are no longer able to conduct inquiry or discourse with intellectual authority. That very obvious point is often overlooked. Nonetheless, it explains why no ethical system based on moral theology can contribute to ethical discourse in universities or the public square.

Religious moral philosophers often give the appearance of relying on objective reason in addition to sacred texts and seem to have some capacity to conduct discourse outside their religious communities. In fact, however, religious moral philosophers ultimately depend upon God and sacred texts for their *a priori* assumptions. In order to conduct legitimate *secular* ethical inquiry, *religious* moral philosophers would have to identify a *secular* source of knowledge. In a manner of speaking, they would have to become secular moral philosophers. One cannot blame religious moral philosophers for not having a great deal of interest in that career change. They are capable of contributing to secular ethical inquiry and public discourse, but they must be committed to that goal.

For the most part, secular moral philosophers have located the source of truth in the individual. They have rejected the possibility of developing an authoritative ethical system or canon and thereby destroyed the capacity and legitimacy of teaching ethics. Many insist that any universal ethical system must be oppressive. Some secular moral philosophers attempt to develop social ethics, but ultimately they face the fate of analytical philosophers. They have no canon; they can achieve no agreement. They have nothing to advocate but their personal opinions, which leaves them unable to contribute to public ethical inquiry and discourse.

In the 17th century, social scientists began their long history of distancing themselves from moral theology (for all of the reasons why moral theologians cannot speak outside their communities), and from religious moral philosophers (for all the reasons they are religious). On the other hand, secular moral philosophy has become so atomized, so individualized, that it has lost its value. An indication of the indispensability of ethics to the social sciences are the ongoing attempts by politicians, the media, and various activists to bring ethical debate into the center of discourse in the public square. The vacuum created by the academy's ethical nihilism has been filled by moral theologians, religious moral philosophers, and private individuals who take various ethical stands. The arguments that ensue quickly become polarized, redundant, and hostile because they employ deductive reason grounded in contradictory, incompatible, and irreconcilable *a priori* assumptions. Social scientists and society need a system of mature secular ethical reasoning. Social scientists must at least try to solve this problem.

However, moral theologians and religious moral philosophers, and especially orthodox religious leaders have interpreted the first amendment in terms of a logic of separation of religious and ethical matters. This logic insists that religion *and ethics* are a private matter to be resolved in the privacy of homes and freely chosen religious communities. This is the same logic that produced the enormous inadequacy of the principle of tolerance in 16th and 17th century English political life. The principle of tolerance was too passive to provide a useful basis for designing laws and institutions that assured peace and security. Habeas corpus, for example, is a far more assertive principle than tolerance. It led ultimately to the restructuring of government into various branches that separated power and required different branches of government to protect citizens from violations of power by other branches.

Moral theologians, religious moral philosophers, and especially orthodox religious leaders present an enormous threat to social scientists attempting to develop mature secular moral reasoning. So long as religious leaders and activists define all ethical assertions as subject to the logic of separation contained in the First Amendment, they undermine social ethical development and conduct. Importantly, they do not only undermine ethical development among citizens who are not religious, they also undermine the development of mature ethical reasoning within their faith communities. Religious leaders have long been troubled by the dichotomy between their ethical teachings at church and the ethical conduct of church members in public, political, and commercial life. The problem is quite obvious. However ethical a person might be when arriving at work, attempts to assure ethical conduct in the work place encounter the same old problem. How does one conduct ethical discourse that leads to agreement, commitment, and action if there is no agreement regarding the *a priori* assumptions of the ethical system being used to conduct the conversation?

Religious leaders, moral theologians, and moral philosophers have been playing an ethical and intellectual charade since the Protestant Reformation, pretending that they provide forms of ethical reasoning and an ethical canon that can guide inquiry, discourse, and conduct in the university and public square. They do not. Their systems and canon divide the public square into contentious camps that argue over irreconcilable differences. They obstruct rather than build public ethical consensus. They must end this pretense, expand their understanding of the First Amendment to include *a logic of engagement,*[16] *and must join with* secular moral philosophers to develop mature secular moral reasoning and a canon of secular social ethics that can guide civil society and the social sciences.

As long as moral theologians and religious moral philosophers cannot walk across campus and conduct discourse that contributes to inquiry and teaching in the social sciences, they cannot inform ethical discourse in the public square. They can still fill the vital role of contributing to ethical discourse in their faith communities, but they must, inevitably, limit their ethics to their faith communities. They must, inevitably, exclude topics of general interest in society. Because the arguments structured by religious moral philosophy cannot be carried to the public square, religious moral philosophers cannot teach, in a meaningful, applicable way, the ethics that must guide corporate or medical or social or political policies which exist in the public square.

Moral theologians and religious moral philosophers have long defended their disciplines from secular moral philosophy. It is time for both to recognize that as citizens, as members of the larger society which includes their faith communities, they have as much at stake in the development of *mature, secular* moral reasoning as secular moral philosophers and social scientists. They do their faith communities and society grave harm by maintaining their hostility to mature secular moral reasoning.

On the other hand, secular moral philosophers must change how they think and conduct inquiry. Their nihilism creates an ethical vacuum in the university and public square that is filled by contradictory religious views, contradictory secular views, and grimly naive, immature ethical assertions. If that is their permanent condition, we must wonder what place they have in the university, for their products are humiliating to themselves and the university. As long as secular moral philosophers cannot walk across

[16]Joseph Cardinal Bernadin, *The Catholic Church and the Ethics of Life*.

campus and conduct discourse that contributes to inquiry and teaching in the social sciences, they cannot inform ethical discourse in civil society and their discipline is doomed to irrelevance. Their hostility to attempts by social scientists to develop a system of mature secular ethical reasoning can be treated sympathetically and refuted rationally. It must be rejected.

The conduct of encyclopaedists, on the other hand, is impossible to predict. It all depends on who they really are. We have seen that encyclopaedia lost its intellectual underpinnings during the first half of the 20th century. Still, it continues to influence public rhetoric and the development of public policy in spite of having no voice in the university and no capacity to survive rational scrutiny. I have treated its advocates sympathetically, claiming that they operate from self interest and old habits largely because religious and secular moral philosophers have failed to provide a mature secular ethical system capable of guiding inquiry and discourse. English and American economists, corporate and financial leaders, and the media have employed this view to great effect. Some orthodox Christians sects have employed the Puritan (Calvinistic) tradition to vest moral authority with wealth, thereby consciously or unconsciously contributing to economic and ethical elitism. The Catholic hierarchy, with its aristocratic roots and increasing preoccupation with brute authority, has provided considerable support to this view. I am inclined to believe that the conduct of the elite results more from the absence of mature ethical development in our culture than from inherent ethical flaws. We will see. Redefining economic inquiry and national economic policy in terms of an ethically grounded economic *telos* will challenge all of these leaders ethically and cognitively. Not to be ignored, it will place at risk long standing, financially beneficial relationships among religious, media, and intellectual leaders with corporate leaders and financiers.

Teaching Mature Secular Ethics in Education

Martin Buber reminds us of the wonderful gift in the Jewish tradition that teaches young people to find a master and maintain that relationship as long as they both live. In an extraordinary little essay titled "Teaching and Deed," Buber gives us a sense of the role and urgency of the teacher:

In these recurring encounters between a generation that has reached its full development and a generation that is still

> developing, the ultimate aim is not to transmit a separable
> something. What matters is that time and again, an older
> generation, staking its entire existence on that act, comes to a
> younger with the desire to teach, waken, and shape it; then the
> holy spark leaps across the gap.[17]

Teaching anything, but especially ethical reasoning, is a sacred trust and a great, vital profession.

Clearly, educators must pay special attention to their own ethical development and the ethical development of their profession—the shared values to which they all commit and that they all commit to teach. The older generation (of which I am a part) has ignored Buber's warning that their whole existence depends upon their reaching full development and then coming to the younger generation with a desire to teach, waken, and shape it. We still face the task of reaching full development.

Although Turiel observed that teaching impacts ethical development, he did not explain why. Vygotsky's theory of learning accounts for Turiel's findings. Vygotsky agreed with Piaget that there are stages and ages of cognitive development. However, he considered the biological explanation of cognitive development seriously inadequate. He recognized that children benefit from carefully structured and even quite informal learning experiences provided by parents, family, neighbors, older children—anyone in their social surroundings. One of the terms he used to describe these sessions was *mediation*. Before his death in 1934, at age 38, Vygotsky corresponded with Piaget, arguing about this very issue.[18]

Vygotsky considered cognitive development similar to any other kind of learning. One does not expect children to learn mathematics simply because they become old enough to do so. The vast majority of children cannot *spontaneously* (Piaget's term) learn mathematics upon reaching some age. The fact that some can must not be confused with the expectation that all can. The vast majority of children who learn mathematics learn it because they are taught it. And that was Vygotsky's point. Adults must teach children how to form and use mature conceptual constructs, what he called *scientific concepts*. He admitted that children

[17]Herberg, Will (ed.); *The Writings of Martin Buber*; (p. 319).

[18]See chapter notes in *Thought and Language*.

must be the appropriate age and have had appropriate experiences to learn genuine concepts, but he insisted that most children who are the appropriate age and have had appropriate experiences cannot spontaneously generate age appropriate concepts. Only after children have received the necessary mediation, only after they have been taught to develop concepts, can they independently or spontaneously develop concepts appropriate to their age and experience.

The necessity of instruction to development explains why so many adults are not able to function at higher cognitive levels: they have not been taught to. And it explains why so many adults cannot function at higher levels of moral reasoning: they have not been taught to![19] I am not saying that all adults can master calculus or become sophisticated ethicists. I am merely saying that far more adults are capable of far more highly developed cognition and moral reasoning than actually occurs. But adults who need instruction must rely on researchers who develop knowledge and teachers who teach it.

Teaching Ethics to Educators

There is an obvious dilemma facing professionals who must develop high levels of moral reasoning. It is the same dilemma that MacIntyre, like Aristotle, described in the context of an apprentice learning a craft. When apprentices first attempt to become fine woodworkers, for example, they do not know what good means, what their work *ought to look like*. They cannot see or feel the difference between fine and careless work. They do not even know what would be good enough during their early stages of learning. The dilemma is this: How can anyone strive for the good unless they know what the good is? Aristotle's answer was that they must find a master.

However, as MacIntyre stresses, the master woodworker must be accomplished at more than the craft. The master must be committed to teaching, and must be committed to teaching *according to the standards of the craft*. An apprentice enters into a relationship with the master that is most fundamentally described as trust. The apprentice agrees to accept the master's standards, the master's instructions regarding what is good ultimately as well as what is good enough along the way. But the implicit

[19]It also explains why many adults think and act unethically: they have been taught to.

assumption made by the apprentice is that those standards will be accepted by the community of woodworkers.

Anyone who would teach education to teacher apprentices enters into a relationship grounded in trust. These students implicitly agree to accept our standards assuming that if they do the work necessary to meet those standards, what they learn will count when they begin their professional work. They deserve to know that if they entrust themselves to this graduate program and this professor and achieve what is expected of them, that achievement will be accepted in the profession. That is what happens in medicine and law and natural science. That sacred trust is as inherent between those who teach prospective teachers as it is between school teachers and their students. And it is also inherent between young teachers and veteran educators.

Young educators must be able to anticipate that their more experienced colleagues can provide them with the conceptual frameworks and intellectual tools required to conduct mature moral reasoning and examples of mature ethical conduct. Young educators must receive from education's inherited culture moral conclusions and tools to which they can commit in order to become the kind of professionals who can reason competently as they mature in their profession.

I have outlined the framework of a system of mature secular ethical reasoning. I have not attempted to articulate its canon, although I have established a method that can be used to develop it and standards for it. The full development of this ethical system and its canon requires a major ethics research and development project, supported by a major ethics teaching project. The ethics project must develop the social ethics that professionals must follow as members of school communities and that they can teach to children. However, the necessity of a social ethics project is not obvious when we talk merely about professional ethics. It becomes far more obvious when we think about the ethics that children need to succeed in school.

Teaching Secular Moral Reasoning and Ethics in Public Schools

As soon as we accept that moral reasoning is as indispensable to the social sciences as mathematics is to the natural sciences, we necessitate the teaching of moral reasoning and ethics in public schools. This necessity increases when we consider how the ethical development of children impacts their conduct in schools. We have already noticed that in their early teens children cease to accept the ethical teachings and expectations of adults and begin to rethink ethics for themselves. Most importantly, they restructure everything they know, everything they have been taught about ethics, into their new system of moral reasoning. Their new system is at best immature for it develops two canons, one that applies to the individual and his or her friends, and another that applies to everyone else. But has we have seen, even that development is not guaranteed. Instruction impacts development. So we must ask, who is providing the instruction? Clearly, schools are not.

Some students receive enormous help from parents. But a significant number of students, and in many schools the vast majority of students, receive ethical instruction from their peers, the popular culture, and the media. Children can get lucky with their peers, if, for instance, a child's best friends have received mature ethical mediation from parents or other adults. But when children must rely on each other, they have less chance of developing mature ethical reasoning and content than they would have of figuring out geometry or trigonometry by themselves. Other than an amazing cultural indifference to mathematical illiteracy that is unique in developed countries, American adults do not assault young people with misinformation regarding the structure and content of mathematics. But they bombard children with ethical nihilism, tolerate and sometimes glorify the most destructive, unethical conduct, and employ forms of ethical reasoning that vitiate the minds of children. Some video games are problematic, but they are the topics the media is comfortable talking about. Far more significant are the inept structures of moral reasoning and conduct of journalists and the profoundly unethical conduct glorified in otherwise very well made, well acted, attractive films. This is not to say that the media can or the popular culture should change. Rather, educators must act upon what we already know: *most children have no chance of developing the mature ethical reasoning they need to study the social sciences and the ethical canon they need to function successfully in school unless educators teach them.*

We can relieve some of the tension inherent in this conversation by stressing that we do not intend to interfere with the religious ethics taught in faith communities or the private ethics taught in homes. We are interested in the secular intellectual ethics students need to study the social sciences and the social ethics they require to contribute to a safe and secure learning environment. We do not concern ourselves with the private ethical conduct of students. But we must concern ourselves with the ethical conduct of students in the intellectual and social context of schools. But still we must anticipate fierce opposition. Our greatest defense lies in understanding the opposition and in developing an ethical system and canon that wins consensus within the education community, the university, and the public square.

Clearly, it is beyond the scope of this book to develop the content of social ethics to be taught in public schools and schools of education. But again, we can frame the issue. In chapter six, we discussed the meaning of love and refuted a post modern claim that different experiences demand individual definitions of love. We relied on Buber's concept of I-Thou relationships and Johann's concept of *intersubjectivity* to frame ethical inquiry and teaching in the assumption that we must treat all persons as full participants in their own humanity and not as objects of the interests or needs of the elite or powerful. I might add that Buber and Johann help us overcome the tendency to pursue silly, materialistic notions of equality, as if all people are born with equal talent or equal intelligence or equal drive. It helps us understand that we are all born with equal humanity and that we must all work to develop our own humanity and the humanity of our culture. Justice and dignity emerge as far more compelling and rewarding virtues than materialistic equality.

It is fortunate that mature moral reasoning promises so much to individuals, the social sciences, and society, for it takes enormous work and requires enormous change in how most of us think about humanity and ethics. Mature moral reasoning engages us as persons and energizes our psychological and sociological development. It offers a profound, invigorating alternative to the goal of becoming an autonomous individual. It replaces that goal with the goal of becoming mature, empowered, and engaged persons who are active, contributing members of families and communities. Autonomy produces narrow intellectual and ethical virtues and shallow personal development. Its greatest promise is that I can become myself privately, fully developed in isolation from others. Mature ethical reasoning engages us psychologically and sociologically and permits thorough and deep personal development. Its greatest promise is that I can become myself profoundly, an authentic person engaged with every other human. Mature secular moral reasoning is indispensable to the full development of social scientists as individuals, professionals, and as members of the human family. Similarly, it is indispensable to the full development of citizens and society.

Opposition to Ethics in Public Education

The importance of the information we discussed in Part I grows in proportion to the conflicts inherent in our development and use of secular ethics. Even when we limited our use of ethics to guiding research and practice in the social sciences, we anticipated considerable conflict. But when we suggest that educators have a responsibility to teach secular ethical reasoning and the ethical canon that applies to both intellectual and social conduct, we anticipate a maelstrom.

Opposition to the development of secular ethical reasoning in the social sciences is located almost exclusively in the university and among politicians and pundits. To a great extent this opposition is intellectual and is grounded in intellectual problems. Solving those intellectual problems seems to be the key to neutralizing that opposition. Economists, moral theologians, religious moral philosophers, and secular moral philosophers have the opportunity to meet and identify economics' ethically grounded *telos*. Such a meeting and the eventual success of such a project is not hard to imagine.

Public education, on the other hand, is a uniquely popularized social endeavor. The U.S. Constitution does not mention education. Consistent with the Tenth Amendment,[20] education has largely been treated as a state and local matter. Every state has established locally elected boards of education to govern public schools, with varying degrees of state vs. local control. One might argue that the popular governance of public schools has contributed to the gap between research and practice by causing practitioners to be more interested in responding to the concerns of the public than to research. From that view, it only makes sense that researchers and university faculty would seek to distance themselves from practitioners. I have chosen to avoid those conversations, and focus instead on education and educators and the intellectual solutions we must find to build an authentic, effective professional community. But we cannot ignore the vast popular opposition to educators' establishing intellectual authority and especially to educators' establishing secular ethical reasoning and teaching a secular ethical canon. All of the opposition we discussed earlier in terms of the social sciences can be

---

[20] "The powers not delegated to the United States by the Constitution, nor prohibited by it to the States, are reserved to the States respectively, or to the people."

expected to weigh against secular ethics in education. To that must be added local, popular opposition.

States did not immediately develop public schools and have never attempted to develop a uniform system of public education. Private schools predate public schools and have maintained an important role in many states. In addition, states have long accommodated the First Amendments's demand for the separation of church and state with the desire of some church leaders to provide religious schooling as an integral part of a child's school day. States have accommodated these differences, choices, by crafting compulsory attendance laws that permit parents and churches to maintain private and parochial schools. Until recently, those alternatives defined the term *school choice* and by requiring private financing left public schools as the predominate source of education for America's children.

More recently, the moral decline in American society in general and in America's public schools in particular has caused parents and the public to point out that public schools do not provide a viable choice for the majority of parents and children. They complain that it is absurd to permit the only publicly financed choice for youth education to be conducted in a manner that does not meet the needs of Americans or America. Too many schools are not safe. In too many schools, children do not learn. In too many cases, public education seems to have lost its way intellectually and ethically. And when that is the condition of one's local school, parents and politicians insist that parents must have a choice. Their complaints resonate throughout society.

Our analysis of the history of moral theology and philosophy and the enormous changes created by the Protestant Revolution has taught us that moral theology and religious moral philosophy cannot guide ethical inquiry or teaching in the public square. On the other hand, when we note the vast inadequacy of ethical reasoning and teaching in education and public schools, we note that the failure lies with secular moral philosophy. The United States Constitution separates church and state, and the tradition of academic freedom has permitted secular moral philosophers wide latitude to solve ethical problems independent of religion. In spite of the enormous public support for moral philosophy represented by the maintenance of departments of moral philosophy in virtually every major state university and all of our great private universities, secular moral philosophers continue aggressively to offer up ethical nihilism. They persist, in spite of the undeniable fact that no one listens.

On the other hand, moral theologians and religious moral philosophers have maintained astonishing silence rather than object to the inadequacy of secular moral philosophy. Their silence and the inadequacy of secular moral reasoning have created the ethical chaos that plagues public schools.

Our knowledge about the indispensability of ethics to education and the limits of religious moral philosophy and the ineptitude of secular moral philosophy must embolden and empower educators to withstand the challenge of ethical nihilists and dogmatic natural and social scientists who would demand that no ethics be taught in public schools. We must oppose orthodox dogmatic religious parents and church leaders who would demand that the only ethics taught in public schools be their ethics. We can withstand those challenges. In fact, we can be so clear and united in our logic that we can discuss these issues rationally and maintain our position. We can respect them while rejecting their views. Some of our opponents may become furious with us, but we cannot help that.

Educators have nothing for which to apologize to dogmatic moral theologians or dogmatic ethical nihilists who insist that we must teach the ethics they believe or that we cannot teach any ethics at all. We have nothing for which to apologize to parents who would impose their indifference to ethics and learning on public schools. However, the longer we continue to conduct our profession without mature secular moral reasoning and to teach curricula devoid of mature secular moral reasoning and ethical content, the more we must apologize to students, parents, the community, and the academy.

Educators must build a system of mature secular ethical reasoning and teach mature secular ethics in public schools. And we must develop sophisticated expectations regarding the right of parents to choose alternatives to public schools.

Recognizing the long tradition and value of private and parochial schools, we must encourage their continued existence. As we have seen, sound religious instruction benefits our society in ways that appear to be irreplaceable. Still, it is simply impossible to provide religious instruction in public schools. Private, parochial, and public education serve society in different but essential ways. These educators and their supporters must recognize and support each other, for none alone can provide what together they all provide. They must do everything they can to support each other in pursuit of education's *telos*, in support of the education of all children.

In terms of the choices being made by parents whose children currently attend public schools, educators must focus on the kind of schools we conduct, what we insist upon from parents and students and professionals, and the kind of alternative choices these schools suggest. Parents who want their children to learn intellectual and universal secular social values, insist that their children be safe, and demand that educators both challenge and help their children to excel must be welcomed in and satisfied with public schools. Similarly, parents who have not benefitted from schooling but are willing to trust public educators, must have that trust honored and met. Educators must do a great job with their children.

Let parents who demand that their children be permitted to conduct themselves with a total disregard for other children or who have no regard for the quality of learning or who do not believe their children should work hard and who want to impose those dreadful values on public schools, let them be the ones who exercise the right to seek alternatives. Let orthodox dogmatic religious zealots who insist that their ethics are the only ethics schools can teach start their own schools. And let the teachers and administrators who share those views join these parents in choice schools.

What we must take with us from this chapter is the confidence we gain by solving a 700 year old intellectual problem and the major points that comprise that solution: that educators must develop our ethically grounded purpose and commit to it as our source and standard of knowledge, that to do so educators must develop and teach professional and social ethics, and that mature secular ethical reasoning is indispensable to the social sciences.

Education's Source and Standard of Knowledge

Earlier we acknowledge that our *telos* cannot be a statement that describes what we know how to do. It must describe what ought to be. But we have not yet answered the question, What ought to be in education? What is education's *telos*? What we do is educate children. Our *telos* must speak to our professional commitment regarding the education of children. It cannot be to educate children to the best of our current knowledge or our current professional or individual ability because that goal would make research and development unnecessary. It might be to educate children to the maximum of their ability. But that statement is also inadequate.

In the past, many educators have insisted that our goal is to educate all children to the best of their ability, but, in the end, that apparently challenging goal became a slogan that was used to justify any result. The teacher taught perfectly, used perfect research, and the children learned according to their ability. That goal did not guide research and practice; it justified *any* research and practice. Any statement of purpose that does not focus on children and guide research and practice must, like any other inadequate ethical principle, destroy itself in practice.

On the other hand, ethical statements that are so detached from our lives that we cannot apply them to our actions are useless. So although our *telos* cannot be simply to do what we know how to do, it cannot demand that we do what we do not know how to do. Our understanding of ethics and its indispensability to the social sciences has allowed us to describe the intellectual solution to the problem of identifying our source of knowledge as distinct from what we must do.

The system of ethical reasoning we borrowed from Aristotle provides the solution to the problem of the relationship between our *telos* and what we must do to achieve it. We can note, without being discouraged, that there is a profound difference between our commitment to strive for our *telos* and being expected to do what we do not know how to do. The structure of our ethical system reminds us that our *telos* is our ethically grounded purpose, our ultimate goal. Our *telos* is quite different from the virtues that lead to it or the vices that lead away from it. Having noted the indispensability of ethics to the social sciences, we may not be surprised to notice that the structure of ethical reasoning we have used provides the structure of inquiry in the social sciences. By employing this ethical structure as our structure of inquiry, we must notice that our *telos* does not tell us what we know and are obligated to do to achieve it. We make the distinction between our goal and what we know how to do formally and concretely. In the past, both sides of this coin have been abused. We have described our purpose without commitment, and we have criticized each other for not doing what none of us knows how to do.

For years, school superintendents have tried to ground their leadership in mission statements and grand strategic plans. Both produce ethical statements that declare what the district is committed to do. But superintendents have been unable to translate their mission statements and strategic plans into policies and develop them as institutionalized conduct. The major event surrounding mission statements and strategic plans has been the printing process that placed them on the back cover of district publications. They have not guided curriculum, pedagogy, or assessment. Why? Because various epistemological barriers to intellectual authority have made these tasks impossible.

Identifying the content of our *telos* is not the problem. The problem is identifying our *telos* in such a way that it attains the authority and stature required for it to direct research and practice. What we discover is that no statement can win the authority required to direct research and practice unless three conditions are met: 1) The statement must be a rational, objective, universally applicable ethical statement, 2) Educators must bring mature ethical reasoning to their consideration and commitment to it, and 3) Educators must integrate it into how they think and what they do. The challenge educators face regarding the adoption of and commitment to an ethically grounded purpose cannot stop with identifying it or even with understanding that it is an ethical statement that requires developing the ethical maturity needed to commit to it. These are significant tasks, but they are not enough. Educators must make their source of knowledge, their *telos*, function as their ultimate standard of knowledge.

When educators confront each other with contradictory claims about the efficacy of different programs, their disagreements include both what the programs ought to achieve and what the programs actually achieve. They disagree regarding the purpose and responsibility of education; and therefore they disagree regarding the purpose of programs. Consequently, they have no capacity to make meaningful comparisons of results. What educators must do is agree that their *telos* functions as their source of knowledge by establishing it as their standard of knowledge. Different educators may design two different instructional programs, but they must agree regarding what they are attempting to do. If they are attempting to achieve the same goal, and one design is demonstrably more efficacious than the other, *it must win*. By clarifying and agreeing about desired outcomes or standards, educators clarify the criteria for the evaluation of educational research and practice.

First they agree on and commit to their *telos*. Then they begin to analyze their conduct, which means they evaluate their research and practice. But what is their criteria, their standard for evaluation? Why, their *telos*, of course. Research and practice that leads to their *telos* is *effective* and research and practice that leads away from their *telos* is *flawed.* As in ethical reasoning, they are not terribly interested in flawed research and practice other than to identify them and eliminate them from their conduct. More interesting and challenging, they compare various forms of effective research and practice to determine if one is significantly more efficacious than the other.

So what is education's *telos*? Again, it is not the task of this text to fully develop an ethical system or to answer specific ethical questions. That is the task of the ethics project I have mentioned. But clearly, education's *telos* must focus on children, be just, and guide research and practice. As such, the options are somewhat limited. Because it is ethically grounded it will have to be a statement that challenges educators to provide quality education to *all children*, that challenges educators to assure that all children learn well. The problem with using outcomes and standards as our *telos* is that they are expressed in lengthy documents. Our *telos* should be a universal ethical statement that is as brief and comprehensive as possible. In any event, the identification of education's *telos* must be part of the ethics project.

Educators must *develop* a structure of inquiry that establishes their *telos* as their source and standard of knowledge and conduct their evaluation of research and practice in reference to that standard. If that sounds just too obvious, I should note that it solves the 700 year old problem regarding the source of knowledge in secular moral philosophy and, by extension, in the social sciences and education. It overcomes the problems that confounded scholastic philosophers by explaining that moral philosophy and the social sciences depend upon *ethical development* and that ethics cannot be found in ontological locations, not in the ideal, the individual, or nature. And it solves the 350 year old problem in the social sciences by re-equipping inquiry with an ethical architecture.

Clearly, mature moral reasoning is as indispensable to the social sciences as mathematics is to the natural sciences. Intellectual development in the social sciences depends upon ethical development. Intellectual leaders must develop and teach a system of mature secular moral reasoning and its canon. Although we cannot develop the canon in this work, we were able to discuss the teaching of ethics both to professional educators and public school students.

However, it is a mistake to assume that identifying our *telos* tells us what we must do, how we must teach or design curricula in order to achieve our *telos*. Now we must overcome the intellectual barriers that prevent us from identifying what we know that we must do and what we know that we must not do. For that discussion we turn our attention to cognitive development, the other component of intellectual development and its contribution to the integration of research and practice.

8

The Integration of Research and Practice

By identifying our *telos* and committing to it, we solve our problem regarding the source of knowledge in education. At this point, ethical commitment runs into an inevitable conflict with practical reality. We may commit, as an ethical matter, to do what leads to our *telos* and not to do what detracts from our *telos*. But neither the clarity of our *telos* nor our ethical commitment to it tells us what to do to achieve it. Vygotsky made the essential distinction between our *telos* and the *activities that lead to it* when he discussed the role of *purpose* in learning. He agreed that the learner's sense of a problem provides a critical motive to learn, but he disagreed with psychologists who thought that identifying a problem so clarified the purpose of learning that nothing else was required.

> The experiments of Ach and Rimat, while they have the merit of discrediting once and for all the mechanistic view of concept formation, did not disclose the true nature of the process— genetically, functionally, or structurally. They took a wrong turn with their purely teleological interpretation, which amounts to asserting that *the goal itself creates the appropriate activity* via the determining tendency—i.e, that the problem carries its own solution.[1]

Identifying the *activities* that we must accomplish in order to achieve our *telos* constitutes a distinct intellectual problem and requires its own research and development project.

In this chapter, we continue to develop the epistemology of education by addressing what we must know and be able to do to reach our *telos*. This task requires that we give considerable attention to the development of professional *cognition* as essential to the development of knowledge and skills. Cognition is how we think; professional cognition is how we think as a community. Knowledge is what we think and do; professional knowledge is what we think and do as a community.

[1]*Thought and Language*, (p. 103, emphasis added).

Just as the vast majority of children and adults cannot develop levels of moral reasoning that do not exist in their culture, the vast majority of professionals cannot develop levels of cognition and knowledge that do not exist in their profession. Intellectual leaders must develop and teach mature ethical reasoning and the formal cognitive architecture needed to allow education and educators to reach full intellectual development.

We have already noted the intellectual problems that plague research and practice in education. By treating the individual as the source of knowledge, we demand that each individual decide for himself or herself the goals of education, the method of research, and the method of instruction. Of course, groups of individuals may agree to agree, but if they encounter disagreement, their only recourse is to agree to disagree. There is no intellectual authority in education. As a result, we conduct research that inevitably produces contradictory findings.

One might think that we can solve these problems by employing Vygotsky's and Piaget's theories of cognitive developmental. In a way, that is what we do, but we do it by replacing the anti-epistemology we have called individualism with an entirely different epistemology. Neither Vygotsky nor Piaget helps us improve upon individualism. They help us replace it. Educational leaders must develop working familiarity with both Piaget's and Vygotsky's theories. Piaget's taxonomy is well known to educators. It proceeds from sensory-motor to pre-operations to concrete operations to formal operations. Vygotsky's taxonomy is less known. It consists of three *phases*, each of which has different *stages*. I list only the phases: 1) *Unorganized congeries,* 2) *Thinking in complexes,*[2] and 3) *Scientific concepts.* Important to this discussion, individual opinion does

---

[2]This phase includes five stages. Vygotsky's discussion of these five stages provides profound insights into the advantages and disadvantages that result from the cognitive development of most school age children. For leaders not to know this part of Vygotsky's work probably constitutes mal practice. I might note that the term *complexes* produces references *to complex thinking* which for most American educators is assumed to refer to a high level of cognitive development, not a deeply inadequate phase. I have discussed this problem with Kozulin and we came up with an alternate term, but I have never used it. It is actually easier to help students and teachers associate Vygotsky's concepts with terms such as an "inferiority *complex*" than to replace the term Kozulin used throughout his translation.

not exist in either Piaget's or Vygotsky's taxonomy of cognitive development.

According to Piaget, early on children process perceptions in very loosely structured schematics. That is not the same as professionals noticing that they have difficulty agreeing and concluding that all knowledge is equally valuable regardless of the level of cognition used to develop it. That view is completely incompatible with Piaget's theory of cognitive development. It would require us to agree to something as absurd as physicists needing to teach creationism and evolution as equally *scientific*. Consequently, we cannot merely say that the task of educators is to restructure inquiry and knowledge from concrete operations to formal operations. Eventually we must attend to that task, but first we must agree to quit thinking that educators develop equally valuable knowledge regardless of their effort, competence, or level of cognitive development.

Vygotsky's theory is even less amenable to individualism. As we have seen, Vygotsky agreed with Piaget that there are stages and ages of cognitive development, but he rejected Piaget's claim that cognitive development is essentially a product of biological or genetic capacities and events. We talked about these differences in our discussion of the development of moral reasoning and noticed the importance and usefulness of Vygotsky's understanding of the role that social mediation plays in cognitive and ethical development. What we have not talked about is Vygotsky's description of the stages of concept formation through which children travel. Vygotsky used an experiment worked out by a colleague (Lev Sakhharov) to study children's concept formation in its several developmental phases. I discuss two stages of his taxonomy.[3]

Vygotsky set before young children (age 7-10) blocks that were different geometric shapes, sizes, and colors. Looking at the blocks one would see four different shapes (triangles, balls, squares, and trapezoids), in four different colors (red, blue, green, and white), all of which were four different sizes. The children were asked to put the blocks into four

---

[3]This topic is located in *Thought and Language*, chapter 5, "An Experimental Study of the Development of Concepts." In a footnote that begins on page 103, Kozulin described many of the details of the experiment and how non-sense words were used to assist the subject in forming coherent groups. I have taken some liberty with the details and vastly simplified the topic.

groups. An adult and older children would immediately select a grouping principal: size, shape, or color. Four groups would quickly form, based upon the principle selected: size, shape, or color. They would form groups of four sizes or four shapes or four colors.

But in Vygotsky's experiment that is not what young children did. They did not select a grouping principle *and stick to it.* Rather, they frequently changed their grouping principle. When they had completed placing all of the blocks in four different groups, each group had all of the variety of the original: four different sizes, four different shapes, and four different colors. When Vygotsky asked the children to explain each of their decisions, he found that they made their decisions based upon size, shape, and color, but they frequently changed the basis for their definition of the group when they selected an object. For instance, a child might begin a group by selecting a small *yellow* triangle. Next the child would select a large *yellow ball.* An adult would immediately recognize that the four groups were going to be based on color. But then the child would select a large *blue ball.* When asked why, the child would state the obvious, because it is a *ball*—just like the previous choice. Each selection was similar, in some manner, to the previous selection, but no stable principle guided choice after choice.

Vygotsky pointed out that small children could not produce four coherent groups because they did not begin with a principle that said: I will do this *and I will not do that.* Using additional studies, Vygotsky built upon this insight to distinguish what he called *pseudo concepts* from *scientific concepts.* Pseudo concepts can be described as groups of information that do not distinguish what they include from what they exclude. Scientific concepts (Vygotsky's term for mature or genuine concepts) exercise both decisions: such and such includes what is X and excludes what is not X. Admittedly this is not an entirely new principle. It is very similar to Aristotle's rules of classification. Years ago, when undergraduates uniformly studied Aristotle, one might hear a student mock a recent lecture by rising in the dining hall and declaring in *basso* or *soprano profunda,* The entire universe can be divided into what is this fork and what is not this fork. So we should add the requirement that genuine concepts express meaningful principles of inclusion and exclusion.

Individualism, by definition, prohibits educators from developing and sticking to principles of inclusion and exclusion in the development of concepts. It limits inquiry in education to the development of pseudo-concepts.

Now for those of us who would wish to improve intellectual leadership in education, it seems that we have some promising tasks. We must develop principles that allow us to organize education's knowledge into genuine concepts. These principles must tell us both what is included and what is excluded in our conceptual frameworks. Furthermore, they must be meaningful. In chapter seven we described how to accomplish these tasks although we did not refer specifically to principles of inclusion and exclusion.

By agreeing on our ethically grounded purpose, our *telos*, educators commit to a shared source and standard of knowledge. This commitment provides a set of principles that forces us to include and exclude knowledge: knowledge that leads to our *telos* must be included, knowledge that leads away from it must be excluded. In addition, if two competing views both lead to our purpose, but one is significantly more efficacious than the other, we include the one that is more efficacious and exclude the other. If two views are equally efficacious but one is simpler or cheaper, we include the simpler, less expensive and exclude the more expensive, complex view. The very fact that our adopted views demonstrate efficacy, clarity, and simplicity in advancing our ethically grounded purpose assures that they are meaningful and useful.

Committing to a *telos* and using it as the source of knowledge provides the foundation of intellectual authority we need to include and exclude knowledge. But we still must find a way to identify and agree upon what it is that we must do and not do in order to achieve our *telos*. To identify these activities, we must give attention to the development of mature *cognition*.

The Formal Integration of Research and Practice

One of the great errors in the philosophy of education has been to assume that conducting research and integrating research with practice are two independent tasks. Probably the most familiar example of this error is found in Ernest Boyer's claim that the three major intellectual tasks of professors are discovery, integration, and application.[4] Those terms easily translate into the terms we have used: research, the integration of research and practice, and practice. Clearly, research can be conducted separate

---

[4]*Scholarship Reconsidered: Priorities of the Professoriate.*

from although not independent of practice. And clearly, practice can be conducted separate from although not independent of research. But research and practice cannot be integrated separate from an integrated, *formal design* of research-and-practice. *Research and practice must be integrated formally before they can be integrated in practice.*

Ernest Boyer was a brilliant and enormously influential intellectual leader in education. He was the President of the Carnegie Foundation for the Advancement of Teaching. Money, institutional authority, and intellectual prestige supported his leadership. His call for educational researchers to accept the challenge of integrating research and practice attracted considerable attention, but it has almost completely failed. The exceptions to complete failure that I think one might attribute to Boyer's influence are the increased and important examples of researchers at some of our great universities integrating their research with practice. Some notable examples include:

Accelerated Schools, Henry Levin, Stanford University
Bright Start, H. Carl Haywood, Vanderbilt University
The Coalition of Essential Schools, Theodore Sizer, Brown University
Effective Schools, Lawrence Lezotte, Michigan State University
Mastery Learning, Benjamin Bloom, University of Chicago
The Success for All Project, Robert Slavin, Johns Hopkins University

All of these projects come out of universities and connect with public schools, but *they do not connect with each other*. These scholar/activists have integrated research with practice in what one might call vertically integrated projects.

Now, it might seem appropriate to take the time and space in this text to describe these projects (classical realism and all that), but in fact that discussion would not help us at all. We could describe all of their work and not be any closer to understanding the necessity of integrating research and practice or the intellectual barriers to that goal, because they give these issues no attention at all. They do not seem even to think about and clearly do not attempt to solve the epistemological problems that plague educational research. So rather than discuss their work in detail, it is more helpful to discuss solutions to the intellectual problems that plague the cognitive development of education and educators and then explain in those terms what they do not do and what they could do together. But first, we must develop a clearer understanding of what it means for research and practice to be integrated formally. Again, we look to natural science for insight.

Scientific Paradigms

Thomas Kuhn is the philosopher of science who made the only significant improvement to the epistemology of science since the 17th century when he described the nature and role of scientific paradigms.[5] According to Kuhn, a paradigm is an *intellectual achievement* that provides the organizing principles that unite a scientific discipline's knowledge into a coherent whole and its members into a community of scholars. From the 17th century, scientists understood the enormous contribution that the scientific method and the academies made to intellectual authority in natural science. Kuhn explained the role that such intellectual achievements as Newton's system of the world, evolution, and the theory of relativity had on scientific inquiry and community.

Kuhn is helpful because he points out that we are searching for an *intellectual achievement* that unites us. We are not simply asking everyone to work and play nicely together. We are looking for an intellectual achievement that unites us intellectually and socially. Evolution, for instance, is an intellectual achievement (a paradigm) that unites biological information and increasingly all knowledge in natural science and the entire community of natural scientists.

From Chaos to Order in Education

Kuhn was not particularly interested in the social sciences and education, and he did not address how these disciplines might develop paradigms. However, he gave considerable attention to the fact that in natural science paradigms do not last forever. What scientists do when a paradigm wears out is quite instructive for educators.

One can tell that a scientific paradigm has become exhausted when researchers begin to identify more problems than solutions; for when a paradigm is exhausted, it loses its capacity to direct research. It has contributed everything that it can contribute. The Ptolemaic view of the universe was a paradigm that directed astronomy for hundreds of years, but by the 16th century it was exhausted, and the Copernican revolution

---

[5]*The Structure of Scientific Revolutions.*

replaced it.[6] So, what do the scientists in a discipline whose paradigm has been exhausted do to find a new one?

When a scientific paradigm becomes exhausted, various members of the scientific community suggest *different* intellectual achievements, different *theoretical models* that can unite inquiry and practice. That is a very important term: *theoretical model*. A theoretical model has the *same structure and content* as a paradigm. It is the same thing with one very important difference. A paradigm is a theoretical model *that has been accepted by the entire community* as its new foundation of inquiry. According to Kuhn, a scientific community makes a paradigm shift when its existing paradigm is exhausted and a new theoretical model wins the acceptance of the community. How does a theoretical model win the acceptance of the community? It competes with other theoretical models that are advanced by different groups of scientists. *The one that prevails becomes the new paradigm.* When the entire community agrees that one of the theoretical models is more explanatory, gives greater direction to research and practice, and provides researchers and practitioners with more useful solutions than any of the other competing theoretical models, the victorious theoretical model is declared the winner. It is the intellectual achievement that is accepted as the discipline's *paradigm*.

It is important for educators to notice that when a scientific community's old paradigm has been exhausted and different theoretical models compete with each other, the scientific community is split. That is the condition of theoretical physics today which has something like five different theoretical models competing to provide the *unified theory*, the theory of everything. The condition of inquiry in physics is somewhat like the condition of inquiry in education today, with two important differences. First, physicists notice that there are fundamental incompatibilities between the theory of relativity and quantum mechanics. They notice that they do not have a paradigm. Second, physicists find the conflict in their structure of inquiry intolerable. Yes, they are able to develop important, useful knowledge following each theoretical model, but they know and are disturbed by the fact that where the two models should meet, they do not. They cannot be integrated, and physicists see

---

[6]That a new paradigm completely replaces the old paradigm is a subject of debate among philosophers of science. We need not enter that debate to draw from Kuhn's work insights that assist us.

that incapacity as a fundamental flaw in the structure of inquiry in their discipline. That is why five different theoretical models are being advanced and some scientists who are acknowledged to have the greatest minds in the world are risking their intellectual lives pursuing one or another of these views.

Articulating Theoretical Models in Education

Paradigms have received little attention in education because education does not have one. However, the point is not that education does or does not have a paradigm. The point is that educational leaders must figure out how educators, as a community, can integrate research, integrate research and practice, and conduct discourse that leads to agreement, commitment, and action. Epistemological claims that explain and support the continued fragmentation of inquiry and the deep divide that separates research and practice in education cannot contribute principles of inclusion and exclusion that are essential to the development of genuine concepts. They cannot contribute to the development of formal operations in education. They must be rejected and educators must construct theoretical models and seek a paradigm.

Until we commit, as a community, to formal definitions of inquiry, and organize research and practice into some kind of coherent, principled whole, it is impossible for education or educators to reach full development. Unlike physicists who find the absence of a unified theory disquieting, educators protect the rights of individuals to think as they please as if no more were at stake than what one is going to fix for dinner. But upon what basis can educators even begin to organize our research and practice into integrated wholes? It makes no sense to begin by trying to get educators to commit to one theoretical model. Attempting to *declare* one best view would be impossible, just as it is impossible for theoretical physicists merely to declare the one best unified theory. However, like scientists whose paradigm has become exhausted, we can identify our four or five competing views, our theoretical models. We can set those theoretical models and their advocates in competition, and quite possibly one can emerge victorious and unite both knowledge and educators. Both theoretical models and paradigms provide a formal architecture that guides inquiry and practice. They tell us what we can do and how we can do it. We must vastly improve inquiry in education by organizing inquiry and knowledge into competing theoretical models.

Before we discuss paradigms and theoretical models in education, let me explain what we are doing that is different from what happened in natural science. Scientists consciously developed an authoritative epistemology during the 17th century. Since then, each branch of natural science has committed to *intellectual achievements* that unified their theory and practice. The most notable modern paradigms have been Newton's system of the world and Darwin's theory of evolution. In the 1950's, Kuhn noticed and described the role that paradigms play in scientific inquiry and defined their components. Kuhn noticed the role that paradigms played in scientific inquiry. He did not invent paradigms; he noticed and described them.

We are going to work with Kuhn's definition of paradigms and theoretical models and translate his definitions into terms that are more useful in education. In a manner of speaking, we must be more creative than Kuhn, for many intellectuals would claim that it is impossible for education to develop a paradigm or theoretical models. We must invent *the structure* and *the components* of paradigms and theoretical models appropriate to inquiry in education. We then use this invention to identify the intellectual achievements that are capable of operating as theoretical models in education. Our purpose in the following discussion is to describe and explain the components of paradigms and theoretical models in education. In describing these terms, we identify the major intellectual achievements in education that seem capable of being developed as theoretical models.

However, I do not claim that the terms I use to define paradigms and theoretical models in education can be used in other social sciences. I started with Kuhn's language, and only changed it when I consistently found myself using other terms. Other social scientists should also start with *Kuhn's language* and only change it as other terms become more useful. Leaders in the social sciences must develop the structure and language of paradigms and theoretical models before they can identify the theoretical models that exist potentially in their disciplines. The economic systems employed in England and America, France and Germany, and China seem to constitute competing theoretical models. But without a formal, objective definition of theoretical models in economics, it will be impossible to identify or analyze them. At the outset, I think social scientists benefit from using Kuhn's language as the formal architecture that can guide inquiry in all of our disciplines. Although I changed some of his terms, I did not abandon his formal framework.

Paradigms and Theoretical Models in Education

Although Kuhn's *The Structure of Scientific Revolutions* has been essential to my thinking about theoretical models and paradigms, identifying what he considered the components of a theoretical model required my doing some work with his text. Kuhn has been criticized for not settling on one definition of paradigms and theoretical models. Rather, throughout his text he built a conceptual framework for the term by adding dimensions to the framework and loading it with content or examples. But he never quite achieved the Aristotelian and Vygotskian requirement of taking the defining stand: it incudes this and excludes everything else. In addition, Kuhn thought about paradigms and theoretical models as they function in natural science. Some of his terms are not useful when used to think about knowledge in education. Therefore, I have had to make two different sets of decisions: 1) I had to decide how to describe Kuhn's definition of theoretical models and 2) I had to decide what terms to use to describe theoretical models for use in education. But again, I did not abandon the formal architecture Kuhn provided.

I have selected five terms that seem to include the major insights Kuhn expressed in his discussion of paradigms and theoretical models. According to my reading of Kuhn, components of a paradigm/theoretical model include: 1) Fundamental Assumptions, 2) Problems and Solutions, 3) Methodology, 4) Instrumentation, and 5) Laws.

One can easily locate these terms in Kuhn's text. However, in using them to study various theories of learning and pedagogy with teachers and graduate students, I found that some of them cause considerable confusion. In attempting to explain the logical relationships among them, I found myself so frequently using other terms that I adopted these other terms for use in education. The terms I use to define paradigms and theoretical models in education are: 1) Fundamental Assumptions, 2) Advantages/Disadvantages, 3) Methodology, and 4) Instrumentation.

The most obvious difference between the two lists is that the second does not include *laws*. My experience with educators revealed deeply ingrained habits of treating laws in the absolutist manner of the obedient citizen or the totally relativistic manner that calls all statements hypotheses. Rather than take on those habits, I have avoided them by eliminating the term. This decision may have to be revisited, especially if one theoretical model is able to win the support and commitment of educators, but until then, the term seems more distracting than helpful.

The other difference is that *Problems and Solutions* appears to have been replaced by *Advantages/Disadvantages*. Actually, I divide *Problems and Solutions*. I use *Advantages/ Disadvantages* to redefine *Problems*, and I use *Methodology* to redefine *Solutions*. What Kuhn meant by *methodology*, I treat as a separate epistemological issue and discuss in chapter nine. These changes become far more clear in the discussion below and probably need only be mentioned to resolve questions that might be raised by readers who are familiar with Kuhn's text. Again, I have not abandoned Kuhn's formal architecture. I have merely translated some of his terms into language that is more helpful in education.

In order to understand these terms, it is helpful to recall what theoretical models do. Like paradigms, theoretical models are intellectual achievements that organize and direct inquiry. Kuhn's epistemological achievement was to describe the formal architecture that permits us to think about how we think in our discipline. When students study science, they actually study the current prevailing way of doing science, the scientific paradigm. It is possible to learn the current scientific paradigm using concrete operations, but almost all students who have completed quality undergraduate and graduate programs in natural science have studied Kuhn. They know that they are studying a paradigm and that the paradigm can change. They know that physicists are working to develop a new paradigm.

But when students study education, they have no prevailing view to study. Indeed, they do not even have an organized body of knowledge to study. Students of science are taught both how to think in science and what to think. Science as a discipline provides both an epistemology and canon (or acknowledged body of knowledge) as *starting points* for students. But students in education are expected to figure out how to think and what to think in education, to invent their own epistemology and canon. Now that may seem really neat, very liberating and all that. But when we recall that it is impossible for most students and professionals to develop higher levels of cognition than exists in their discipline, we realize that the lack of cognitive development in education constitutes an enormous barrier to the cognitive development of students and professionals.

The task of this text is not to fully articulate all or any one of the theoretical models that could be elaborated in education, but merely to establish definitions and examples of each component. Fully articulating all theoretical models for all subject areas is a task that must be accepted by educational leaders and funded by the federal government, states, and major foundations. Now we discuss the four components of theoretical models in education.

Fundamental Assumptions

Fundamental assumptions are best understood as the fundamental assumptions of cognitive psychology—the theory that explains how people, especially children, learn. They provide the principles upon which various theoretical models are based. When we begin to develop theoretical models, we must be sure that the statements we select as fundamental assumptions are grounded in cognitive psychology and not in methodology. Methodological statements, as we see below, cannot guide the development of the rest of a theoretical model. Indeed, if we employ methodological statements as fundamental assumptions, they force us into concrete operations rather than structuring formal operations. Methodological statements are concrete and factual rather than abstract and logical.

Contradictory and incompatible *fundamental assumptions* define the starting points of *different theoretical models*. Furthermore, *fundamental assumptions must provide abstract conceptualizations of learning that logically reveal specific advantages and disadvantages that children bring to learning.*

Examples of statements that qualify as fundamental assumptions include: the behaviorists' belief that learning is a behavior that results from conditioning,[7] Piaget's belief in the role that biological development plays in cognitive development, and Vygotsky's belief in the impact that

---

[7]Some statements associated with behaviorism (i.e., that humans and all other living organisms learn the same way, that the internal operations of the mind cannot be observed and therefore are irrelevant, and that only behavior is the proper object of inquiry about learning) provide the *a priori* assumptions of behaviorism. They say nothing about how children learn. They contribute starting points for basic research, but they cannot contribute to applied research.

social mediation[8] has upon language development, cognitive development, and learning.[9]   The incompatibilities between behaviorism's and Vygotsky's fundamental assumptions reveal the two major theoretical models in education.

To identify fundamental assumptions, we first identify the major assertions in cognitive psychology that explain how children learn. Second, we organize those concepts into compatible groups.   In identifying these groups of compatible theoretical statements about how children learn, we identify different theoretical models.   Each group of compatible theoretical statements provides the foundation of its own theoretical model.   Third, we make sure that we select only those statements that reveal advantages and disadvantages that children bring to learning.[10] Inherent to selecting a fundamental assumption about learning, we ask, What does this statement reveal about *children*?

[8]Although Vygotsky developed the seminal research on mediation, he died very young and was unable to develop methodology that supports the theory. Reuven Feuerstein has developed this theory and added highly developed methodology. It makes no sense to be interested in Vygotsky or Feuerstein without knowing the work of the other.

[9]Readers unfamiliar with cognitive psychology might find this discussion frustrating. Let me recommend a few works—see the bibliography for details. For behaviorism, I recommend the brief but excellent treatment offered by Phillips and Soltis in *Perspectives on Learning*, or for a fuller explication of this theory, Bower and Hilgard's *Theories of Learning*. Singer and Revenson's, *A Piaget Primer*, provides an excellent introduction to Piaget; and Evans, *Dialogue with Jean Piaget* provides Piaget's own words. For Vygotsky, there is only one work: Alex Kozulin's translation of *Thought and Language*. For Feuerstein, a great starting point is "The Theory of Structural Cognitive Modifiability" in *Learning and Thinking Styles*.

[10]They also reveal advantages and disadvantages that adults bring to learning which is interesting but not the topic of this work. Most adult learning theory is based on descriptive research, not cognitive psychology. It explains a lot of social issues that surround adult learning environments but virtually nothing about adult cognitive development, concept formation, and mastery of content.

Advantages and Disadvantages that Children Bring to Learning

Advantages and disadvantages flow logically from the fundamental assumptions of various theories. If one supposes that children are born with various degrees of intelligence and that little can be done to alter their capacity to learn, the advantages and disadvantages are obvious: intelligence is an advantage and lack of intelligence is a disadvantage. But there is a huge problem with that view. It leaves educators with virtually nothing to do. As a practical matter, why would we accept it? Theory must guide research and practice. It cannot do that if it destroys hope.

Similarly, when one considers the imperative of biological maturation in Piaget's theory of learning, it is obvious that children who mature early have an advantage. However, since the ages at which biological maturation occurs constitute a fairly narrow range, at least theoretically the advantages and disadvantages of biological maturation are not terribly impressive. These fundamental assumptions and their advantages and disadvantages are not helpful, for they do not explain learning or children in a way that tells researchers what to study or teachers what to do to increase learning. An additional fundamental assumption found in Piagetian theory (as it has been developed by his followers) reveals more useful advantages and disadvantages. This fundamental assumption claims that when children have achieved a new level of development, they spontaneously function at the higher level of cognition assuming that they have had the *experience* needed to trigger that cognitive functioning.[11]

This fundamental assumption gives researchers and teachers something to work with. Children who have reached a new stage of development and who have had various experiences have considerable advantages in school and can expect success. On the other hand, children who have reached the new stage of development but have had virtually no experience bring huge disadvantages with them to the classroom. Researchers can study how to reproduce in classrooms, field trips, and

---

[11] Singer and Revenson make more of the role of experience in Piaget's theory than I have found in his writing. Clearly, his theory makes more sense with their interpretation of the impact of experience, but for those who know his work and his arguments with Vygotsky, this claim may seem inaccurate. I have used their elaboration of his work because I admire their contribution to making Piaget accessible to a wide audience. Their influence has led many to believe that Piaget made as much of experience they do.

extracurricular activities the experiences that successful students bring to learning. Teachers and parents can focus on increasing the variety and quality of children's experiences in order to increase their ability to learn. This is an example of fundamental assumptions and advantages and disadvantages explaining learning in a way that tells adults what they can do to enhance learning.

As we have noted more than once, Vygotsky communicated extensively with Piaget and agreed that there are stages and ages of cognitive development, and, like Singer and Revenson, Vygotsky placed great importance on experience. However, he disagreed with Piaget regarding the importance of *spontaneity* to children's actualizing cognitive potential. He insisted that even if children have matured biologically, the vast majority need mediation or teaching in order actually to develop.

Using Vygotsky, we can develop a highly explanatory theoretical model.[12] Children who mature early have advantages. And children who have extensive experience have advantages. And children whose parents or other adults mediate their development of language, concepts, and intellectual and social ethics (metacognition) have advantages. And children who have all of these positives working for them have enormous advantages.

Similarly, children who mature late have disadvantages. And children who live dull, narrow lives, who experience little, have disadvantages. And children who have lived lives isolated from adult mediation of the development of language, concepts, and intellectual and social ethics have disadvantages. And children with all of these negatives working against them have what appear to be insurmountable disadvantages. And yet, these disadvantages are not all that insurmountable, at least theoretically, because the analysis *structured* by theoretical models forces us to explain

---

[12]Piaget and Vygotsky's theories can be integrated with some work deciding what is kept and what is dropped. Feuerstein studied under Piaget, but his work resembles Vygotsky's more than Piaget's. After leaving Russia, Kozulin came to the U.S. where he completed his translation of *Thought and Language*. He then moved to Israel to join Feuerstein. Haywood, has worked with Feuerstein and several Russian scholars. By combining their work in what I call the Vygotsky/Feuerstein model, educators can articulate a constructivist theoretical model that could provide education's paradigm.

the sources of advantages and disadvantages and logically points toward solutions.

Every time we identify a fundamental assumption about how children learn, we ask, What does this reveal about the advantages and disadvantages children bring to learning? As theoretical models become more fully articulated, practitioners are able to notice advantages and disadvantages children have and ask, What do we know about why this occurs? In other words, we can ask, What fundamental assumptions in cognitive psychology explain this advantage or disadvantage.

Even this introductory discussion of the structure and content of theoretical models allows us to notice an essential benefit that comes from subjecting various theories of learning to the analysis structured by theoretical models. It allows us to organize information about various theories in a way that integrates and directs research and practice. A fundamental assumption that does not reveal advantages and disadvantages is not, by definition, explanatory or helpful. It cannot direct research or practice. We dismiss it. On the other hand, a fundamental assumption that reveals important, frequently observed, or too frequently unnoticed, advantages and disadvantages in students, is highly explanatory and helpful. It can direct both research and practice in a compelling and integrated fashion. We make it a central part of our theoretical model. The fundamental assumptions about how children learn that describe the role of social mediation in the development of thought and language, for instance, may not tell teachers what to do in all cases. However, it explains the advantages that some children and the disadvantages that other children bring to developing language, learning to read and write, and learning to develop scientific concepts in *all disciplines*.

On the other hand, conflicting fundamental assumptions generate very different explanations of advantages and disadvantages. An invaluable task that the proponents of various theoretical models can perform for education and the public is fully to articulate all of the various advantages and disadvantages that flow from their fundamental assumptions. Disadvantages describe the difficulties children have and challenge researchers and teachers to overcome them. Advantages describe the opportunities that children bring to learning and challenge researchers and teachers to maximize them.

Both the advantages and disadvantages that children bring to learning *challenge* researchers and practitioners. *They both* constitute what Kuhn called *problems*. I point that out to stress that I have not abandoned Kuhn's formal conceptualization of paradigms and theoretical models but also to note that this structure provides an intellectual achievement that may not be obvious. It eliminates the entire debate that treats the pursuit of excellence and the pursuit of equity as mutually exclusive, as choices that must be made. Rather, this formal architecture (especially when used to articulate the Vygotsky/Feuerstein model) treats excellence and equity as virtually identical constructs that are located on a single theoretical continuum. Researchers and practitioners must be able to identify and explain all of the advantages and disadvantages that children bring to learning. Both advantages and disadvantages present problems for educators, because they both demand that educators respond appropriately to them. Educators must maximize advantages and overcome disadvantages. As students overcome disadvantages, they develop advantages that must be maximized.

Methodology

Inseparable from the task of identifying advantages and disadvantages is developing *methodologies that maximize advantages and overcome disadvantages*. One thing should become quite clear in this discussion: disadvantages do not prevent a child from learning. Disadvantages only hinder a child's learning if educators do not recognize them or if they do not know what to do about them. Similarly, advantages do not guarantee that children will achieve excellence. Students only benefit from advantages if educators recognize and consciously maximize them. Of course, children can do well in class because of various advantages they bring to learning, but that is not the same as teachers recognizing their advantages and maximizing them. Indeed, advantages explain why some students learn. But as a research issue, as a profession, educators must be able to recognize when a student's ability to learn is explained by what children possess independent of any influence educators have had upon them. That is no different intellectually from being able to recognize a student's inability to learn that is best explained by what children possess independent of any influence educators have had upon them. Educators must be able to explain why children learn and why children do not learn, regardless of the source. And we must be able to maximize advantages, not merely take credit for them; just as we must be able to overcome disadvantages, not merely blame others for them.

The question that this discussion demands is, What are our solutions, the methodologies, that teachers can use to maximize advantages and overcome disadvantages? Methodology is what a teacher does when working with children within a theoretical model: in preparing the curriculum or lesson, in teaching, or in assessment. Different advantages and disadvantages challenge educators to construct different solutions or methodology. It is in fully articulating the advantages/disadvantages revealed by a fundamental assumption, and the methodologies that maximize advantages and overcomes disadvantages, that theoretical models integrate research and integrate research with practice.

Recall that Piagetian fundamental assumptions deal with biological development, experience, and spontaneity. Children who have matured, have enjoyed extensive experience, and who spontaneously function at high cognitive levels obviously can be expected to perform very well in school, especially when given appropriate freedom. Thus for these students, providing freedom to choose what they do and how to do it sometimes maximizes their advantages and therefore constitutes an effective methodology.

On the other hand (but staying with Piaget), if a student has not matured cognitively, the teacher must design instruction at a level of cognitive development at which the student can function. If students cannot function at the appropriate cognitive level for their age, the teacher can add experiences. Ultimately, if they follow the logic of Piaget's cognitive psychology, teachers must wait for students' biologically determined cognitive development to occur. In this case, Piaget's theory does not suggest terribly helpful methodology.

Vygotsky's theory calls for a different response to students who mature early, have enjoyed extensive experience, and demonstrate spontaneous cognitive functioning. Even these students benefit from mediation of concept formation as tools that permit the formation of even more sophisticated concepts. His theory calls for much more work with able students than merely giving them the isolation that permits spontaneity.

And Vygotsky provides very different methodologies for students who have reached the appropriate age to function at a new cognitive level, have had experience, but who do not demonstrate the ability to function at the appropriate cognitive level. Vygotsky insists that teachers must teach students to function at the new cognitive level by mediating their development of the *language* that is essential to concept formation and the *concepts* that are essential to the formation of the concepts we want them to form.

Regardless of the sequence of development in which a researcher or practitioner is operating, *the methodology* demanded by Vygotsky is that we teach a child to function at cognitive levels which they are old enough to learn. By teaching students the language they need to function with a particular concept and specific operations, by giving them repeated opportunities to use the operation and coaching them when they get stuck, teachers dramatically impact the student's *development* and *knowledge*. Teachers and students are not left waiting for the student's brain spontaneously to get it.

In order to develop complete methodologies we inevitably answer in considerable detail such questions as: What are the methods of teaching that are inherent in each theoretical model and constitute the core teaching activities of each theoretical model? Similarly, as we compare and contrast theoretical models, we identify the teaching methods that are *incompatible* with each theoretical model. We also identify teaching methods that are theory neutral, that teachers can use in any theoretical model without working at cross purposes.

To be quite frank, I am not sure what to think about theory neutral methodology. It may be that they are not theory neutral at all, but simply that we have not discovered the theory that explains them. We need cognitive psychologists to explain why these methods work. In any event, educators must have enough sense to use what works even if they cannot explain why it works, and at the same time protect the integrity of theoretical models by not treating methodology as if it were cognitive psychology. The fact that formative testing/re-teaching works and cannot be explained by any specific principles of cognitive psychology does not make it theory or fundamental assumptions. Formative testing/re-teaching is a methodology.

Instrumentation

Instruments are the tools that bring precision to or make methodology more efficient. Instrumentation tends to be more easily recognized and appreciated by science teachers than others, because natural science cannot be conducted without instruments. With the development of computers, educators can anticipate improved instrumentation. It is a component of Kuhn's paradigm that educators should seek to develop and so I mention it here. Furthermore, the chaos that has plagued educational research and practice has prevented educators from developing instrumentation. We discuss these issues under research and development in chapter ten.

Clearly, fully articulating all of the complete, coherent theoretical models in education will require an enormous amount of work. To be complete, a theoretical model must identify all of the fundamental assumptions that can be combined within one model, articulate all of the advantages and disadvantages that these fundamental assumptions reveal in all children, and identify all of the existing methodologies that can be used to maximize those advantages and overcome those disadvantages. To be coherent, all of the fundamental assumptions, advantages and disadvantages, and methodologies must be deeply connected in a logic that is capable of including appropriate items and excluding inappropriate. The goal of the cognitive development project to which I often refer is to fully articulate the complete, coherent theoretical models that exist potentially in education and set them and their advocates in competition to see which produces the most efficacious research and practice.

Cognitive and Social Development

By structuring inquiry and the analysis of various theories in complete, coherent theoretical models, we achieve the formal integration of research and practice. By definition, theoretical statements about how children learn are developed, analyzed, and applied in one conceptual framework. Researchers and practitioners are not allowed merely to claim that such and such explains learning. Cognitive psychologists, confining their work to psychology can make such claims, but when psychological assertions are brought into education, they must be developed either as their own or as part of an existing theoretical model.

The structure of theoretical models forces educators to apply theoretical statements to practice. When we describe fundamental assumptions in isolation from what they reveal about children, we tend not to notice weak explanations of how children learn. But when we demand that every fundamental assumption be elaborated in terms of the advantages and disadvantages that children bring to learning, we force ourselves to connect learning theory with children. And when we demand that descriptions of the advantages and disadvantages that children bring to learning be connected to descriptions of what teachers can do to maximize advantages and overcome disadvantages, we integrate theory and practice. Theoretical models tie theory to children and practice both formally and practically. They do it formally, because they provide the architecture, the formal structure, that demands that integration. And they do it practically because when we have completed the work of describing what we know and do within this formal structure, we cannot help but have enriched practice.

We can now notice a critical error that many educators make when confronted by formal operations. They treat formal operations and formal knowledge as if they are just too abstract, as if they do not apply to practice. They completely lose the meaning of Piaget's developmental taxonomy and replace the concept of formal operations vs. concrete operations with the concept of abstract information vs. concrete information or theory vs. practice. It is easy for teachers to prefer concrete solutions over abstract theory. Consultants and professors win the confidence of graduate students and professionals when they promise, "I am a practical person. I offer to you solutions, things you can use today, not a bunch of abstract, useless theory." Indeed, practical solutions deserve our attention, and useless theory should be ignored. But it is folly for professionals to prefer concrete operations over formal operations in developing or learning professional knowledge.

Concrete operations do not permit us to create, compare, or evaluate systems. They only permit us to work within a system. Concrete operations force us to choose specific programs and implement them. Concrete operations force central office leaders into the kind of top down management that building administrators hate and teachers find insulting. Why? Because when central office administrators function with concrete operations, they can only select specific programs they find attractive and implement them. They cannot objectively compare and evaluate alternative programs. Leaders stuck in concrete operations have great difficulty noticing when they select contradictory programs.

Similarly, concrete operations only allow teachers to use a particular program or approach. They do not allow teachers to think about how they think about teaching and learning. As long as intellectual leaders in education employ concrete structures of knowledge, most teachers and administrators must remain incapable of developing and using formal operations when they think, conduct research, implement practices, attempt discourse, or study learning theory and pedagogy.

Stuck in concrete operations, graduate students, teachers, and administrators study learning theory in terms of what they believe. A teacher steeped in behaviorism studies developmental learning theory and constructivism *from the point of view of* behaviorism. To the extent that those theories are similar to behaviorism, the teacher evaluates them as good. But to the extent that they are inconsistent with behaviorism, they are wrong. The flip side is true when teachers steeped in developmental theory and those steeped in constructivism study behaviorism or developmental theory. Obviously, that kind of study is never going to permit teachers to learn new theories objectively—from *the point of view* of the new theory. Teachers and administrators who hold different views cannot conduct discourse that leads to agreement, commitment, and action. Unable to agree and commit, teachers and administrators cannot contribute to each others' knowledge and cannot agree on the criteria for the evaluation of programs, practices, or personnel.

Again, we have touched upon a topic that deserves enormous attention, in this case the importance and difficulty of establishing prior commitment to the criteria for the evaluation of programs, practices, and personnel. It is easy to establish casual agreement to such criteria. Most teachers and administrators agree to anything in order to put an end to interminable meetings. But establishing commitment that sustains the use of such criteria to support *negative* evaluations of favorite programs or any personnel is a different matter. Without going further with this digression, suffice it to say that it is impossible to conduct this kind of discourse and reach agreement unless participants can function at the level of formal operations and have available a formal cognitive architecture. If we can only understand other views in terms of our own view, we function at the level of concrete operations. Stuck in concrete operations, educators cannot learn or conduct discourse in a manner that leads to agreement, commitment, and action.

When teachers and graduate students use theoretical models to structure and guide their inquiry into learning theory, they do not begin with their conclusions. They begin with an open, formal structure that permits them to think about various theories and methodologies objectively. They compare, contrast, and evaluate different learning theories and methodologies first in terms of their coherence and completeness and second in terms of their comparative efficacy in contributing to education's *telos*. They become capable of discourse that leads to agreement, commitment, and action. They can learn from each other, build deep knowledge, and commit to the criteria for the evaluation of programs, practices, and personnel.

Notice, when using theoretical models to guide the study of different learning theories, the formal structure does not allow us to stay in the lofty realms of abstract theory. It forces us to identify the fundamental assumptions about learning that we derive from cognitive psychology, and it forces us to relate that theory about learning to children in such a way that it reveals advantages and disadvantages that children bring to learning. And it forces us to identify methodology that maximizes advantages and overcomes disadvantages. It is a formal structure that forces us to restructure what we know about learning and teaching in a way that is more powerful and more explanatory than is possible using concrete operations.

Concrete operations simply cannot deliver the intellectual tools educators need to structure, guide, and integrate research, practice, and discourse. When we consider that the threshold age of concrete operations occurs at age seven and of formal operations at age 11, it is rather embarrassing even to consider insisting that knowledge in education should be structured by concrete operations. It is tantamount to saying that educators must think like seven year old children! But when we recall that only 30% or so of adults achieve the capacity to use formal operations in any aspect of their knowledge, we realize that there is more to developing formal operations than merely getting older. Clearly, in order for educators to develop formal operations, intellectual leaders must develop and teach formal operational structures. We cannot expect individual researchers and practitioners to function at higher levels of cognitive development than the cognitive development of the profession.

The Application of Theoretical Models in Education

Let us assume that educational researchers and practitioners agree to structure knowledge in theoretical models. We would then face the enormous task of articulating the theoretical models that exist in education. As I mentioned earlier, physicists have something like five theoretical models that are competing to integrate knowledge in physics. Education clearly has two: behaviorism and constructivism. But constructivism has been developed in two dramatically different ways. At least two theoretical models could be developed out of current constructivist writing, but the act of articulating constructivist thinking in theoretical models might resolve those differences. Karpov and Haywood appear to have resolved some of those differences.[13]

Earlier I mentioned the excellent work done by small groups lead by brilliant individuals such as Haywood, Sizer, Levin, Lezotte, and Slavin. We can now discuss why their work is structurally flawed even though much of their work will probably endure in one theoretical model or another. They have very little influence on each other and consequently they exert no intellectual authority on researchers and practitioners as a whole. It is not at all unusual for their programs to be challenged in practice by completely inferior views *and lose*. Their lack of intellectual authority is based on the same problem as their inability to connect: they have not addressed the integration of research and practice at the formal level. Consequently, they have developed their projects in such a way that integrating them would be impossible. Rather than speaking to the discipline with one voice, our very best researchers ignore, contradict, or refute each other. If their disagreements were articulated through a rigorous effort to build clarity, that would be one thing. But most of their disagreements result from different starting points that have been selected rather casually, or differences that have no substantive basis in cognitive psychology. Some continue to cling to notions that unresolved differences exhibit valuable diversity, which would be a compelling argument if anyone could demonstrate how casual, accidental intellectual diversity (chaos) enhances the development of knowledge and cognition in education.

Organizing educational research and practice into theoretical models provides these researcher/activists with the opportunity to identify, in a substantive manner, where they agree and where they disagree. Organizing educational research and practice into theoretical models does not extinguish different theories and pedagogies. It articulates different theories and pedagogies in more substantive, rigorous terms than have been used in the past. When the different theoretical models have been articulated, then our best researchers and everyone else can know whose work is grounded in the same cognitive psychology and pedagogy, and whose work is fundamentally different. Those that are compatible can

---

[13]See: Karpov, Yuriy V. and H. Carl Haywood; "Two Ways to Elaborate Vygotsky's Concept of Mediation: Implications for Instruction."

work together by committing to the same theoretical model, and they can compete in terms of education's *telos*.

Organizing educational research and practice into theoretical models does not eliminate the need for research. Rather, it clarifies and focuses research. Unanswered questions must remain, for they provide the life blood of research and human development. We do not seek to eliminate questions. We seek to organize research and knowledge authoritatively. We seek to state as a community: 1) This is what we know and are responsible to act upon. 2) This is what we are studying confident of finding answers. 3) This is what we do not even know how to study. Teachers and administrators inevitably encounter circumstances in which they have no idea what to do, and in many of these cases they must do something. But like physicians and physicists, they must have a greater capacity to say, We just don't know.

Members of the Educational Community

In the natural sciences, when a particular theoretical model is adopted as a discipline's paradigm, two things occur simultaneously: the winning theoretical model becomes the discipline's paradigm and the group of scholars who make the commitment to it becomes a community. When a scientific community accepts a paradigm, the fundamental intellectual *and social* issues required to integrate research and to integrate research and practice are resolved. All who do chemistry, for instance, do it within the same paradigm, whether they are conducting research, working as practitioners in the chemical field, teaching chemistry, or studying chemistry.

According to Kuhn, the five major tasks of a scientific community are to: articulate a paradigm, extend knowledge within the paradigm, teach the content of the paradigm, conduct practice consistent with the paradigm, and learn the paradigm. These five tasks define an intellectual or professional community's roles. The professionals who fill these roles must see themselves as members of their profession's intellectual community. Everyone involved in any of those tasks, by definition, is a member of the same community. But in education, members of the groups that perform these tasks tend to see themselves as living on different planets from members of the other groups and on different continents from other members of their own group. In order to form an intellectual community in education all of these professionals must change. Educators must become the kind of people who see themselves as members of the same community. Even this rather straightforward topic is complicated in education.

The intellectual community that forms education is actually quite complex. It consists of members of various intellectual communities by virtue of the fact that teachers teach different disciplines: language, mathematics, natural science, history, social science, and so on. Even elementary teachers who have not majored in any discipline other than education act as members of each of the disciplines that they teach, especially language and mathematics. However, educators must be members of the discipline they teach secondarily and members of education primarily. All educators must become members of the education community and make a deep commitment to that community. Mathematicians who teach mathematics to future mathematicians have only one intellectual community to join, the community of mathematicians. But mathematicians who teach mathematics to future public school teachers and especially mathematicians who teach future public school teachers *how to teach mathematics to public school students* must join the education community.

We have described the education community's membership, and it is actually quite startling. It consists of all educational researchers, all university professors who teach teachers, all students of education who are preparing to teach, all school teachers, and all school administrators who guide, direct, lead, or evaluate teachers and educational programs. All of these professionals and students are part of and must commit to the education community. But what exactly do we mean by commitment?

The Character of Professional Commitment

We describe learning communities as consisting of those who articulate and extend knowledge of the theoretical model (researchers), those who teach the theoretical model (university faculty), those who study the theoretical model (teacher candidates), and those who conduct practice consistent with it (school administrators and school teachers). In addition, we have described the components of theoretical models and the enormous work that is required merely to articulate the various theoretical models to say nothing of learning to use each in practice. One might assume that just getting all of that done requires so much commitment that there is nothing more that needs to be said about the topic. But it is important to notice that the scientific community assumes that all of those tasks have been completed, and yet commitment remains a crucial element beyond those achievements.

When Kuhn talked about community commitment, he focused on two points. First, supporters of a paradigm cannot simply demand commitment. Theoretical models and paradigms must *win* the support of researchers and practitioners. The commitment must be a rational act won on rational grounds. Second, once a group of scientists commits to a view, they face the emotional challenge of sticking to their commitment in the face of serious intellectual challenges. In order to test a paradigm, its adherents must be able to bring tremendous intellectual and emotional resources to the challenge. At various points they face questions that can only be answered with long, drawn out work. That is why I mentioned earlier the current state of theoretical physics in which some physicists are staking their entire professional careers on developing the content of five different versions of the unified theory. It may turn out that none is right. At best, all but one are wrong. And yet, they must commit.

Even when a scientific community has committed to one paradigm, its members must sustain inquiry across generations. If scientists abandoned whole theories or even lines of inquiry just because a generation of them could not solve some problems, natural science would not have advanced in the way that it has. Indeed, some scientists have spent their entire careers pursuing a line of research that proved wrong. It could not produce the expected results. And yet their contributions have been acknowledged as essential to the advancement of learning in their discipline, because those who followed learned that a particularly appealing line of inquiry did not work and why it did not work. Natural scientists work as partners. That is why almost all scientific discoveries are best understood as first community achievements and only secondarily as individual achievements.

Educational researchers must also be willing to dedicate their whole careers to solving certain problems. Only with that kind of commitment can researchers test the full potential of a theoretical model. On the other hand, when researchers discover a methodology that maximizes an advantage or overcomes a disadvantage, practitioners must be committed to learning and using that solution. They cannot go on doing what does not work because they find the new solution difficult to learn. Refusing to learn new solutions must be understood as a major breach of trust to children, the public, and their community.

Furthermore, commitment must be understood in its dual aspect: as an ethical commitment among all educators to their *telos* and to a given theoretical model. All educators must commit to education's *telos*, and each educator must commit to one of the sub-communities organized by theoretical models. And both commitments must be so strong as to cause educators to do what they know is right even though it is difficult.

Commitment among natural scientists is grounded in curiosity and a determined search for truth. It competes with boredom and ignorance, neither of which offers much attraction.

Commitment among social scientists must be grounded in our *telos*, our ethically grounded purpose, in our desire and determination to build a good and just society. Our goals and work ultimately connect with and depend upon an ultimate sense of meaning. Our commitment competes with nihilism. Nihilism encourages us to forget the future, focus on the now, on immediate self-gratification. It encourages us to do what is easy and selfish. These are powerful opponents. They are far easier and provide far more immediate gratification than commitment to unselfish work for an abstract, distant future, for humanity rather than for me, for justice rather than for self-interest. It is not at all clear that secular psychology and sociology can provide the motivation for an ethical commitment that demands so much unselfish work. Christianity can provide that motivation, but Christianity is divided and hostile to secular society. It is not possible to address these fundamental religious and psychological questions in this text, but they clearly are urgent questions. Answering them requires the participation of some of our finest young minds. It offers these scholars an awesome and compelling adventure. Their work could assure that educators who have benefitted from the formal and social integration of their communities will possess the psychological capacity to commit. Problematically, it is not at all certain that psychologists and secular moral philosophers can establish the eternal hope upon which this kind of commitment ultimately depends. If they cannot, religious communities that combine eschatological hope with deep concern for secular society will offer their members enormous competitive advantages as professionals in general and especially as intellectual leaders.

We have come a long way in this journey. We have noticed that when we locate complete coherent theoretical models within the ethical structure of inquiry that we described in chapter seven, they provide the formal conceptual architecture that integrates research and practice in education. The ethical structure establishes our source and standards of knowledge and provides the foundation of intellectual authority that demands that we identify what we know works and are obligated to do and what we know does not work and are obligated to avoid. Theoretical models structure research so that it connects to children and to practice.

By selecting and committing to one theoretical model or another, members of the education community organize themselves into at least meaningful sub-communities. And by placing all of these sub-communities into competition aimed at achieving our *telos,* educators act as a single intellectual community. Those are major epistemological achievements. However, to match the epistemological achievements and intellectual authority of natural scientist, we must solve one last set of problems. We must agree on research methodology and invent some institutional form of intellectual authority. We turn now to those discussions.

9

Institutionalizing Intellectual Authority

I have claimed that any epistemology must account for the source and standards of knowledge, the architecture of inquiry and knowledge, and the method of inquiry. In addition, I have noted that once we have accounted for all of the components of an epistemology, we must address how that epistemology can be institutionalized. The institutionalization of an epistemology is essential so that the intellectual authority it makes possible can actually occur and be sustained. In this chapter, I complete the description of education's epistemology by discussing research methodology. Then I discuss institutional solutions to the implementation of intellectual authority, a topic that does not constitute a component of an epistemology.

Our discussion of methodology is rather straightforward because our work with epistemology provides answers to methodological questions. For instance, we resolve the major arguments that undermine the integration and use of qualitative and quantitative research. In addition, we discuss the role of deductive reason and argue that we need to give more attention to teaching it to educators. Neither discussion contains surprises. Both use epistemological insights we have developed earlier to clarify and concretize our understanding and integration of research tools that have been developed in other disciplines.

On the other hand, our discussion of the institutionalization of intellectual authority produces some surprises, which is probably good news to the reader. The discomfort with intellectual authority expressed by genealogists in general and advocates of critical theory in particular captures an important concern. We certainly do not want to invent and empower an institution that treats the task of sustaining its power and influence as if it were the purpose of the social sciences or education. Again we look to natural science for insights. We notice that the royal societies and academies that were so important during the early centuries of the modern era have been replaced by more democratic, less formal institutions. First we discuss methodology, then authority. We end this chapter with a brief discussion of how education's epistemology accommodates change.

Research Methodology in Education

Research methodology in education suffers two major obstacles: first, by lacking an effective epistemology, virtually every research project begins and ends with substantial credibility problems. Second, philosophical nihilism has contributed to the careless application of some very competent research methods developed in other disciplines. Qualitative analysis and quantitative analysis are prime examples.

In this discussion, I merely attempt to frame the topic of educational research, not resolve the details. I emphasize the roles and relationships of the major forms of inquiry that I believe enhance research within theoretical models: deductive reason, quantitative analysis, and qualitative analysis. Earlier, we discussed hermeneutics and critical theory noting that for all of their value in theology, history, and literary criticism, they are not helpful methods of inquiry in education, unless, of course, one is studying education's history or literature.

The Role of Deductive Reason in Education

Deductive reason developed a bad reputation during the Enlightenment when it was treated as contradictory to empiricism and identified as one of the causes of intellectual backwardness during the Middle Ages. And yet it remains an essential tool in intellectual life, whether conducted in the public square or in the academy. It provides the heart and soul of pure mathematics. Ironically, natural scientists tend to extol the virtues of empiricism and look askance upon the primitive methods of medieval inquiry; but by virtue of their almost universal deep training in mathematics, they have preserved the deductive tradition. It is important to rekindle appropriate, conscious interest in deductive reason in the social sciences.

When we analyze or debate an argument developed with deductive reason, we ask, Does the speaker present an argument that takes us from point A to point B in a manner that is internally consistent and necessary. Point A, or the beginning of the argument, defines the topic/problem and the assumptions upon which the argument is built. Deductive reason has two essential parts: its premises and its conclusion. Most of what can be challenged rationally in a deductive argument are contained in the definition of the problem and the premises, not in the conclusion. If we agree with the statement of the problem, and if we agree that the premises proceed logically and that they eliminate all other possibilities, and if we agree that the conclusion proceeds logically from the premises, then we are bound to accept the conclusion. Unless, of course, it is morally reprehensible. Or unless an equally compelling logical argument produces a more desirable result. Most importantly, if the argument does not build *necessary* relationships from one point to another along the way, then the conclusion is not *necessary*, it is merely one of many possible conclusions. The topic may be worth studying further, but the conclusion is probably not worth arguing about.

When do we use deductive reason? In research, we use deductive reason when we design or evaluate research proposals. Many doctoral candidates have been sent back to the drawing board because their proposals were logically inconsistent. Similarly, benevolent foundations reject research proposals that are logically flawed. Proposals are written to get the support needed to conduct empirical studies, which means that they are written before empirical evidence has been gathered. The only rational standard these proposals can meet are the standards of deductive reason.

Although deductive reason is requisite to the design of empirical studies, it cannot produce *measurable predictions of what will happen* in practice. The education community must demand that researchers go beyond deductive reason and actually conduct the empirical studies that permit them to predict and measure what various programs and practices accomplish.

Inevitably, of course, teachers and administrators encounter innumerable situations that research cannot explain. Every day, practitioners must act without guidance from research. Importantly, in many of these situations, it is in the interest of everyone that teachers and administrators decide as a community how to act. Just where a line can be drawn that distinguishes what teachers and administrators ought to be able to decide for themselves and what demands community agreement and commitment could occupy many studies. But clearly, these discussions require intellectual attention and tools. Deductive reason is an essential tool in these discussions.

Adapting the Scientific Method in the Social Sciences

The scientific method is undeniably powerful when doing what it was designed to do. Problems with the scientific method become evident when it is used inappropriately. Distinguishing the appropriate use of the scientific method from inappropriate uses requires intellectual attention. However, we have clarified so much of our thinking about how to think about knowledge and inquiry, that answering this question is surprisingly easy. Indeed, it seems too obvious.

The scientific method helps us understand *what is*, not what ought to be. It is appropriate to use the scientific method to verify the results of pilot or existing programs—what exists. The scientific method allows us to answer such questions as: Can the program do what it claims it can do? Can its achievements be replicated by other professionals in all of the settings to which it may be generalized? And can it accomplish what it claims more efficaciously than competing programs?

Once a theory about learning or teaching has been subjected to legitimate applied research, it must become some kind of curriculum, instructional program, or assessment. Each must make some claim to assist teaching and learning. Whatever that claim is, it must be measurable. If it is not, either the claim is spurious on the face of it or the program has been inadequately developed. It might very well be that a theory of learning has been elaborated in an impressive instructional program, but it may require additional applied research to sort out assessment problems. Ignoring or otherwise failing to develop adequate program assessments constitutes a grave research and development error. Practitioners and the public have every right to make that demand on research. And that means they have every right in the world to reject claims from research and development that fail to deliver complete, ready to use programs. All this nonsense about certain programs dealing with such rarefied phenomena that they defy assessment or operate on some plane too pure for accountability must be rejected as unprofessional and intellectually inadequate. We are a profession, not a bunch of mystics.

The natural sciences have given the Western intellectual tradition its greatest achievements in the study of observable phenomena. In our evaluation of educational programs and practices, we must use everything we can learn from natural science about inductive reasoning, empirical method, verification of observable phenomenon, and the use of mathematics in quantitative analysis. We must form hypotheses and analyze results. We must verify that what is attempted conforms in substantial ways to what is intended. If we observe serendipitous events, we must not assume that we have accounted for them. We must expand our studies to include these new events until they have become not merely positive but also predictable. And so on.

We must use the scientific method, but we must not get sucked into the indifference of scientific inquiry. Our demand for efficacy related to our *telos* brings rigor and accountability to research and development in education. It also demands that what we strive to achieve is ethically sound. We seek to do what is right excellently. These are enormously important standards, but they demand change. Educators must give up our tendency to accept research and personal claims that do nothing. We must accept the rigor of the scientific method. We must demand that researchers and administrators demonstrate the ability of programs to contribute to the achievement of our discipline's *telos*. Natural scientists have developed powerful research tools that are readily available to social scientists. But we must use them appropriately. Importantly, there is one area of the study of *what is* in the social sciences that proves intractable to the scientific method.

The Integration of Qualitative and Quantitative Analysis

The essential role of mathematics in science accounts for the term quantitative analysis and its identification with the scientific method. Social scientists often attempt to prove they conduct real science by giving the same role to mathematics in their research as do natural scientists. However, the relationship between social science and mathematics is not as natural as the relationship between natural science and mathematics.

Inevitably, social scientists must discover the forces that drive social phenomena. These phenomena, the world of humans, are enormously complex and unstable. They are subject to historical, anthropological, sociological, and individual forces that must be rooted out in order to understand what is going on. These subtle characteristics and hidden forces must be discovered so that researchers know *what to study*. At the outset of such studies, researchers must admit that they know something interesting is going on but are so unsure of its character and source that they dare not jump to any conclusions. They must investigate the phenomena from as open and unbiased a point of view as is possible. The method of research used to sort out the complex character and hidden forces in social phenomena is called *qualitative analysis*.

Unlike scientists using the scientific method who must form hypotheses, scientists using qualitative analysis must avoid hypotheses and tests of hypotheses. Common sense and empiricism permit us to say, If I hadn't seen it, I never would have believed it. The anthropologists and sociologists who invented qualitative analysis have taught us to say, If I hadn't believed it, I never would have seen it. Or more to the point, If I had not hypothesized it, I never would have observed it. The essential attitude in qualitative analysis is open expectancy. The essential task is to observe everything. The essential skill is to be able to look without looking for anything.

Not surprisingly, qualitative analysis generates enormous amounts of data. The analysis of this kind of research does not use statistical methods. There is nothing to measure. These researchers try to identify organizing principles or tendencies among their unbounded observations. Sociologist and anthropologists who have introduced me to this method assure me that collecting, organizing, and making sense out of these kinds of data are far more difficult and time consuming tasks than anything they ever did in quantitative analysis. Yet many researchers accuse this method of being soft, of lacking rigor.

The argument that ensues is important to note but not helpful for it falls victim to semantic rather than substantive confusion. This confusion is best revealed in the arguments opponents give for why the methods they decry should be abandoned:

> Quantitative analysis should be abandoned because it cannot escape its compulsive demand to place mathematical and structural rigor above any regard for useful knowledge. It is always an impediment to developing useful understanding of social phenomena.

> Qualitative analysis should be abandoned because for all its interest in the illusive, mysterious, undefined forces in the human condition, it can never accept responsibility to predict and be accountable for anything.

In their defense, qualitative researchers argue that their research is rigorous, indeed, terribly difficult. But that is not what quantitative researchers mean by rigor. Rigor means that when research is replicated, it produces the same results as the original study. Rigor means that the researcher can predict what will happen when practitioners do something. Qualitative researchers lose the argument on rigor every time, because qualitative research is not designed to predict anything. Indeed, it is designed not to predict so that researchers can discover subtle characteristics of and hidden forces in social phenomena.

On the other hand, quantitative researchers defend themselves from the accusation that they study precisely irrelevant stuff by pointing out that their research is rigorous, that it predicts. They completely miss the point that if they use predictive methods to discover the subtle characteristics and hidden forces in social phenomena, they fall victim to seeing only what they believed at the outset of their research.

The solution to this conflict seems to lie in recognizing that social phenomena require two very different stages of research. In the first, researchers must conduct unbounded observations. This stage has no need for and must avoid the biases inherent in quantitative analysis. In the second stage, researchers must design studies that sort out the salience of the forces identified in the first stage and develop interventions that overcome or exploit these forces in the social setting. This kind of research cannot be conducted without quantitative analysis.

The question that must be resolved about qualitative research and quantitative research deals with how they contribute to each other, once again, how they can be integrated. And the answer seems plain. Qualitative research must be used early on to identify the forces or issues in a field of study. However, once those variables have been identified, quantitative research must be used to assure predictability and accountability in the programs developed to improve the social setting studied. An example might be useful.

Parents have an indisputable impact on the capacity of students to learn, but educators do not understand the character of that influence. Educational researchers have not identified and characterized the activities of parents that contribute to the success of children in school. We do not have adequate knowledge of the parent behaviors that help prepare children to begin school. We have even less knowledge regarding these behaviors during the years children attend school, especially during secondary schooling.

When we consider how little we know about these influences, it becomes obvious that we cannot begin a research project aimed at identifying and evaluating these influences by using deductive reason to form hypotheses that predict what those influences are. To identify those influences, researchers must first go into homes to talk to and observe parents of successful and unsuccessful students. They must interview family members, neighbors, and anyone else who influences children. They might even ask various adults to keep journals to help them notice and recall what they do when they interact with their children. Those are the essential tools of data collection in qualitative research: open ended (rather than hypotheses bound) observations, journals, and interviews. The major contribution of qualitative research in such a study would be to identify all of the various parental behaviors that constitute the positive and negative influences (variables) that assist or detract from student success in school.

Ultimately, however, quantitative research would have to be used to determine which of these variables are salient, worth attempting to assure all children receive, and which are spurious. Then the researchers would have to develop programs that provide these influences to students, programs that can be used in schools, and programs that parents can learn to use. Probably the most essential task of this phase of the research would be to discover which influences schools can provide and which influences parents only can provide. Clearly, those questions require a research methodology that can produce measurable predictability. Qualitative research must be used to identify the major parental influences or variables; quantitative research must be used to validate programs designed to meet the needs of students.

It should be easy to use the scientific method appropriately in the study of social phenomena. Our rule is as simple as, Use it when we know what we are studying and have tasks that demand predictive research. Of course, we must also avoid the naturalistic fallacy by not treating these phenomena as necessary in themselves, but rather evaluating them and the efficacy of our programs in terms of our *telos*.

It is also easy to use qualitative analysis appropriately. We use it to discover the subtle characteristics and hidden forces in social phenomena, but we stop when those discoveries are made. We do not use qualitative research to produce predictive conclusions. And we clearly do not use our comfort with or awareness of qualitative research to build arguments against achieving program predictability and accountability.

None of this discussion has explored new ideas. But it has advanced the cognitive maturity of our thinking about research methodology, for it has provided principles that declare when we use one method (and not the other) and when we use the other method (and not the prior). We have developed these concepts so that they express what is included and what is excluded, and we have shown how they must be integrated to provide a complete research model.

We have accounted for education's source and standard of knowledge, its architecture of inquiry and knowledge, and its research methodology. We can see that educators are capable of integrating research, integrating research and practice, and conducting discourse that leads to agreement, commitment, and action. We have accounted for intellectual authority in education by accounting for the intellectual development and competence of educators. Specifically, we have assured *intellectual development* by accounting for *ethical and cognitive development* in education and educators. And we have explained how educators can form a professional community. But we have one last topic to visit. We must wonder how all of this intellectual development can be institutionalized. During the 17th century, the Royal Society of London and the French and German Academies worked together to assure that Newton's epistemological laws were followed. But we rarely hear of these institutions today. Once again, in order to begin thinking about an intellectual challenge in education and the social sciences, we investigate solutions in natural science. And once again, we discover that we learn a great deal, but we must adapt what we have learned to the unique character of our disciplines.

Intellectual Authority in Natural Science

To understand what has happened with intellectual authority in the natural sciences, it is helpful to define pure, basic, and applied research, for they depend upon very different kinds of authority. Basic research is often defined as research that is conducted without an applied aim in mind. According to this definition, the sole purpose and only justification required for basic research is the advancement of knowledge. The only motivation required is curiosity. In reality, however, basic research often includes research that addresses problems that have been identified in scientific practice or even in the corporate world. What makes it basic is not that it has no practical motive but that it has no known approach. It creates a whole new line of inquiry or body of knowledge. On the other hand, applied research has a very clear and practical use. It would be helpful to have words to describe these three kinds of research. At the risk of confusing long established connotations, I would suggest that we use the term *pure research* to denote research that has no known application and is conducted for the sole purpose of advancing knowledge. I would use *basic research* to denote research that is original in creating new structures of inquiry or forms of knowledge with some practical application in mind. For example, some scientists conduct pure research in material science, but most of the original work in material science is funded by industries that are looking for solutions to well described problems. This research is not pure, but it is certainly basic. Finally, I would use *applied research* as it has always been used, to describe research that is conducted to transform basic research into the products it has made possible.

When we talk about research and development, I think it is helpful to assume that we are talking about basic research and applied research and development. These distinctions help us understand who funds the research, who can make proprietary claims to the research, and what national policies apply to the dissemination of the research. We do not pursue those discussions, but that is an example of why the distinctions are important. To our end, we must notice how basic research is integrated with applied research in the natural sciences and commerce, for that is the process that ultimately establishes the intellectual authority of natural science when it is bound to commercial purposes.

Research and Development in Natural Science and Commerce

Government, university, and commercial research centers conduct both pure and basic research in natural science. All of these researchers, regardless of how different their settings may seem, conduct research that is formally integrated. They all operate with the same epistemological and logical assumptions; they are part of the same intellectual community. They use the same knowledge and methods, and their discoveries flow back and forth protected from careless alteration. Indeed, the integration of natural science and commerce has been one of the most persuasive explanations for the recent economic success in the United States.

Problems and solutions flow coherently from the university to commerce or from commercial research centers to the university. And it is that coherence, the ability of practical questions to flow to research centers and new knowledge to flow to practice, that has enabled commercial leaders to form the systems that carry findings in basic research into product development.

It is important for educators to know about the systems that make it possible for research problems to flow back and forth between research and practice in natural sciences and commerce. For one thing, we do not have these systems, and it seems clear that we need them. But more is at stake, for these systems link both research and practice to the market place, and the market place has virtually replaced any other institutional source of intellectual authority in the applied sciences. This development is revealing, worth copying, and demands attention from social scientists. By accepting the authority of the market place, natural scientists have brought an enormous amount of financial support to their endeavors.

Again, we must do some work with these systems, for nothing that the natural sciences do seems to travel whole cloth to education or the social sciences, but they provide vital insights. So much has been written and discussed about the major systems that integrate natural science with commerce that I need to provide only a quick, general discussion and one example.

The percentage of pure research that is conducted at universities and government sponsored institutes rather than in corporations seems to be increasing. As we have seen, natural scientists, especially those doing pure research, publish their findings *internationally* and call for replications in order to validate new knowledge. Obviously, such a requirement presents problems to corporate research centers that must justify their existence to shareholders, because it means that the value of their discoveries accrue to the whole world and do not enjoy proprietary protection. There is enough risk involved in applied research and product development to stretch the capacities of businesses. To expect them also to fund pure research over which they would have no proprietary claim is impractical.

There is no single path that describes how knowledge moves from basic research to profitable products, but one example is especially effective and revealing. In the model made famous at the Massachusetts Institute of Technology (MIT), both knowledge and people transfer from the university to business. That model has also been used at Stanford University, most famously with its links to Silicon Valley.

In the MIT model (which I simplify), graduate students work with brilliant scientists and pursue promising lines of inquiry, make major discoveries, and then personally carry that information to the business world. They either join existing companies willing to pay for their expertise or they start their own companies, funded by venture capital. To sell their discoveries to an existing company or to venture capitalists, researchers must have some notion of the application and financial value of their discoveries.

We have identified three major systems that operate in the relationship between science and commerce: university and government sponsored basic research, established businesses willing to sponsor applied research, and venture capitalists willing to fund applied research in start up companies. But there is far more to notice. Applied research takes a promising idea and develops it into various potential products–thus the term *product development*. Each of these products is tested in the lab, a stage often referred to as *alpha testing*. Alpha testing is used to improve and validate product efficacy. Next, the product is placed in a real world setting, one for which it was developed, and is tested in that environment, a stage often referred to as *beta testing*. Once the product has been developed and tested, it must be mass produced. The organized effort to design and develop mass production is called *production engineering*. Finally, marketing, sales, delivery, and service systems must be designed and developed to exploit potential markets. Each of these systems requires considerable time, expertise, and funding, and each involves risk. An example might be helpful.

Let's say a graduate student doing basic research in bio-medicine makes a discovery that indicates a diagnostic test for mad-cow disease might be developed. Fabulous! Beef producers will no longer have to destroy herds based upon exposure. A blood test will reveal which animals are infected and which are not. Upon graduation, she presents her findings to pharmaceutical companies and venture capitalists. Subsequently, she makes a deal that places her in a lab designed, equipped, and staffed to conduct applied research. Importantly, whether she joins an established firm or goes with venture capitalists, she will benefit either from internal support systems of the corporation or from the cottage industries of accountants, attorneys, and management consultants connected to venture capitalists.

In the early phases of the applied research she and her team actually develop and establish the efficacy of a test for mad cow disease. Typically, the testing procedures will be quite complex, so once the general method is established the team must work to reduce the complexity of the test. From requiring all kinds of equipment, the test is simplified to requiring only a small amount of blood and a two step process in the lab. Very important, but not a product ready for market.

To be effective, the test must be inexpensive and completed at the ranch. Both buyers and sellers of cattle are put off by uncertainty. If buyers have any reason to doubt the health of cattle, they do not want to buy them. If sellers can verify the health of their herds, they can command greater value. But they need a simple test, not a laboratory event.

Product development continues until a product is developed that is appropriate to the market. Most ranchers can take blood from their cattle, keep samples separate, and conduct an inexpensive one step test. Clearly, there is a systemic demand for early, inexpensive, and simple testing. Plus there is enormous profit potential in early inexpensive testing. So product development continues until an inexpensive, one step test has been developed.

The one step test is developed in the lab. But *researchers* still face two challenges, either of which can be expensive. First, they must move from alpha testing to beta testing. They must conduct beta testing where they expect their product to be used, in this case, on ranches. Once the product passes beta testing, they must develop mass production processes outside the lab. Even in established pharmaceutical companies, this step often requires the development of all new production facilities. Production engineers must invent the mass production process and build the mass production facility that will be cost effective and maintain high quality control.

The scientific systems and stages of research and development include: basic research, applied research that develops useful technology, product development in the lab that produces specific products, and production engineering that makes it possible to mass produce the product. But the task of bringing products to market and ultimately assuring a profit does not end there.

Next comes market development which also requires an in-determinant amount of time and money. Any new product is designed to be sold. Which means that buyers must not merely be found, they must be closed. Potential customers do not write checks. Admittedly, this example does not provide an interesting discussion of the challenges that companies often face when they attempt to develop new markets. Developing a test or cure for any major disease encounters far more risk during development than marketing. But one can easily imagine the risks that would apply to marketing other products or if two products competed in the same market place. But even without competition, there is considerable expense involved in developing the delivery, training, and other customer services related to bringing a new product to market.

Bringing new products to market requires *financial commitment to an in-determinant set of costs*. Only after markets have been developed and enough checks have been written to reach the break even point, does the venture become profitable. And those profits must be sustained in order for investors to see a profit.

Both the scientists who invent the knowledge that can generate a new product and the investors who fund those efforts must have a high tolerance for risk. The risk that such ventures present is not merely that they might fail to develop a product that works or fail to engineer an efficient production process. A group might succeed in all of those tasks yet fail because another group got to the market first.

Financial Support of Commercial Research and Development

Educators might rightly conclude that the *financial* systems and the sophisticated commitment of investors that support the entire research and development process contribute the most impressive aspects of the link between research and commerce in the United States. Clearly, whether starting her own company or joining an established company, the graduate student turned entrepreneur must make sure that the organization she selects has the financial backing and sophistication required to see the project through market development. Otherwise her product and effort can fail, not because she and her team could not achieve their goal, but simply because they ran out of money. Educational research desperately lacks both funding and sophisticated support. This topic is so important to everything we must do to integrate research and integrate research and practice that we benefit from looking even more closely at the financial support enjoyed by research and development in commerce.

Both established industries and venture capitalists have had to learn the value and necessity of every step of the research and development process. They have had to develop financial support systems that are designed to provide adequate resources up front, add resources along the way, and most important, stay the course. Venture capital is rewarding on four major fronts: 1) The investment is in people and new companies which means the investor is participating directly in the development of jobs and the economy, not in securities speculation. 2) There is a great deal of excitement in picking, supporting, and following to the end the development of new ideas and new companies. 3) There is also big time risk, for investors know that they can lose their entire investment. 4) There are huge rewards when the venture works.

The development of sophisticated financial systems to support venture capital has made possible the unparalleled growth of start up companies in the United States. Importantly, Congress and regulatory agencies have limited participation in venture capital to sophisticated investors or to sophisticated venture fund managers. Direct investment by unsophisticated investors has pretty much disappeared.

A typical venture capitalist invests 500,000 to a million dollars, distributing the risk in various investments that average around $50,000 per venture. The sophistication and complexity of venture capital and the support systems that accompany the investment has increased dramatically in the last 10 years. Sophisticated venture capital provides a major competitive advantage for the United States' economy. It creates new products, businesses, and jobs. What is rather amazing is that financiers enter the bargain understanding that they must support each phase of product development and then step up to support market development. All of this is of great interest to educators because they need to replicate, in some form, all of these systems.

Importantly, no economist considers venture capital investments a drain on the economy, neither the expensive research, development, and marketing systems they support, nor the immensely expensive support systems provided by attorneys, accountants, and management consultants. Even ventures that fail are recognized as an important part of the economic system for they contribute to the broad base of ideas required to assure full exploitation of human potential. They create the competition that brings energy, excitement, and urgency to product development. Economists, politicians, and investors recognize that without risk, there can be no rewards or *progress.*

Competition and the Market Place vs. Competition in Society

It is interesting to notice that the market place contributes intellectual authority to natural science when it is conducted with a commercial purpose. Nature still provides the source of knowledge, but the market place adds its own demands. Applied researchers and production engineers do not depend merely on their own intellectual interests in designing products. They must meet the demands of the market place in terms of attraction, simplicity, quality, and cost. However, the market place has limited authority. Accountants adeptly factor in profit margins to decisions regarding production quality, cost, and service. The market place does not provide a perfect source of authority on issues such as quality and safety, but it seems to be more efficient and effective than governments. Educators must give some attention to the authority, efficiency, and effectiveness of competition and the market place because we can learn from it. Many politicians and pundits make deeply flawed claims that all of education's problems can be solved by increasing competition.

A fundamental principle of market economics is that transactions are conducted between *a willing buyer and a willing seller*. Competition forces sellers to pay attention to the demands and interests of buyers because it provides buyers a choice and sellers the freedom to win buyers through quality and cost. Theoretically, competition forces scientists and engineers to integrate quality and cost into the standards of product development and production engineering.

However, when buyers face decisions in which they are not truly free to choose what they will buy, the concept of the willing buyer is marginalized or destroyed. Most obviously, in order to be a willing buyer, one must have money. Relatively few buyers ever purchase their dream car or their dream house any more than they have their dream job or discover a dream hobby. Rather, people seem to operate within the anchor points of what they consider the worst realistic possibilities in their lives and the best realistic possibilities in their lives.[1] The closer they operate to the best realistic possibilities in their lives, the more satisfied they seem to be. And, as Maslow taught us, anchor points change as people gain or lose realistic access to various needs.

The market place is most effective when transactions involve *preferences*, things that the buyer can do without. But it becomes highly dependent on the general economic system and national wealth when it must meet the *basic needs* of people. Air and water must be free, because humans cannot live beyond minutes without air and hours without water. Fortunately, nature provided an abundance of air and water. But market principles have not protected nature's gift. It is becoming increasingly apparent that throughout the world, national economic policies have permitted production engineers and business leaders to destroy the quality

---

[1]Patricia C. Smith, et al; *The Measurement of Satisfaction in Work and Retirement: A Strategy for the Study of Attitudes.*

of air and water. As a matter of national economic policy, the costs of reclaiming these essential sources of life have been passed on to the public. The market place has not been able to intervene in that dynamic. Even today, the earth's overall capacity to produce clean air and water is being eroded due to the inadequacy of market ethics.

Competition and the market place seem to be most effective in managing fundamentally insignificant transactions. It does not really matter what kind of car I have, if I have a car that safely transports me to work, my kids to school, and so on. There is a staggering range of housing available to the vast majority of citizens in developed countries, but far too many live in conditions that jeopardize their safety and health.

The social sciences are interested in creating the principles, laws, and institutions essential to human life, development, and dignity. Economics concerns itself with developing the systems that produce wealth and distribute that wealth justly. Competition and the market place seem to have an enormous capacity to generate wealth, but they seem to be unable to distribute wealth justly or to assure the security, safety, and dignity of all people and the earth. It seems that economists must figure out how to maximize the obvious contributions of competition and the market place, but not permit those constructs to completely define the purpose of economics.

This distinction between the capacity and limits of competition and free market economies creates substantial intellectual challenges. These are the challenges to which George Soros[2] and Lionel Jospin[3] refer when they insist that we benefit from market economies but cannot endure market societies. It seems that we can use market principles to generate wealth, but we cannot use market principles to distribute wealth or to assure that all members of society have access to quality air and water, food and shelter, health care, and education.

Educators in particular are sensitive to the economic conditions that prevent many school districts from providing clean and safe classrooms or adequate textbooks, materials, and equipment. We know that children who live in poverty bring a variety of disadvantages to learning. We

[2] "Toward a Global Open Society," *The Atlantic Monthly*, January, 1998.

[3] "Survey: France," *The Economist*, June 5 - 11, 1999; (p. 6). Mr. Jospin was elected prime minister of France in June, 1997.

accept the challenge to identify those disadvantages and produce methods of instruction that solve them. But we realize that we probably cannot even identify all of the psychological, social, ethical, and spiritual disadvantages these children bring with them to school, and we certainly cannot solve all of them. Therefore, we can neither tolerate the view that economists, politicians, and business leaders are innocent, nor permit them to continue to ignore the consequences of the poverty they create.

We reject Marxism and its planned markets and oppressive, dictatorial governments. But we agree with scholar activists such as Leonardo Boff when they point out, "Poverty is not innocent, not produced by nature, not what God wants. It is the result of a process that produces wealth and poverty side by side."[4]

It is not the purpose of this text to solve these vast intellectual problems. But we can point out that because these problems are the proper topic of the social sciences, their solutions must depend on intellectual development that consists of both ethical and cognitive components. Economics must employ an ethically grounded purpose as its source of knowledge and it must develop complete, coherent theoretical models that compete in terms of its *telos*. Our discussions of mature secular moral reasoning tell us that economists can craft an objective, universal ethical statement that defines the *telos* of economics in all countries, for all people. However, the activities that achieve that *telos* cannot be imposed. They must be designed in theoretical models that compete. But where education can articulate different theoretical models and let them compete within states or even large school districts, economic models must be organized by nation and accommodated internationally.

Competition in economics cannot be understood as competition among individual citizens. It is competition among nations and their scholars, politicians, and business leaders who must work together fully to develop and implement their economic model. England and America seem to have implemented a common economic model. France and Germany have resisted that model, accepting free markets, but insisting that labor and broader social concerns must be given equal status with capital–maybe even higher status than capital. China clearly has resisted Western free market models but has suffered from the inadequate production of wealth.

---

[4]*The Path to Hope: Fragments from a Theologian's Journey* (p. 69).

China may be more vigorously and openly engaged in studying and solving economic problems, both intellectually and practically, than any countries in the West. Intellectual integrity and the commitment of all economists and politicians to the *telos* of economics must produce interest in and support for these various endeavors. National and international trade policies, for instance, must be just and provide a level playing field upon which these models and countries can compete. Economists, politicians, and the media must develop the capacity to think about economics at the level of formal operations. Using formal cognitive operations, they can describe the role of economics' *telos* and report on the competition being waged among theoretical models employed in various countries in terms of that *telos*.

Intellectual Authority in Education

Understanding theoretical models helps educators distinguish basic research from applied research. Theoretical models integrate research and practice. That is one of their most important achievements. At least in education, then, it is useful to use the term *basic research* to refer to research that is conducted outside theoretical models and *applied research* to refer to research conducted within theoretical models. This distinction is controversial, for it treats education as an applied social science. It claims that as a discipline education is not well suited to basic research. It is more like engineering than physics, medicine than biology. Education relies on biophysics, chemistry, and biology to provide the basic research about that nature of learning that is possible to produce in natural science—a body of knowledge that at least currently can best be described as sparse. And education relies on cognitive psychology, a field that has been more useful than natural science but certainly not adequately conclusive or authoritative. For better and for worse, these are the disciplines capable of providing *basic* learning theory to education.

I recommend that educational researchers define themselves as applied researchers and commit to one or another theoretical model. One task is to link basic research produced in natural science and cognitive psychology with the applied knowledge generated within theoretical models. When a team of biophysicists or psychologists makes a discovery that they think could have great ramifications for education, they cannot merely publish articles in educational journals claiming all kinds of practical applications. They must build a connection with educational researchers working within theoretical models.

Similarly, when educational researchers encounter problems that confound current theory, they must communicate with natural scientists and cognitive psychologists to request that basic research be conducted that addresses those problems. Thus a reciprocal relationship may be established between educational researchers who are grounded in the practical problems that teachers encounter in the classroom and researchers in natural science and psychology who are equipped to conduct basic research and generate whole new theoretical frameworks.

Educators may feel diminished by the thought of abandoning basic research, but the opposite is true. Indeed, making this distinction provides rather startling insights into the way educational research is currently conducted. We have noticed that educational research cannot be integrated and it cannot be integrated with practice. But if we ask what kind of research does not have to connect to any other research or to any product, the answer is clear: pure research. It is absurd to say that all educational researchers should be conducting pure research, and no one makes that claim. But when we consider what is actually happening in educational research and notice that there is no formal integration of research or of research and practice, we must admit that it is not merely metaphorical to claim that, more often than not, educational researchers conduct pure research.

If educational researchers were to consider the vastness of the enterprises that must be established in order to link research with practice, they might properly feel overwhelmed rather than diminished. We have described the number and complexity of institutions and systems that link basic research with product development in the natural sciences and commerce. Educational researchers and practitioners would benefit from demanding the development and financial support of similar systems in education.

Research and Development in Education

What is particularly discouraging about the state of research and development in education is that the various systems that are so fully developed to support R & D in natural science and commerce do not exist in education. The impoverishment of education that has occurred in the last twenty years makes it impossible even to imagine how an adequate financial system would be developed to support the intellectual and support systems educational research so obviously needs. The 1997 U.S. Department of Education's appropriation for research, development, and dissemination was $128,567,000. Of that, $53,782,000 was budgeted to the National Education Research Institute (NERI), $56,000,000 to the Regional Labs, and $18,785,000 went to dissemination.[5] The federal government's contribution to educational research (excluding dissemination) was $109,785,000.

Most of us find it hard to consider a hundred million dollars as an inadequate sum for anything. To put these numbers in perspective, we might look at the support Congress gives to highways. On March 12, 1998, the Senate authorized a six year highway budget of $214.5 billion. That amount exceeded the administration's request by $45 billion. Later in March, the House of Representatives increased the authorization to $217 billion. The House version included $9.5 billion for 1000 *high priority* projects. But these high priority projects were funded with no research or outcome standards. States were to be given an enormous amount of money to fund research by messing around, pure research by individuals or companies who had to meet no standards of experience, training, or successful track records. As one competent newspaper noted, "Since these projects—ostensibly to demonstrate new ways of building highway systems—do not come out of a state's overall allocation of federal highway money, they are pure pork."[6]

It is difficult to compare federal funding for the construction of highways to federal funding for educational research and development. Even the $45 billion add-on to the administration's request is difficult to sort out. But $9.5 billion over six years for completely uncoordinated messing around with new ways of building highways? We can compare $110 million a year for research and development in education to $1.5 billion per year with a six year commitment for pork in highway construction. There is no question, more money could be made available for educational research.

[5]Vance Grant, U. S. Department of Education, National Education Library.

[6]*The Economist*, "Hey, big spenders! The budget and Congress," March 28 - April 3rd, 1998, (p. 26).

We can agree that federal support for educational research and development is embarrassingly inadequate and still agree that when evaluated in terms of the contributions that educational research makes to the country's public school classrooms, it is difficult to justify even current levels of funding. Again, I am not saying that there is no good research. I am saying that good research is not adequately impacting public school classrooms. And I am saying that educators are not entirely innocent in this situation. We contribute to and sustain an intellectual tradition that makes a travesty of research and undermines the integration of research and practice. We face some fairly easily described challenges with virtually no capacity to respond as a discipline.[7] We can complain that our discipline has been impoverished and therefore cannot be expected to function professionally, but we have no convincing answer to politicians and citizens who claim that to increase the public's investment in public education would only throw good money after bad. Indeed, if one were to ask teachers where a billion dollars of federal money could best be spent to improve education, they would respond, as they always have, to classrooms and teachers, not to research and development.

We face a chicken and egg dilemma. Let us assume that Congress decides that the major role the federal government should play in supporting youth education is the funding of research and development and that states should be responsible for program implementation, training, and assessment. What would happen to the public's investment in educational research if nothing changed? Educational researchers at the NERI, regional labs, and universities would conduct basic and applied research with virtually no reference to each other and no ability to distinguish pure research from applied research. As we noted earlier, in education the independence of pure research is exercised in both basic and applied research. Education completely lacks the essential processes of applied research and development: integrated product development, production engineering, and market development. Setting aside the quality of the knowledge produced by research, attempts to link it to practice produce their own problems. In education, product developers

[7] One of education's most consistent errors is to ignore problems that we could rather directly solve, problems that impact the learning of a majority of children, and focus instead on the intractable problems that inhibit the learning of a relatively small percentage of students.

exercise the same independence as researchers. They expect to interpret the meaning and implications of research according to their own individual views and routinely exercise the right to change research as they see fit. Textbook publishers have a keen eye for educational fads, but routinely interpret them independent of any research base. I do not mean to pick on education's textbook publishers, just to point out that they too act like educators.

Nearly everyone in education seems to assume that research must be *adapted* rather than carefully, and rigorously implemented. Adaptations destroy the integrity of the original research and make it impossible to evaluate its efficacy in various settings. Uncontrolled adaptation of research destroys the relationship between research and practice, the capacity of researchers to determine the efficacy of their products, and the intellectual authority of both research and practice.

If the federal budget provided $1 billion per year for educational research and development as it is currently conducted, the research purchased by that investment would have nothing but an accidental relationship to programs or products developed for schools. The products presented to the states would have very little added value based upon all of the money spent by the nation's taxpayers, because product developers act according to their individual preferences. The value of research and development systems is realized when their findings improve practice, when deep knowledge is brought to programs, products, and practices. However, as long as product development functions independent of research, educational researchers cannot quantify the value their work adds to educational practice or even argue in the abstract that it adds any at all.

If educators are going to demonstrate that they can add value to education through research and development, they are going to have to become an authentic intellectual community. Which means that our previous discussion of education's epistemology has enormous implications for research and development. Not only must we identify and commit to an ethically grounded purpose that we must treat as our source and standard of knowledge, we must organize research and development as well as practice according to the formal architecture of theoretical models. Then we can discuss research development systems in a meaningful way. Those systems include:

- Basic research.

- Applied research that brings basic research into appropriate theoretical models.

- Applied research that responds to needs identified by researchers and practitioners within a theoretical model.

- Research and development that carefully builds the findings of basic and applied research into specific instructional products that are so well developed that classroom teachers can use them as they are presented. In other words, practitioners should not face major research tasks in order to implement new products. Products should be so highly developed that they only require training to be used, not additional research by practitioners.

- Marketing systems that introduce products to practitioners, provide the information practitioners need to make sound purchasing decisions, and deliver the training practitioners need to use products effectively.

- Sophisticated investors who demand accountability from all of the systems requisite to bringing products to market and who stay the course through the entire research and development process.

- Well funded school districts that have the purchasing capacity to support a financially viable market place.

All of these research and financial systems have been identified in commercial research and development or are obvious extrapolations from that model.

Competition in Education

As we have seen, there is some trepidation involved in committing to an ethically grounded *telos* rather than a practical purpose. An ethically grounded *telos* describes what educators ought to do, not merely what we know how to do. The advantage of an ethically grounded *telos* is that it guides both research and practice. Rather than avoiding the influence or distractions of moral philosophy in order to achieve rigor, the social sciences must develop and use mature moral reasoning in order to assure rigor. But still we must order both research and practice so that they aim toward our *telos* while operating in reality. That is precisely the role of competition. Understood properly, competition does not threaten educators. Educators must not reject competition because we fear losing. Rather, we must embrace competition because it assures us, parents, and the general public that we are doing all that can reasonably be expected of us.

By organizing research and practice into complete, coherent theoretical models, educators make it possible to explain research and practice to parents and the public. Competition among theoretical models produces information that teachers and administrators can use to improve what they do and to reassure the public that they are doing the best that can be done. That competition provides essential information to guide practitioners and reassure the public are not points to be obscured or denied. These are among the most important contributions of this whole project because they allow educators to win the confidence and support of parents and the public.

The problem with the current demands for competition in public education is that they fail to provide a rational or fair basis for conducting the competition. I doubt that I need to provide the details of differences in funding, families, and leadership that are so often ignored in current calls for competition. Indeed, there is probably no more uninformed, inexplicable, indefensible view being expressed today than the notion that competition alone holds the answer to the problems that plague public schools. As we have seen, even commercial enterprises, with all of their intellectual and financial support, fail. Competition in the market place produces failed products and bankrupt companies. Competition produces winners and losers.

Public schools already have winners and losers. The problem is that the winners and losers are children. Society cannot tolerate a system of public education that is designed to produce children who are losers side by side with children who are winners. Such a system is not innocent, it is not natural, and it is not God's will. We must change the terms of competition in education so that research and practice compete and best practices win and lesser practices lose. We must end the conditions that create winners and losers among our children. Importantly, this is an ethical issue, not an innocent description of reality in a blood in tooth and claw world. Many parents, assured of their children's ultimate success, might demand that schools continue to produce children who are winners and losers. But they could never insist that schools assure that their children become losers. The only defense they can mount for such a view depends upon the moral reasoning of children in their early teens.

Again, this distinction between the appropriate terms of competition goes to the heart of the distinction made by Soros and Jospin when they insist that we can have a competitive market economy, but we cannot have a competitive market society. We must have competition in schools, but the competition must be waged among ideas and programs, not children.[8]

When we ask what we can do as a profession to assure that we wage productive competition, the answer seems clear. Competition must be waged among schools that have adequate funding to implement the theoretical models that seem most able to meet the needs of their students. The information gathered in the context of this competition must be used as feedback that allows teachers to improve their teaching and students to improve their learning. It must not be used as a tool to sort and select winners and losers among students.

Sophisticated Financial Support for R & D in Education

As we have seen, in the natural sciences and commerce, sophisticated financial systems do not merely tolerate, they demand that enormous attention be paid to the various phases of product development and marketing. Not only does education lack the structure of an intellectual community, it also lacks the clearly identifiable systems capable of carrying out all of these tasks. Furthermore, it completely lacks the sophisticated financial support needed to create and sustain them. The only effective political pressure for the financing of public education is generated by the National Education Association (NEA) and the American Federation of Teachers (AFT), which many citizens and politicians decry as nothing but unions. In fairness to the NEA and the

---

[8]I have benefitted enormously from competition, and I think that competition can provide wonderful opportunities for students to develop character and confidence and to add intensity to their work. But I also think that competition and sportsmanship are fundamentally virtuous activities that are as poorly understood as ethics in general and require considerable intellectual attention to guide competent activities in schools.

AFT, their job is to support the interests of school teachers, not to create or finance research institutions for education. Rather than blaming the NEA and AFT for not doing what is not their mission, it seems more useful to acknowledge that education needs to develop sophisticated national, state, and local political and educational leaders who can win the financial support of taxpayers for the various systems needed to bring together research and practice.

Sophisticated national, state, and local political and intellectual leaders won the taxpayers' support for the buildup of the peace time military, the federal highway program, and the space program. Politicians, the media, parents, and citizens must abandon the silly notion that educational research and development can gain the support it needs from local elections. Educational research and development address national challenges and must be supported nationally. The nation's security, prosperity, and domestic tranquility depend upon the improvement of education. Educators must show the way, and politicians must stand up and be counted for support and leadership.

A consortium that includes the NEA, AFT, American Association of School Administrators (AASA), and National School Boards Association (NSBA) is called for. Of course these groups have cooperated in the past and even formed formal coalitions. What I am recommending is that they join together to provide intellectual leadership that demands coherent research that is integrated with practice. Within that context, they can establish the moral and intellectual authority required to support their efforts to bring increased financial support for educational research and development.

Politicians unfriendly to public education may insist that public education must prove itself worthy of such funding before it is granted. That demand is sensible or absurd depending upon what educators are expected to do to demonstrate their worthiness. If educators must change their outcomes, i.e., improve student performance, in order to escape impoverishment, that demand is absurd. On the other hand, for educators to insist that the public should increase its investment in public education's research and development as it is currently practiced is equally absurd. However, if education's leaders and researchers commit to changes that alter how research is conducted and how research is integrated with practice, then the public must support those efforts.

The chaos in educational research, the lack of intellectual authority, and the unceasing disappointments in public education undermine attempts to increase financial support for any facet of education. These challenges call for considerable sophistication among educational and political leaders. Educational leaders must be able to deal with systemic design and epistemological issues if we are to make a convincing argument for the enormous increase in financial support we need. And political leaders must be able to grasp the need for funding and garner the will to support the funding of the whole research and development system needed if we are going to re-vitalize research and improve practice.

While the national educational organizations work to build support for increased funding for youth education, educational researchers and practitioners must begin to change how we think and how we conduct practice. We must begin to break down the intellectual barriers that prevent us from integrating research, integrating research and practice, and conducting discourse that leads to agreement, commitment and action. We must change. But as Michael Fullan, Andy Hargreaves, and others have taught us, educators in most universities and public schools are not amenable to change. I argue that the fundamental irrationality that plagues inquiry in education undermines change. Since change is such an important and problematic issue upon which increased funding ultimately depends, it is helpful to notice how the new epistemology restructures and facilitates change.

Re-Thinking Change in Education

Change has been an important intellectual topic in education for a number of years. It is particularly interesting to us because during attempts at leading or participating in change, educators come face to face with the deep intellectual problems that our epistemology attempts to solve. As we discussed in the introduction, the deliberations that educators conduct when attempting to address change often lead to deep, unresolvable conflict. Such conflict ends in a truce in which we agree to disagree because we conclude that we can never agree on anything. Unknowingly, we assent to a deeply problematic epistemological conclusion about the nature of knowledge in education. We do not say that we are never going to agree on this *unless we get some help with intellectual conflict resolution.* We conclude that the problem resides in the nature of knowledge in education, not in intellectual skills and certainly not in epistemology.

As we have seen, that conclusion is not only unexamined, it destroys inquiry, discourse, and intellectual authority throughout education. It precludes the development of professional knowledge and therefore precludes professional skill and stature. Furthermore, it leads to some astoundingly impractical and ineffective approaches to leading change in education. The inadequacy of current thinking about change is made evident by the fact that there are very few examples of successful change occurring where disagreement exists. More significantly, educational leaders have demonstrated no capacity to replicate or generalize the change processes used in those few instances where disagreement has been overcome.[9] Since deep disagreement is a nearly inevitable condition in schools of education and public schools, the fact that attempts at change inevitably fail where disagreement exists is no small matter. It means that the vast majority of educational settings in which change is needed are intellectually unsuitable to change.

The inadequacy of our understanding of change is also manifested in the schizophrenic attitude we have regarding the nature of change. These two personalities reveal themselves depending upon whether the change we are discussing is expected of students or professionals. There is no problem with change if we expect it of students. But there are deep, deep problems when we expect it of professionals. If there really are two distinct kinds of change, we need to identify them and develop new words for them. If there are not two distinct kinds of change, something is seriously wrong with how we think about change.

The Irrational Context in Which Change is Attempted

Behaviorists have associated learning with changes in behavior. More recent learning theory associates learning with development, which is certainly a kind of change. In particular it associates learning with the ability to develop cognitive constructs. All of this is change, and we expect it of students daily. We also expect students to change their attitudes or conduct *before they return to class*, which, as a practical matter, can be interpreted to mean that we expect them to change quickly.

---

[9]This is one of the most important findings of the Effective Schools Project and has been extensively reported by Larry Lezotte.

Such expectations of students by teachers and administrators provide a startling paradox when we compare them to our expectations of educators' capacity to change. We expect students to change in the same way that many American teenagers change when they cross the threshold from age 15 to age 16 and rush off to take their automobile driver's test and win their driver's license. We expect them to encounter change as a matter of excited fulfillment, of growing up, of becoming empowered. After all, we adults know that learning to read and to solve mathematical problems are even more empowering achievements than learning to drive a car.

But when we think about educators' dealing with change, we shift concepts. We replace insights regarding learning and development with metaphors that depict death and dieing, grieving or healing. We have three and six and twelve step processes for implementing change. It reminds us of becoming sober or getting divorced or losing a parent. We know that it is hard and that it takes time. We have to take time and talk to one another, but mostly we have to be sure to take time.

The problems with change in education are grounded in the irrational (anti-rational) views we have called encyclopedia and individualism. These unexamined quasi or anti epistemologies undermine how we think and how we conduct research and practice. The reason change is hard is that both what is being changed and what it is going to be changed to, the status quo and the innovation, are supported by deeply irrational or a-rational positions. This irrationality makes it impossible for educators to conduct the kind of rational discourse or provide the rational arguments and empirical evidence that support change in a manner that is persuasive to all of the participants.

To understand the problems with change in education, we must agree that there are innovations in education that are so efficacious that the arguments for them should be persuasive to all educators. That point helps us understand that the problem is not the absence of quality programs or arguments for them. The problem is that educators have not established an authoritative source of knowledge. Individualism prohibits educators from conducting rational discourse. And that is why, regardless of the evidence that establishes the quality of a program, it is impossible to convince all of the participants in a change that it is the right or best thing to do.

That is why educational leaders are reluctant to attempt to lead even modest changes in educational settings where participants hold contradictory views. When leaders do attempt to lead such change, they typically implement the change in so limited a fashion that only those who agree to the change at the outset are invited to participate. Often, these voluntary changes are called pilots so that leaders do not have to lose face over their inability to design wider implementation strategies or endure the shame that attends their inevitable failure.

A pilot is a legitimate sounding step in change, and sometimes it is genuinely appropriate. Like beta testing, pilots provide an essential stage in program development. But when the expected results of a pilot merely confirm what has already been confirmed, conducting another pilot as a wise component of change merely postpones the inevitable. The pilot is conducted. The change produces the predicted results. Now it is time to extend the change. And to the absolute shock of the innovation's supporters, some of their colleagues ignore the compelling evidence of the pilot. They exclaim, Well, be that as it may, I disagree. Or they point out that there was some minuscule flaw in the design of the pilot, a flaw that makes it impossible to generalize the pilot's conclusions to their classrooms. The indisputable epistemological assumption of individualism demands: *No one knows better what the students in an individual classroom need than the teacher in that classroom.* The point is, pilots, even compellingly successful pilots, are not persuasive in a discipline that is fundamentally a-rational.

It is a mistake to assume that educators stubbornly resist fundamentally rational innovations. That is not the case either. In a discipline that conducts a-rational inquiry, even the best innovations cannot escape the inherent irrationality in which they were developed. This does not mean that there is no logic to them, but that virtually any argument, however specious or absurd, against an innovation is as persuasive as any argument, however thorough and sound, for an innovation. Because educational research and pilot studies are conducted as part of an intellectual system which is incapable of resolving conflict, incapable of integrating research, findings of research can have no authority when presented to practitioners. In a way, practitioners are compelled to reject the findings of research. Because all research projects begin with the assumption that they are not and need not be related to any other research, there is no rational basis for any study to win wide support. That is why practitioners experience forceful attempts at change more like death and dieing than learning and empowerment. And it is why practitioners respond to gentle attempts at change with indifference.

How Education's Epistemology Accommodates Change

Because the new epistemology integrates research and practice formally rather than as an artificial, add on task, it dramatically alters the nature of change for it alters the structure and commitment of the educational community. Not only do the members of a theoretical-model-grounded-community commit to the intellectual assumptions of the model, they also commit to education's *telos*, which means that they conduct research and practice in terms of that *telos*. They are committed to the same source and standards of knowledge, the same organization and structure of knowledge, and to the same method of inquiry. They agree regarding what practitioners know and do not know, which means that they agree about what they *must* do. In addition, researchers know what problems practitioners cannot solve. In this kind of community, what researchers seek to discover, practitioners are waiting to find out.

I am not describing some utopian intellectual dream. What I am describing is exactly what happens in science, especially practice driven sciences such as medicine and engineering. Physicians know what they know and what they do not know. They are morally and legally obligated to do what the discipline knows, and they anxiously await answers to what they do not know. Engineers do not engage innovations in physics or chemistry with long, agonized, twelve step change processes. They use them to solve problems or develop new products.

If all educators were committed to the same purpose but organized in competing communities defined by different theoretical models, the difference between education and science would be that education would still not enjoy the clarity and unity that is achieved by committing to a single paradigm. We would still need that ultimate intellectual achievement, the victory of a theoretical model and its acceptance as our paradigm. Until then, researchers must develop innovations within theoretical models and deliver them to members of the community organized around each theoretical model. Only when one theoretical model prevails and all educators commit to *a paradigm* can education enjoy the intellectual and practical unity of science. Then change can move through the entire community much as it does through the entire scientific community.

It is no small matter, then, that the epistemology I am proposing requires the integration of research into coherent theoretical models and requires practitioners to form a professional community by committing to one theoretical model or another. Although establishing such a community requires enormous work on the part of researchers, it assures that their work matters. And although it requires practitioners to commit to the model and commit to change, community assures them of access to a body of research that is dedicated to solving the problems that they encounter with their students. In such a community, change is treated as an integral, anxiously anticipated part of the professional's life. In such communities, change is not a very interesting topic. Research is interesting. Major breakthroughs in cognitive psychology or pedagogy are interesting. Keeping up with the literature is not only interesting, it is a professional imperative. But in a genuine intellectual community guided by a powerful epistemology, the nature of change is neither troubling nor interesting.

In many respects, I claim that education can adopt virtually the identical *communal structure* that physicians and engineers enjoy. I merely acknowledge that we must start by solving the epistemological problems that prevent us from integrating research, integrating research and practice, and conducting discourse that leads to agreement, commitment, and action. Some of these problems have roots in the 14th century. Others have only been understood in the 20th century. We must identify our source and standard of knowledge, organization and structure of knowledge, and method of inquiry. We must organize competing communities around the different theoretical models that are sufficiently compelling to earn the commitment of professionals who fill all of the major roles in education: researchers, university teaching faculty, school administrators, and school teachers. We must let these communities compete. If one theoretical model demonstrates that it is significantly more explanatory, that it produces significantly better results in student achievement, it must win the support of the entire educational community.

We have solved a 700 year old epistemological problem and created a structure of inquiry that integrates knowledge and provides the intellectual and communal bonds required to form a community of scholars and practitioners. Implementing these solutions demands such enormous change and can be expected to create such intense intellectual conflict, that leaders can be expected to reject the project before attempting it. But that would be an enormous error for the new epistemology permits us to make change a natural part of our professional lives.

10

Conclusion

In the introduction, we described the kind of schools parents and citizens want for children and the levels of achievement that the new world economy demands of students. Because children must learn more than was required in the past, educators must change what they do rather quickly. But when principals and teachers discuss innovations or attempt to improve their schools on their own, they encounter unresolvable conflicts. Typically, educators work to resolve those conflicts; but in time, they conclude that they cannot agree. After a few repetitions of that experience, educators conclude that they cannot agree on anything. The sensible response to that conclusion is to conduct research and practice individually or in groups of like minded folks. That is what educators have done, and on the surface it seems sound.

However, throughout this text we demonstrated that the conclusion that educators cannot agree on anything is a profound and deeply problematic epistemological assertion. Educators do not merely notice that they cannot agree. They claim that the nature of knowledge in education is such that individuals must see reality through lenses shaped by their individual genetic and experiential make up. They inevitably disagree, and those disagreements are unresolvable.

Adopting this epistemological view has enormous ramifications for the intellectual development of education and educators. It prohibits educators from thinking about the intellectual problems that prevent them from conducting discourse that leads to agreement, commitment, and action. It prevents practitioners from noticing that educational researchers have reached the same conclusion and therefore do not even attempt to integrate educational research. Rather, researchers do their own thing, which produces research that is so fundamentally incompatible that it cannot be integrated. Further, it is impossible to integrate contradictory research with practice. This fact becomes evident when practitioners attempt to resolve differences by checking the research. Instead of finding clarity, they find deeply contradictory conclusions, regardless of the topic. Instead of resolving disagreements by checking the research, practitioners exacerbate conflicts.

Rather than noticing that both research and practice suffer from severe intellectual problems, educators have just kind of found themselves in a situation in which they assume that they cannot agree on anything. Researchers publish articles that few researchers and fewer practitioners read. Teachers go to their classrooms and do their own thing. Principals feel safest in their offices. And superintendents prefer each others company to the company of building staff. Everyone seems to be hiding out. However, the enormous impact of education on the lives of citizens and the capacity of commerce has made education one of the two or three most visible and controversial topics in developed nations. Educators cannot hide.

We have also seen that because educators conduct research and practice as individuals, they have no capacity to speak to each other with intellectual authority. Since educators cannot speak to each other with intellectual authority, they cannot speak to the public with intellectual authority. Parents, politicians, and pundits have noticed that educators disagree with each other, and they have decided that they can disagree with educators. Not surprisingly, some politicians and parent activists have sought to institutionalize their capacity to disagree with educators by developing various governance and finance initiatives that create publicly supported schools that are completely independent of educators. Vouchers provide the most dramatic example, but charter schools and home schooling do much the same thing.

More complex to notice, the same intellectual problems that have caused educators to conclude that they cannot agree on anything about learning and teaching have caused them to agree that they cannot agree on anything about the ethical development of children. Nor can they agree about the social ethics that have deteriorated in public schools. Religious activists have noticed this weakness and some have attempted to bring their ethics into public schools. They have also sought new laws that provide public support to schools that teach their religious views and operate independent of public school educators or any oversight by the public. They want the separation of church and state in governance, but they seek to knock down that wall of separation in order to gain public dollars.

Educators have become more and more frustrated and humiliated by these events. To make matters worse, many state legislatures have lost interest in fighting to fund public schools. In many states, public schools have been impoverished, but public school educators have been asked to do more and more for children. The challenges that confront educators are vast and the forces that undermine the intellectual authority and professional status of educators are great. In this text, we have taken a long look at how public education arrived at such a debilitating condition.

As I pointed out in the introduction and demonstrated in the text, in order to develop *intellectual leadership*, educators must develop *intellectual authority*. To do that they must attend to their *intellectual development*, both as a community and as individuals. One of the more important observations we have made is that education is a social science, like economics, sociology, and political science. We discovered that intellectual development in the social sciences depends upon three essential activities: ethical development, cognitive development, and community development. Ethical development requires *mature secular* moral reasoning. Cognitive development requires the design and use of a formal cognitive architecture that organizes inquiry and structures knowledge. Community development is grounded in ethical and cognitive development but includes both a focus on the individual and a focus on the community.

It is more than a little controversial to claim that education and the other social sciences as well as most discourse in the university and the public square must be guided by mature *secular moral reasoning*. I confronted that controversy head on by reviewing the Western intellectual tradition. I acknowledged that Western civilization derived part of its unique character from the influence of Jewish and Christian theology, especially the eschatological hope of Christianity and the humanism demanded by the last seven of the Ten Commandments. I described the astonishing events that permitted Christianity to be the only Roman institution that survived the Germanic peoples' conquest and plunder of the Roman Empire. And I described the impact that Western Christendom, a unified religious culture that persisted for a thousand years, had on Western civilization. Religious activists who insist that Christianity must play a central role in sustaining American and Western culture will agree that without Christianity it is indeed impossible to explain where we came from and in many ways who we are. But they tend to underestimate or ignore the impact that the Protestant Reformation had on Western civilization.

The Protestant Reformation ended the unity of Western Christianity and ushered in religious diversity that shook the foundations of Western political and civil life. We discussed the Thirty Years War, a religious war that devastated Europe, and the English-American political revolution that first established secular principles of political authority and then separated religion from politics and the state. It invented a new, secular political theory. Importantly, we noted that the events that drove religion out of political and public life were perpetrated by Catholic and Protestant religious and political leaders, *not by secular intellectuals.* The diversification of Western Christendom was achieved by theologians and religious leaders. Religious diversification necessitated the development of secular ethical reasoning and a canon of secular ethics capable of guiding inquiry in the university and discourse in the public square. We have adopted a complex but decisive and unapologetic view of the relationships among religion, natural science, and the social sciences.

Religion derives its truth and intellectual authority from God, sacred texts, and for Catholics, tradition. But various religions draw different conclusions about God (the relationship of humans to God, the nature of sin, the capacity of humans to gain salvation) through various interpretations of sacred texts, and of course the Catholic reference to tradition which includes papal and ecclesiastical authority. These religious communities disagree so profoundly on theological and ethical issues that they must be assured freedom to protect their ability to be different. The state cannot endorse or advance any one religion to the detriment of any other religion. Similarly, religious authority is confined to religious communities that citizens are free to join, leave, or ignore. Obviously, no single religious view can be allowed to impose its ethical views on the university, public schools, or the public square.

On the other hand, we have noticed that Christianity's greatest contribution to Western civilization may not have been the Ten Commandments. It may have been the eschatological hope that the promise of eternal life gives humans. Early in Western history, that promise provided the psychological and sociological motivation for Western people to develop and follow ethical principles that express humanism that was unique among world cultures of the time. Today it may be unarguable that Western societies must develop a system of mature *secular* ethical reasoning in order to build ethical consensus in the university and public square. But it is not at all clear that devoid of eschatological hope Western societies can sustain the social ethics that distinguished their development. Psychologists and sociologist have quite a challenge responding to that question. It may be that they will be forced to seek help from *secular theologians* if I may use that term. I think of secular theologians as non-denominational intellectuals who could develop the formal architecture needed to permit religious theologians and members of faith communities to think about, compare and contrast, and ultimately evaluate all religions. They might also hold all faith communities *intellectually* accountable to standards that enhance the lives of their members and society, permitting a legitimate place for God in Western intellectual and public life. That may turn out to be the unique contribution that the divinity schools at great secular universities such as Harvard and Chicago have already begun to play in American society.

Natural science, on the other hand, derives its truth and intellectual authority from nature and the commitment of all scientists to the epistemology of science. We have noted the tremendous impact that the epistemology of science has had on the authority, independence, and stature of natural scientists since the 17th century. We have also noticed that there is no particularly interesting conflict between religion and natural science unless theologians or natural scientists mix their epistemologies, i.e., theologians attempt to use religious epistemology to conduct science or scientist try to use the epistemology of science to conduct religious inquiry. Creationism is an example of the former. But even Newton was susceptible to the latter which did not ingratiate him with Anglicans and Presbyterians.

Social science has conflicted with and been confused by religion and natural science because it has not figured out its source of truth and therefore its basis for intellectual authority. During the Middle Ages, what we today call the social sciences were included in moral philosophy. Scholastic moral philosophers could not conduct inquiry independent of theology. That was not a problem for them, because they lived in a world with a single Christian view. But the Protestant Reformation ended that world and the comfort of scholastic philosophers. Social scientists adopted their new name in order to distance themselves from moral philosophy and scholastic philosophy which disappeared except in departments of moral philosophy in some Catholic universities.

But for all the distance that they attempted to place between themselves and moral philosophy and their intellectual ancestors, social scientists have not been successful in resolving the epistemological problem that scholastic philosophers encountered after the death of Aquinas.

The necessity of identifying a source of knowledge that was different from God and sacred texts became evident when medieval Christian scholars had to accommodate the vast store of Greek, Roman, Arabic, and Jewish knowledge that flooded Europe shortly after the close of the Dark Ages. Aquinas developed a variation of Aristotle's rationalism that at least theoretically put reason on a par with faith and made the West safe for reason. But Aquinas was a theologian, and his *a priori* assumptions were inexorably tied to Christian dogma. Scholastic philosophers used Aquinas' method and were free to develop reasoned views that did not depend upon faith and sacred texts for their assumptions. But as we have seen, freedom has as much to with ability as opportunity, and scholastic philosophers were not able to develop a source of knowledge that could match the intellectual authority of faith and sacred texts. It is not that they did not try, but the problem is quite dicey. In any event, the Protestant Reformation put an end to Christian unity. Quite suddenly, scholastic moral philosophers had to develop secular ethics to guide public life. This challenge was especially urgent for philosophers working in what today we call political science, because religious diversity compromised the old principles of political relationships which had provided the ethical foundation of laws. These principles were said to have come from God, but when theologians, intellectuals, rulers, and the people ceased to agree on what God said, the principles that came from God became subject to unresolvable disputes. Intellectuals began to look for secular *a priori* principles that could guide the development of laws. Scholastic philosophers had developed a two hundred year track record of unsuccessful attempts to develop secular *a priori* principles. They had not been able to identify a secular source of knowledge for ethical principles.

The leaders of the English-American revolution of the 17th and 18th centuries developed the principles that guided the development of laws, but they did not solve the source of knowledge problem. Relying on Christian humanism to assert the rights of man, they developed legal mechanisms such as the right of habeas corpus, the separation of church and state, and democracy to assure peace and justice. The length of that revolution, nearly 200 years, gives evidence of the methods they employed, trial and error guided by common sense and a fairly clear sense of purpose.

Of course, trial and error works and it worked for these revolutionaries. But in addition to working, it is notable for being inefficient. Trial and error wastes time and money. Educators do not have the time and money to waste on an inefficient mode of inquiry. Social scientists must develop intellectual solutions to the problems that plague our disciplines. Educators, in particular, feel that pressure. And as we have seen, we cannot use the epistemology of religion which guided moral philosophy in the West for a thousand years. And we cannot use the epistemology of science.

Science conducts inquiry into *what is*, into *nature*; and nature provides science with its source of knowledge. The social sciences conduct inquiry into *what ought to be* in society. In general, social scientists know that we seek a society marked by justice and peace, but what is our source of knowledge? How can we establish intellectual authority for our disciplines? Our answer has focused on two major achievements: 1) Identifying an ethically grounded purpose (our *telos)* and employing it as our source and standard of knowledge, and 2) Developing the formal cognitive architecture that allows us to identify activities that achieve that purpose. To identify and win commitment to our *telos*, social scientists must develop a system of mature secular ethical reasoning. To employ formal operations, social scientists must develop the formal architecture unique to each discipline.

We have established that more adults can learn mature moral reasoning and the canon of a mature ethical system than can develop either on their own. Similarly, more adults can learn to use a formal cognitive architecture and to function with formal operations than can design and develop either on their own. Intellectual leaders must therefore be able to develop and teach mature secular moral reasoning and formal cognitive operations.

This fairly recondite discussion is not terribly attractive unless we keep in mind students and what is at stake for them. All educators (researchers, teaching faculty, school administrators, and school teachers) are responsible for the education of *all children*. We must educate virtually all children to levels never before required. That is a new goal, and it demands new methods that we must discover. As a practical matter, education must make deep changes. And because we are responding to events that have already become evident in the world, because changes in the world economy already provide enormous opportunities for citizens who can participate and devastating consequences for those who cannot, education must change fast.

However, it is impossible even to think about how education can change fast if educators continue to conduct research and practice as individuals or in small groups of like minded people who, only by chance, agree with one another. The intellectual structure of that arrangement destroys change because it destroys ethical and cognitive development. It destroys attempts to integrate research, integrate research and practice, and conduct discourse that leads to agreement, commitment, and action. It destroys intellectual development, and it destroys intellectual authority. It thereby destroys intellectual leadership.

During the course of this work we have experienced a very interesting shift in how we think about education's goals. While retaining our interest in preparing all students to thrive in the new world economy, we have also noticed that students cannot learn the social sciences unless they develop the capacity to conduct mature secular moral reasoning. And they cannot develop the ethical conduct required to succeed in the social settings of school and work unless they learn the content of a mature secular ethical system. Educators cannot leave students' development of mature secular ethical reasoning or conduct to chance. Like adults, far more children can learn mature ethical reasoning and the canon of a mature ethical system than can develop either on their own. Similarly, we have learned that a significant majority of students, like adults, cannot learn to function with formal cognitive operations unless they are taught both a formal architecture within each discipline and the formal operations essential to it. *The intellectual and social development of students depends upon their learning mature ethical reasoning and formal cognition.*

Now there are two goals to challenge educational researchers and practitioners. They demand the intellectual development of education and educators, and they demand change with all due speed. Educational leaders must design, raise funding for, and conduct two major research and development projects: 1) An ethics project that develops a system of mature secular moral reasoning and its canon, and 2) A cognitive project that develops the architecture of formal cognition and its operations. These projects must do more than satisfy the curiosity of researchers.

They must develop programs that practitioners can use and training that facilitates that use. They cannot send incomplete products to practitioners, requiring them to conduct substantive research and development in order to make the products useful.

I have described mature secular moral reasoning in a manner that indicates that an ethics project could be successful. It could develop a system of mature secular ethical reasoning that could win consensus in the public square. Importantly, this project inevitably must aim to develop a system of ethical reasoning that can be used by all social scientists, not just educators. The ethics project's purpose must be to provide the intellectual tools needed to identify the ethically grounded purpose of each of the social sciences and the canon of social ethics that guide discourse and conduct in the university and the public square.

Each of the social sciences must develop its own *telos* (which provides evidence that each constitutes a distinct discipline), but each must be able to use the same system of mature secular moral reasoning. Therefore, this project must anticipate interest from and participation by members of all of the social sciences. In addition, all ethicists have an enormous stake in the development of mature secular moral reasoning and a canon of social ethics. The ethics project must also anticipate interest from and participation by moral theologians, religious moral philosophers, and secular moral philosophers. It should be quite a project.

On the other hand, the cognitive project seeks to identify the *activities* social scientists require to achieve their *telos*. Each of the social sciences must develop its own activities, its own knowledge, skills, and tools required to achieve its *telos*. Each must therefore develop the formal architecture that organizes and structures its knowledge and skills in a manner that employs formal rather than concrete operations. The first phase of the *ethics project* must aim to develop a mature system of ethical reasoning that can be used by *all social scientists*. The second phase of the ethics project must be conducted in each of the social sciences because each of the social sciences requires its own *telos*. But *the entire cognitive* project must be conducted within each of the social sciences. It makes little sense for economists and educators to seek common activities. However, once economists, sociologists, anthropologists, and political scientists have developed the formal architecture and formal operations that guide inquiry, those achievements must alter the content of public school curricula in those disciplines.

Education's cognitive project, then, must develop the formal architecture needed to organize inquiry and structure knowledge required to achieve our *telos*. As we have seen, concrete operations allow us to know and be able to do things. But they do not allow us to think about, compare and contrast, or evaluate what we do. Stuck in concrete operations, if educators happen to analyze or evaluate what others do, they can only do so in terms of what they themselves know. To the extent that what someone else does is similar to what we do, we evaluate it as sound. To the extent that what they do is different from what we do, we evaluate it as unsound. Such analyses and judgements humiliate everyone.

The structure of complete coherent theoretical models that I have offered provides the formal cognitive architecture required for educators to conduct their cognitive project. It demands that we identify the schools of cognitive psychology that inform education by identifying the coherent fundamental assumptions about learning that cognitive psychology has to offer. Even if cognitive psychologists cannot agree on these constructs, educators must. By identifying these sets of coherent fundamental assumptions about how children learn, we identify the various theoretical models that exist potentially in education. By identifying the advantages and disadvantages that children bring to learning as revealed by these fundamental assumptions and then by identifying the *existing* methods that teachers can use to maximize student advantages and overcome student disadvantages, we fully articulate these models. The task of articulating even one complete, coherent theoretical model is so vast as to seem overwhelming. However, if we consider the energy and resources that we currently waste because we do not work together and if we imagine the amount of work that we could accomplish by working together, this task begins to look far less daunting. There is a bit of a knack to defining fundamental assumptions and identifying the advantages and disadvantages that flow logically from them. Once those skills have been developed, however, identifying *existing* methodologies that maximize advantages or overcome disadvantages is a rather straightforward intellectual task.

The methodological challenge comes when we attempt to find *new* ways to maximize advantages and overcome disadvantages. In order for education to be a profession, it must be guided by knowledge. In order to be guided by knowledge, we must be able to say: This is what we know; this is what we do not know but are studying with a realistic expectation of finding answers; and this is what we currently do not even know how to study. We must accept the challenge of knowing and using proven methods and developing new methods.

These tasks describe the first phase of the cognitive project. In the second phase, all educators (researchers, teaching faculty, school administrators, and school teachers) must select the complete coherent theoretical model to which they will commit. Educators will thereby form sub-communities that consist of members of all the major roles in education. These sub-communities will compete to identify the theoretical model that makes the greatest contribution to achieving education's *telos*. Hopefully, one theoretical model will prevail in all instructional settings and become education's paradigm.

This work calls for three major projects: the ethics project, the cognitive project, and the community project. I have described the first two projects, but it seems prudent to wait on the third. It is impossible to predict what might have to be done to establish communal bonds among educators after the ethics and cognitive projects are completed and their products implemented. Both require so much commitment, that they may by themselves form a professional community.

Both of the projects I have described will require significant financial support and an enormous amount of work. Each must be highly developed before it will be prudent for superintendents and principals to commit to the second phase of the cognitive project, the phase where they must select one theoretical model or another.

Over time, some teachers and administrators and even university professors may have to move to different schools or districts to work within a theoretical model to which they can commit. For some, that move may constitute a great burden. We must develop employment policies and salary schedules that permit teachers to move to districts or schools where they can participate in the theoretical model they prefer without suffering unnecessary family and financial burdens.

If we do our job well, education, the other social sciences, and moral philosophy will do the most important, exciting, and productive research in the 21st century. Physics, biology, electronics, and all forms of technology will pale in comparison to the impact that secular moral philosophy, education, economics, sociology, and political science will have on the lives of individuals, communities, and nations. After all, natural science and technology can only improve our physical space and give us mechanical conveniences. Moral philosophy and the social sciences can show us the full potential of human existence. Only they can work to assure dignity and justice for all humans in all lands. Secular moral philosophy and the social sciences have the capacity to attract the very best young minds to our professions, earn the respect of the public and the academy, and receive an enormous increase in financial support. But we must focus on cognitive and ethical development. We must bring intellectual authority to our research and practice. And we must learn to work as international intellectual communities that identify the ethically grounded purpose of our work and compete to achieve that *telos*.

Some educators may find such promise intimidating. Some may question their capacity to succeed in a profession that demands significant intellectual development. Reuven Feuerstein[1] makes an important observation about teachers being confident in their ability to learn. He claims that in order for teachers to believe that children can learn, they must believe that they can learn. A few years ago I was talking with Alex Kozulin, Vygotsky's translator, who works with Feuerstein in Israel. I asked him how they select teachers to receive training in Feuerstein's work, which at the time I thought might be difficult for many teachers to learn. Kozulin replied with one question, "Are they going to be teaching children?" In other words, researchers, university faculty, administrators, and teachers must believe that we can learn just as we must believe that students can learn. And we must believe that we can learn well.

But like Vygotsky, Feuerstein and Kozulin know that we can learn far more if we receive help than if we are left to do it on our own. Intellectual leaders must attend to helping all of the members of our profession gain confidence in our ability to learn and to providing practitioners with products that are efficacious and complete—that are ready to be used. It is not unusual for leaders quite unconsciously to ask teachers to learn a new program when actually they are asking them to finish developing it. Obviously, it is a huge error to infer anything about

---

[1] *Don't Accept Me as I Am: Helping "Retarded" People to Excel.* Unfortunately, Feuerstein's early works are out of print. This work has brought his theory into special education to the benefit of many children, but it has also caused many educators to think that his work is designed only for children with special needs. That conclusion is wrong and works to the detriment of a vast number of children and teachers.

the ability of teachers to learn from their willingness to conduct such research.

That being said, I have claimed that the new epistemology is simple and powerful, but I never said that developing it or implementing it and the new knowledge it will generate will be easy. I had good reason for stressing that our *telos* is an ethically grounded purpose. Once professional educators accept that we have an ethical responsibility to students that is described by our *telos* and manifested in our commitment to our community, we cannot ignore our duty to learn and to do what we know works simply because it is hard. We can advance different views, demonstrate that they would be more effective than others, but we cannot refuse to engage new knowledge or the challenge to grow simply because it is hard. We must all commit. And that commitment must be allowed to motivate us to work hard, maybe harder than we have never worked before. For only then can we learn just how much we can learn, just how much we can do.

We are free because we are able to work hard and because we are able to understand the difference between ethical and unethical professional conduct. This freedom makes us responsible and accountable for our decisions. Ability, responsibility, and accountability, there is more than a dull rhyme to those words. They describe our burden and our hope.

Bibliography

Ahmann, J. Stanley and Marvin D. Glock; *Evaluating Pupil Growth: Principles of Tests and Measurement*, Third Edition; Allyn and Bacon, Inc., Boston; 1967.

Aquinas, Saint Thomas; *Summa Theologica*; Great Books of the Western World, Encyclopaedia Britannica, Inc; Chicago, 1952.

Argyris, Chris; *Overcoming Organizational Defenses: Facilitating Organizational Learning*; Allyn and Bacon, Boston; 1990.

Aristotle; *Nichomachean Ethics*; In Great Books of the Western World, Robert Maynard Hutchins, General Editor, Encyclopaedia Britannica, Inc, Chicago; 1952.

Bacon, Francis; *Essays, Advancement of Learning, New Atlantis, and Other Pieces*, eighth printing, Richard Foster Jones, editor; The Odyssey Press, Inc., New York; 1937.

Bellah, Robert N., Richard Madsen, William M. Sullivan, Ann Swidler, and Steven M. Tipton; *Habits of the Heart: Individualism and Commitment in American Life*; Perennial Library, Harper and Row, Publishers, New York; 1985.

Bernadin, Joseph Cardinal, *The Catholic Church and the Ethics of Life*, an unpublished address delivered at Georgetown University, September 6, 1996.

Bloch, Marc; *The Historian's Craft*, Translated by Peter Putnam; Vintage Books, Random House, New York; 1953.

Boff, Leonardo; *The Path to Hope: Fragments from a Theologian's Journey*; Orbis Books, Maryknoll, N.Y.; 1993.

Bower, Gordon H. and Ernest R. Hilgard; *Theories of Learning* (fifth edition); Prentice Hall, Englewood Cliffs, New Jersey, 1981.

Boyer, Ernest L.; *Scholarship Reconsidered: Priorities of the Professoriate;* The Carnegie Foundation for the Advancepment of Teaching, Princeton, NJ; 1992.

Britannica World Language Edition of Funk & Wagnalls Standard Dictionary, Volumes One and Two; Encyclopaedia Britannica, Inc, Chicago; 1960.

Buber, Martin; *I and Thou* (Second Edition); Charles Scribner's Sons, New York; 1958.

"Teaching and Deed" in *The Writings of Martin Buber*; Will Herberg, editor; Meridian Books, The World Publishing Company, New York; 1965.

Burrell, Gibson and Gareth Morgan; *Sociological Paradigms and Organizational Analysis: Elements in the Sociology of Corporate Life*; Heinemann, London; 1979.

Cheyney, Edward P.; *A Short History of England*; Ginn and Company, Boston, MA; 1960.

Coleman, James S.; *The Adolescent Society*; Free Press, Glencoe, Il; 1961.

Culbertson, Jack A.; "Three Epistemologies and the Study of Educational Administration," *UCEA Review*, The University Council for Educational Administration, Vol. XXII, Number 1, Winter, 1981.

Dawson, Christopher; *Religion and the Rise of Western Culture* (Gifford Lectures Delivered at the University of Edinburgh, 1948-49); Image Books, Garden City, New York; 1958.

Descartes, Rene; *Meditations on First Philosophy*, Second (Revised) Edition, Translated by Laurence J. Lafleur; The Library of Liberal Arts, The Bobbs-Merrill Company, New York; 1960.

Dillon, J. T. (Editor); *Deliberation in Education and Society*; Ablex Publishing Corporation, Norwood, N.J.; 1994.

Dornbusch, Sanford M. and W. Richard Scott; *Evaluation and the Exercise of Authority*; Jossey-Bass Publishers, San Francisco, 1975.

Elliott, William Y. and Neil A. McDonald; *Western Political Heritage*; Prentice-Hall, Inc., Englewood Cliffs, N.J.; 1949.

English, Fenwick W. and John C. Hill; *Restructuring: The Principal and Curriculum Change*; National Association of Secondary School Principals, Reston, Virginia;1990.

Epstein, Herman T.; "Growth Spurts during Brain Development: Implications for Educational Policy and Practice;" *Education and the Brain*, The Seventy-seventh Yearbook of the National Society for the Study of Education, Editors: Jeanne S. Chall and Allan F. Mirsky, University of Chicago Press, Chicago Illinois; 1978.

Evans, Richard I.; *Dialogue with Jean Piaget*; Praeger Publishing, New York, 1981.

Feuerstein, Reuven, Ya'acov Rand, Mildred B. Hoffman; *The Dynamic Assessment of Retarded Performers: The Learning Potential Assessment Device, Theory, Instruments and Techniques*; University Park Press, Baltimore; 1979.

Feuerstein, Reuven, Ya'acov Rand, Mildred B. Hoffman, and Ronald Miller; *InstrumentalEnrichment An Intervention Program for Cognitive Modifiability*; University Park Press, Baltimore; 1980.

Feuerstein, Reuven and Mildred B. Hoffman; *Instrumental Enrichment: A Word of Introduction*; Hadassh-Wizo-Canada-Research Institute, Jerusalem.

Feuerstein, Reuven; *Instrumental Enrichment: A Selected Sample of Materials for Review Purposes*; Hadassh-Wizo-Canada-Research Institute, Jerusalem.

Feuerstein, Reuven and Mildred B. Hoffman; "Intergenerational Conflict of Rights: Cultural Impositionand Self-Realization," in *Viewpoints in Teaching and Learning*, Journal of the School of Eucation, Indiana University, Vol 58, No 1, Winter, 1982.

Feuerstein, Reuven, Ya'acov Rand, John E. Rynders; *Don't Accept Me As I Am: Helping "Retarded" People to Excel*; Plenum Press, New York; 1988.

Feuerstein, Reuven; "The Theory of Structural Cognitive Modifiability," in *Learning and Thinking Styles: Classroom Interaction*; Robert McClure, editior; National Education Association, Washington, D.C.; 1990.

Fischer, David H.; *Historians' Fallacies: Toward a Logic of Historical Thought*; Harper Torchbooks, Harper & Row, New York; 1970.

Fowler, James W.; *Stages of Faith: The Psychology of Human Development and the Quest for Meaning*; Haper San Francisco, 1995.

Fullan, Michael G.; *Successful School Improvement*; Open University Press, Philadelphia; 1992.
The New Meaning of Educational Change; Teachers College Press, New York; 1991.
"Staff Development, Innovation, and Institutional Development," in *Changing School Culture Through Staff Development*, Bruce Joyce, Editor; 1990.

Fullan, Michael G. and Andy Hargreaves; *What's Worth Fighting For: Working Together for Your School*; Ontario Public Schools Teachers Federation, Toronto, Ontario; 1991.

Gardner, Howard; *Frames of Mind: The Theory of Multiple Intelligences*; Basic Books, 1985.

Goodlad, John I., Roger Soder, Denneth A. Sirotnik, editors; *The Moral Dimensions of Teaching*; Jossey-Bass Publishers, San Francisco; 1990.

Guskey, Thomas R.; "Integrating Innovations," *Educational Leadership*; 1990.
Implementing Mastery Learning; Wadsworth Publishing Co., Belmont, California; 1985.

Hargreaves, Andy and Michael G. Fullan; *Understanding Teacher Development*; Teachers College Press, New York; 1992.

Hawking, Stephen W.; *A Brief History of Time: From the Big Band to Black Holes*; Bantom Books, New York; 1988.

Hobbes, Thomas; *Leviathan: Or the Matter, Forme, and Power of a Commonwealth, Ecclesiasticall and Civil*; Collier-MacMillan, Ltd., London; 1970.

Hopkins, David; "Integrating Staff Development and School Improvement: A Study of Teacher Personality and School Climate, in *Changing School Culture Through Staff Development*, Bruce Joyce, Editor; 1990 Yearbook of the Association for Supervision and Curriculum Development, Alexandria, Virginia.

Hume, David; *An Enquiry Concerning Human Understanding;* In Great Books of the Western World, Robert Maynard Hutchins, General Editor, Encyclopaedia Britannica, Inc, Chicago; 1952.

James, Henry; *Pragmatism, and Four essays from The Meaning of Truth;* Meridian Books, The World Publishing Company, Cleveland, Ohio; 1964.

Johann, Robert O.; *The Meaning of Love: An Essay towards a Metaphysics of Intersubjectivity;* Geoffrey Chapman LTD, London; 1954.

Joyce, Bruce and Marsha Weil; *Models of Teaching*; Prentice-Hall, Inc., Englewood Cliffs, New Jersey; 1980.

Joyce, Bruce with Barrie Bennett and Carol Rolheiser-Bennett; "The Self-Educating Teacher: Empowering Teachers Through Research," in *Changing School Culture Through Staff*

Development, Bruce Joyce, Editor; 1990 Yearbook of the Association for Supervision and Curriculum Development, Alexandria, Virginia.

Joyce, Bruce and Emily Calhoun; "Changing Interpretations of Change: A Review of *The New Meaning of Educational Change*; Unpublished Review distributed at Colorado Department of Education Three R's Conference held January 10, 1992, in Denver, Colorado.

Kant, Immanuel; *The Critique of Pure Reason, The Critique of Practical Reason, Preface and Introduction to the Metaphysical Elements of Ethics, With a Note on Conscience, General Introduction to the Metaphysic of Morals*; In Great Books of the Western World, Robert Maynard Hutchins, General Editor, Encyclopaedia Britannica, Inc, Chicago; 1952.

Karpov, Yuriy V. and H. Carl Haywood; "Two Ways to Elaborate Vygotsky's Concept of Mediation: Implications for Instruction," *American Psychologist*, the American Psychological Association, Vol. 53, No.1, (p. 27-36) January, 1998.

Katz, Daniel and Robert L. Kahn; *The Social Psychology of Organizations*; John Wiley & Sons, Inc., New York; 1966.

Koch, Sigmund; *American Psychologist*; "The Nature and Limits of Psychological Knowledge: Lessons of a Century qua Science;" Vol. 36, No. 3, pp 257-269, March, 1981.

Kofman, Fred and Peter M. Senge; "Communities of Commitment: The Heart of the Learning Organization," in *Organizational Dynamics*, Special Issue, Autumn, 1993, American Management Association.

Kohlberg, L.; "From Is to Ought: How to Commit the Naturalistic Fallacy and Get Away with it in the Study of Moral Development;" in *Cognitive Development and Epistemology*, T. Michael editior; Academic Press, New York; 1971.
"The Contribution of Developmental Psychology to Education;" *Education Psychologist*, 10, No. 1, 1973.
"Development as the Aim of Education;" *Stage Theories of Cognitive and Moral Development: Criticism and Application, Harvard Educational Review*, 1978.
The Meaning and Measurement of Moral Development; Clark University Press, Worcester, MA; 1976.

Kozol, Jonathan; *Savage Inequalities: Children in America's Schools*; Crown Publishers, Inc., New York; 1991.

Kozulin, Alex; "Book Review: Vygotsky and Education: Instructional Implications and Applications of Sociohistorical Psychology," (Edited by Luis C. Moll, New York: Cambridge University Press, 1990) in *American Journal of Psychology*, Vol 105, No. 3, pp 510-516, Fall, 1992.

"Literature as a Psychological Tool," in *Educational Psychologist*, 28(3), 253-264; Lawrence Erlbaum Associates, Inc.; 1993.

Kuhn, Thomas S.; *The Structure of Scientific Revolutions*, Second Edition, Enlarged; TheUniversity of Chicago Press, Chicago; 1970.

Küng, Hans; *The Council, Reform, and Reunion*; Image Books, Doubleday, Garden City, New York; 1965.

Langer, William L. (Editor); *An Encyclopedia of World History*; Houghton Mifflin Company, The Riverside Press, Cambridge, MA; 1952.

Lewis, C. S.; *Four Loves*; Harcourt/Peter Smith, New York; 1960.

Lezotte, Lawrence W.; "School Improvement Based on Effective Schools Research"; Unpublished Paper, National Center for Effective Schools Research and Development, Okemos, Michigan; 1989.

"Effective Schools Reserch Model for Planned Change"; Unpublished Paper, National Center for Effective Schools Research and Development, Okemos, Michigan; 1989.

"Strategic Assumptions of the Effective Schools Process"; Unpublished Paper, National Center for Effective Schools Research and Development, Okemos, Michigan; 1989.

"Correlates of Effective Schools"; Unpublished Paper, National Center for Effective Schools Research and Development, Okemos, Michigan; 1989.

Lezotte, Lawrence W. and Michelle L. Maksimowicz; *Workbook for Developing A District Plan for School Improvement Based on the Effective Schools Research*; Michigan Institute for Educational Management, Lansing, Michigan; 1989.

Locke, John; *An Essay Concerning Human Understanding*; In Great Books of the Western World, Robert Maynard Hutchins, General Editor, Encyclopaedia Britannica, Inc, Chicago; 1952.
An Essay Concerning the True Original, Extent and End of Civil Government (The second of *Two Treatises of Government* published together in 1690) in *The English Philosophers from Bacon to Mill*, Edwin A. Burtt, editor; The Modern Library, New York; 1939.

Luria, A. R.; *The Making of Mind, A Personal Account of soviet Psychology*; Editors, Michael Cole and Sheila Cole; Harvard University Press, Cambridge, MA; 1979.

Maslow, Abraham H.; *Toward a Psychology of Being*, Second Edition; D Van Nostrand Company, New York, 1968.

MacIntyre, Alasdair C.; *Three Rival Versions of Moral Enquiry: Encyclopaedia, Genealogy, and Tradition*; University of Notre Dame Press, Notre Dame, IN; 1990.
After Virtue: A Study in Moral Theory; University of Notre Dame Press, Notre Dame, IN; 1981.

Mann, Dale, Editor; *Making Change Happen?*; Teachers College Press, Columbia University, New York; 1978.

McBrien, Richard P.; *The Harper Collins Encyclopedia of Catholicism*; Harper San Franscisco; 1995.

Mill, John Stuart; *On Liberty*; The Liberal Arts Press, New York; 1956.
The Six Great Humanistic Essays of John Stuart Mill; Washington Square Press, New York; 1969

Mischell, Theodore (editor); *Cognitive Development and Epistemology*; Academic Press, New York, 1971.

Mishel, Lawrence, Jared Bernstein, and John Schmitt; *The State of Working America, 1998-1999*; Cornell University Press, Ithaca, New York; 1999.

Montaigne, Michel de; *In Defense of Raymond Sebond*; Translated by Arthur H. Beattie; Milestones of Thought, Frederick Ungar Publishing Co., New York; 1959.

Nehamas, Alexander; "Trends in Recent American Philosophy," *Daedalus:* Journal of the American Academy of the Arts and Sciences, Winter, 1997.

Newman, John Henry Cardinal; *An Essay in Aid of A Grammar of Assent*; University of Notre Dame Press, Notre Dame, IN, 1979

Newton, Sir Isaac; *Mathematical Principals of Natural Philosophy*; In Great Books of the Western World, Robert Maynard Hutchins, General Editor, Encyclopaedia Britannica, Inc, Chicago; 1952.

Narrol, Harvey and Dan G. Bachor; "An Introduction to Feuerstein's Approach to Assessing and Developing Cognitive Potential," *Interchange*, Vol. 6, No. 1, 1975.

Organizational Dynamics: Special Issue on the Learning Organization; American Management Association; Autum, 1993.

Phillips, D. C. and Jonas F. Soltis; *Perspectives on Learning*, Second Edition; Teachers College Press, New York; 1991.

Plato; *The Dialogues of Plato*; Translated by Benjamin Jowett; In Great Books of the Western World, Robert Maynard Hutchins, General Editor, Encyclopaedia Britannica, Inc, Chicago; 1952.

Plato; *The Republic*; Translated by Francil MacDonald Cornford, Oxford University Press, London; 1957.

Presseisen, Barbara Z. (et al); *Learning and Thinking Styles: Classroom Interaction*; National Education Association, Washington, D.C.; 1990.

Putnam, Hilary; "A Half Century of Philosophy Viewed from Within," *Daedalus:* Journal of the American Academy of the Arts and Sciences, Winter, 1997.

Reich, Robert B.; *The Work of Nations: Preparing Ourselves for 21st Century Capitalism*; Alfred A. Knopf, New York; 1991.

Rossiter, Clinton; *1787: The Grand Convention*; The MacMillan Company, New York; 1966.

Ruddick, J. and D. Hopkins, *Research as a Basis for Teaching*; Heinemann, London; 1985.

Sarason, Seymour B.; *The Culture of the School and the Problem of Change*; Allyn and Bacon, Inc., Boston; 1971.

Schillebeeckx, Edward; *Jesus: An Experiment in Christology*, Translated by Herbert Hoskins; The Crossroad Publishing Company, New York; 1981.

Senge, Peter M.; *The Fifth Discipline: The Art and Practice of the Learning Organization*; Doubleday/Currency, New York; 1990.

Sergiovanni, Thomas J.; *Value-Added Leadership: How to Get*

Extraordinary Performance in Schools; Harcourt Brace Javanovich, New York; 1990.

Shulman, Lee S; *Harvard Educational Review*; "Knowledge and Teaching: Foundations of the New Reform;" Vol. 57, No. 1, February 1987.

Singer, D and T. A. Revenson; *A Piaget Primer: How a Child Thinks*; A Plum Book, New American Library, Times Mirror; 1996.

Sizer, Theodore W.; *Horace's Compromise: The Dilemma of the American High School*; Houghton Mifflin, Boston; 1985.

Smith, Patrica C., Lorne M. Kendall, and Charles L. Hulin; *The Measurement of Satisfaction in Work and Retirement: A Strategy for the Study of Attitudes*; Rand McNally & Company, Chicago, 1969.

Stenhouse, L.; *Authority, Emancipation and Education*; Heinemann, London; 1985

Soros, George; "Toward a Global Open Society," *The Atlantic Monthly*, January, 1998.

"The National Goals--Putting Education Back on the Road," <u>Kappan</u>; December, 1990.

Tillich, Pual; *Dynamics of Faith*; Harper Torchbooks, New York; 1957.

Tolstoy, Leo; *Anna Karenina*; Constance Garnett translator, The Bobbs-Merrill Comany, Inc, New York; 1978.

Toulmin, Stephen; *Cosmopolis: The Hidden Agenda of Modernity*; The University of Chicago Press; 1990.

Vygotsky, L. S,; "The Problem of the Cultural Development of the Child, *Journal of Genetic Psychology*, Vol 36, pp 415-434, 1929. "The Problem of Age-periodization of Child Development;" Translated by Mary A. Zender and F. F. Zender, *Human Development*, N.17, 1974.
Thought and Language; Alex Kozulin, editor and translator; The MIT Press, Cambridge, Massachusetts; 1993.

Whitaker, Kathy S. And Monte C. Moses; "Does Learning Theory Influence Teaching Practices?" *European Journal of Teacher Education*, Vol. 11, Nos. 2/3, 1988.

Index

Abelard, 42

Ach and Rimat, 197

Advantages/disadvantages, 207, 208, 215

Analytical philosophy, 107, 142-147

Anti-epistemologies, 9, 12

Applied research, 209, 230, 235-239, 245, 248, 249

Aquinas, 35, 36, 38, 41, 42, 44, 46-50, 52, 53, 57, 58, 74, 96, 98, 105, 112, 168, 174, 175, 178, 265, 266

Arian Christianity, 27

Augustine of Hippo, 25, 34-39, 43, 44, 51, 52, 54, 80

Autonomy, 108, 110, 111, 122, 129, 139, 189

Autonomy of pure reason, 108, 110, 129

Averroës, 35

Bacon, 77, 78, 82, 90, 92, 143, 144

Basil, 34

Behaviorism, 209, 210, 218-220

Bernadin, 182

Bill of Rights, 94, 95, 100

Bloom, 202

Boniface VIII, 60, 61

Boyer, E, 201

Buber, 124, 184, 188

Calvin, 63, 67, 69, 117

Charlemagne (742-814), 22

Charles I, 78, 93, 99, 102, 103

Charles II, 93, 99, 103

Charles Martel, 22

Christian unity, 63, 266

Church of England, 63, 68, 69, 95

City of God/City of Man, 25, 59

Classical realism, 109, 110, 124, 202

Clovis, 21-23, 27, 71

Cognitive development, 13, 44, 52, 150, 166, 167, 184, 185, 96, 198, 199, 202, 208-210, 212, 215, 217, 220, 235, 263, 268

Communism, 125, 126

Competition, 59, 97, 115, 205, 217, 226, 239, 241-245, 250-252

Conciliar movement, 62, 63

Constantine, Emperor, 26

Continuous progress of history, 114-116, 120, 121, 125

Copernicus, 64, 88, 89, 91, 108

Counter Reformation, 74

Critical Theory, 135-137, 139, 140, 227, 228

Cromwell, 93, 99, 102, 103

Dansen, 167

Dark Ages, 5, 17, 19-24, 26, 28, 29, 33-35, 37, 40, 50, 69, 72, 86, 88, 132, 266

Darwin, 88, 91, 116

Dawson, Christopher, 29

Deductive Reason, 5, 7, 11, 44-46, 57, 79, 80, 85, 102, 114, 119, 181, 227-229, 233

DesCartes, 87, 106

Donaldson, Margaret, 1

Duns Scotus, 36, 38, 39, 49, 51-54, 98, 106

Elizabeth I, 99

Empiricism, 45, 78-87, 89, 90, 92, 103, 105, 106, 111, 143, 144, 148, 228, 231

Encyclopaedia, 107, 113-115, 117-119, 121-123, 125, 126, 129, 131-134, 139, 142, 148-150, 183

English-American revolution, 266

Epistemology, 6-13, 36, 37, 40, 41, 57, 77-82, 92, 105, 106, 113, 119, 120, 129, 131, 139, 141-145, 148, 155, 157, 159, 160, 172, 179, 197, 198, 203, 206, 208, 227, 228, 249, 254, 257-259, 265, 267, 272
Of education, 106, 157, 197
Of mathematics, 7, 8, 145
Of science, 7, 78-81, 120, 144, 148, 157, 203, 265, 267

Epstein, 167

Ethical (moral) development, 13, 112, 125, 165, 169, 172, 178, 181-184, 187, 196, 199, 262, 263, 271
Pre-conventional, 168, 173
Conventional, 168-171, 173
Post-conventional, 168, 171, 173

Ethically grounded purpose, 156, 164, 165, 193, 194, 201, 225, 244, 249, 267, 269, 272

Fascism, 125

Ferdinand V (1452-1516) and Isabella I (1451-1504), 24

Feudalism, 20, 22, 132

Feuerstein, 209, 210, 212, 214, 272

Free market capitalism, 126

Free will, 39, 51

Freedom, 49, 51, 53, 54, 74, 94, 95, 98, 100, 141, 160, 162, 164, 191, 215, 242, 264, 266, 273

Fundamental assumptions, 70, 122, 150, 207, 209-213, 215-217, 220, 270

Galileo, 82, 89, 102, 108

Genealogy, 107, 112, 113, 118, 129-134, 142, 143, 146, 148, 150

Grace, 37, 39, 49, 51-53

Habeas corpus, 95, 181, 266

Haywood, 202, 212, 221
Hegel, 115-117
Henry IV of France, 69
Henry VIII, 68, 69, 93, 99
Hermeneutics, 40, 135-140,
    228
High Middle Ages, 17, 24, 31,
    33, 34, 40, 43, 45, 54, 55,
    58, 64, 132
Historiography, 8, 11, 131,
    133
Hobbes, 77, 92, 95-106, 171
Hume, 104, 107, 140
Hus, John (1369-1415), 62
Idealism, 36, 37, 41, 51,
    78-80, 109
Individualism, 9-12, 104, 106,
    107, 112, 129, 139, 141,
    142, 146, 173, 198-200,
    256, 257
Inductive, 5, 45, 79, 81, 83,
    85, 114, 119, 230
Infallibility of the pope, 117
Instrumentation, 207, 216
Intellectual authority, 8, 9, 13,
    39, 41, 45, 55, 82, 83, 88,
    89, 105, 111, 121, 139,
    151, 155, 180, 190, 194,
    198, 201, 203, 221,
    225-227, 235-237, 241,
    245, 249, 253, 254,
    262-268, 271
Intellectual development, 13,
    54, 106, 96, 198, 235, 244,
    261, 263, 268, 272

Isidore of Seville, 23
Islam, 23, 24, 35, 56
James I, 93, 99, 102
James II, 93
James, William, 18
Johann, Robert, 64, 124, 135,
    188
Jospin, Lionel, 243, 251
Kant, 54, 80, 106-112, 115,
    130, 134, 143, 155,
    157-161, 165, 166, 171,
    173-176, 178
Karpov, 221
Kohlberg, 164, 166-169, 171
Koran, 56
Kozulin, 198, 199, 212, 272
Kuhn, 85, 203, 204, 206-208,
    213, 222, 224
Leadership, 13, 53, 59, 61, 65,
    140, 147, 193, 201, 202,
    251, 253, 263, 268
    Intellectual Leadership, 13,
    59, 65, 140, 201, 253, 263,
    268
Lenin, 126
Levin, 202, 221
Lezotte, 202, 221, 255
Locke, 77, 92, 95, 96, 98-106
Logic of engagement, 182
Logic of separation, 181
Luther, 63, 65-69
MacIntyre, 42, 50, 106, 109-
    112, 114, 117, 119, 122-
    124, 129, 146, 165, 168,
    186

Manichaean, 36, 38
Manichees, 36-39
Marx, 126
Marxism, 125, 126, 244
Materialism, 67, 80, 109, 117, 125
Mature secular moral reasoning, 13, 74, 144, 164, 172, 181-183, 189, 192, 96, 244, 263, 267-269
Mediation, 185, 187, 199, 209, 212, 213, 215, 221
Methodology, 18, 97, 104, 114, 120, 131, 151, 156, 175, 176, 207-209, 214-216, 220, 224, 226-228, 234, 235
Mohammed, 23
Mojtaheds, 56
Monasteries, 30, 33-35, 40
Montaigne, 91
Moslem, 23, 24, 35, 41, 52, 56, 179
Naturalistic fallacy, 162, 164, 172, 234
Nehamas, 44, 145-147
Newman, Henry, 10
Newton, 47, 58, 82-85, 87, 92, 108, 143, 144, 265
Nietzsche, 9, 111, 112, 129, 134-136, 139, 142
Nihilism, 172, 173, 181, 183, 188, 191, 225, 228
Origen (185-254), 34
Original sin, 39, 40

Paradigm, 58, 85, 203-208, 212, 216, 222, 224, 258, 271
Piaget, 150, 155, 157, 159, 164, 166, 167, 169, 184, 185, 198, 199, 210-212, 215
Plato, 35-38, 50-52, 80, 112, 168, 174
Post-Kantian realism, 109-113, 124, 129, 134
Post-Modernism, 107, 133, 134, 137, 141, 142, 148
Professional ethics, 173, 187
Protestant Reformation, 26, 40, 43, 58, 63, 65, 74, 78, 142, 150, 161, 182, 263, 265, 266
Pure research, 235-237, 246-248
Puritans, 67, 69, 117
Putnam, 145, 147
Qualitative research/analysis, 9, 114, 156, 227, 228, 231-234
Quantitative research/analysis, 83, 156, 227, 228, 230-234
Quine, 145, 147
Rationalism, 40, 41, 44-46, 55-58, 65, 77, 78, 80, 84, 89, 90, 103, 105, 106, 147, 266
Realism, 80, 109-113, 124, 129, 134, 202
Research and development, 156, 165, 179, 187, 193,

197, 216, 230, 231, 236, 239, 240, 246-250, 253, 268

Revelation, 40-47, 51, 55, 90, 105, 106, 108, 111, 179

Richelieu, 63, 71, 72

Royal Society, 82, 86, 235

Sakhharov, Lev, 199

School choice, 190

Scientific method, 6, 7, 9, 11, 80-83, 85-87, 89, 90, 108, 111, 131, 144, 156, 203, 229-231, 234

Singer and Revenson, 159, 211, 212

Sizer, 202, 221

Slavin, 202, 221

Social contract, 97, 98, 100, 101, 103, 168, 171

Social ethics, 19, 141, 142, 150, 179, 180, 182, 187, 188, 193, 212, 262, 264, 269

Solipsism., 106

Soros, 243, 251

Source of knowledge, 7, 8, 12, 13, 40-42, 44, 45, 51, 55, 57, 58, 79-81, 87, 90, 96, 105-107, 109, 114, 119, 120, 129-131, 134, 138-141, 143, 144, 146, 155-157, 161-164, 172, 179, 180, 193-198, 201, 241, 244, 256, 265-267

St. Paul, 39

Telos, 164, 165, 173, 175-179, 183, 189, 192-197, 201, 219, 221, 224- 226, 231, 234, 244, 245, 250, 257, 267, 269, 271, 272

Theoretical model, 204, 205, 207, 209, 210, 212, 213, 215-217, 221-226, 245, 249, 258, 259, 270, 271

Thirty Years War, 24, 63, 69, 70, 72, 74, 93, 96, 115, 142, 263

Thomists, 38, 44, 49, 53, 54

Toulmin, 69, 106

Turiel, 167, 168, 184

Unified theory, 204, 205, 224

Visigoths in Spain, 21, 23, 27

Vygotsky, 44, 52, 136, 137, 165, 184, 185, 197-200, 209-212, 214-216, 272

Western Christendom, 73, 88, 263, 264

William and Mary, 94, 100, 103

Wycliff, John, 61